BI 3083229 2

KT-409-290

LISAA

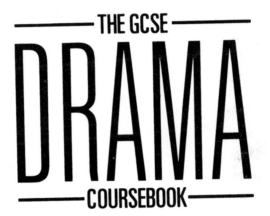

THE GCSE DRAMA COURSEBOOK

Second Edition

THE GCSE
DRAMA
COURSEBOOK

Second Edition

by

ANDY KEMPE

Stanley Thornes (Publishers) Ltd

STANLEY THORNES

Text © Andy Kempe 1997

Original line illustrations © Stanley Thornes (Publishers) Ltd 1997

Illustrated by Francis Bacon, Nick Davies, Bridget Fleetwood, Mark Walker

Picture research by Amanda Davidge

The right of Andy Kempe to be identified as author of this work has been asserted by him in accordance with the Copyright, Designs and Patents Act 1988.

All rights reserved. No part of this publication may be reproduced or transmitted in any form or by any means, electronic or mechanical, including photocopy, recording or any information storage and retrieval system, without permission in writing from the publisher or under licence from the Copyright Licensing Agency Limited. Further details of such licences (for reprographic reproduction) may be obtained from the Copyright Licensing Agency Limited, of 90 Tottenham Court Road, London W1P 9HE.

First edition published in 1990 by Basil Blackwell Ltd.
Reprinted in 1992 by Simon & Schuster Education.
Reprinted in 1995 by Stanley Thornes (Publishers) Ltd.

Second edition published in 1997 by:
Stanley Thornes (Publishers) Ltd
Ellenborough House
Wellington Street
CHELTENHAM GL50 1YW
England

97 98 99 00 01 / 10 9 8 7 6 5 4 3 2 1

A catalogue record for this book is available from the British Library.

ISBN 0-7487-3133-4

UNIVERSITY OF
CENTRAL ENGLAND

Book no. 30832292

Subject no. 373.19 DRA | Kem

INFORMATION SERVICES

* 792   * 792.0712

Typeset by Tech Set Ltd, Gateshead, Tyne & Wear

Printed and bound in Great Britain at Scotprint Ltd, Musselburgh, Scotland

Contents

There are six chapters in the book, each of which starts with a list of the study units within the chapter, and an overview of the work to be covered. The first five chapters are supplemented by two short projects relating to the main thrust of the chapter.

Acknowledgements

The author would like to thank Rick and Jan Holroyd for their help with this book.

The author and publishers wish to thank the following for permission to use copyright material:

Jill Adamson, Charlie Hardwick and Bev Robinson for *Oh dear what can the matter be?*, Amber Lane Press for extracts from Belgrade TIE Co, *Killed: July 16th 1916*; and Leeds Playhouse TIE Co, *Raj*; Alistair Campbell for an extract from his play, *Anansi*, Nelson; Faber & Faber Ltd for extracts from Tom Stoppard, *Rosencrantz and Guildenstern are Dead*; and Christopher Hampton, *Savages*; Guardian News Service Ltd for review by Michael Billington, 'Reality Bites', *The Guardian*, 6.3.96; and television listings, *The Guardian*, 12.5.97; Francesca Hauswirth-Schütt for Hugo Ball, 'Karawane'; David Higham Associates on behalf of the author for Charles Causley, 'Miller's End' from *Collected Poems*, Macmillan; International Creative Management, Ltd. on behalf of the author for an extract from Nick Darke, *The King of Prussia*; Thomas Nelson for an extract from Ben Payne, *The Last Laugh*; Oxford University Press for an extract from Athol Fugard, *Master Harold…and the boys from Selected Plays*, 1984; Penguin UK for extracts from Peter Terson, *Zigger Zagger*, Penguin Books, 1970, Scene 9, pp.48–52. Copyright © Peter Terson 1970; and a page from Raymond Briggs, *Gentleman Jim*, Hamish Hamilton; Random House UK for extracts from Stephen Lowe, *Touched*, Methuen Drama; Bertolt Brecht, 'The Exception and the Rule' from *The Measures Taken and Other Lehrstucke*, trans. John Willet, Methuen Drama; Terry Johnson, *Dead Funny*, Methuen; and John Burrows, *It's a Girl*, Methuen Drama; Solo Syndication Ltd for the front page, headline, 'VE-Day – it's all over', *Daily Mail*, 8.5.45; Times Newspapers Ltd for Benedict Nightingale, 'This much fun must be illegal', *The Times*, 6.3.96. Copyright © Times Newspapers Ltd 1996; The Western Morning News for review by Su Carroll, 'Right royal triumph', *Western Morning News*, 21.3.96.

The author and publishers also wish to thank the following for permission to reproduce copyright photographs:

Associated Press Ltd (p.51); Philip Carter (p.111); Donald Cooper/Photostage (pp.73, 138, 145, 159); Dewynters plc, after Richard Bird's original 1982 poster design/Royal National Theatre (p.217 right); Dominic Photography (pp.123, 147); Mary Evans Picture Library (pp.48, 85, 99); The Fitzwilliam Museum (p.117); Forkbeard Fantasy (p.127); The Ronald Grant Archive (p.87); Sally & Richard Greenhill (p.136); The Guardian (p.82); Reproduced by kind permission of Hamish Hamilton Ltd (p.20); The Hulton Getty Picture Collection (pp.54, 56, 57, 58, 60, 212 left); Trustees of the Imperial War Museum (pp.44, 46, 179); Dafydd Llwyd Lewis (p.131); London Bubble Theatre Company (p.204); Mail Newspapers/Solo (p.66); Mander & Mitchenson Theatre Collection (pp.102, 104); Mansell/Time Inc/Katz Pictures (p.143); McCabes (p.217 left); Barbara Morris and the Sub-department of Film & Drama, University of Reading Bulmershe Court (p.10); Museo Nacional Centro de Arte Reinasofia, Madrid/The Bridgeman Art Library/Giraudon © DACS 1997 (pp.117, 146); National Museum of Labour History (p.188); Rex Features Ltd (p.212 middle & right); The Shakespeare Birthplace Trust (p.16); Humphrey Spender (p.5); Malcolm Stratford (p.125); The Tate Gallery, London (pp.121, 122); Tunbridge Wells Museum & Art Gallery (p. 103); Graham Topping (pp.14, 15, 112); Vaudeville Theatre/John Good Holbrook Ltd (p.217 middle); B. Walters (p.201); Gavin Wilkinson (p.37).

Every effort has been made to contact copyright holders. The publishers apologise to anyone whose rights have been inadvertently overlooked, and will be happy to rectify any errors or omissions.

Preface for teachers

Principles

The first edition of *The GCSE Drama Coursebook* was published in 1990 to meet the needs of teachers embarking on what was then a new examination. In that year 34,649 students left school with a GCSE in Drama. Seven years on, that figure has doubled and the number of students going on to study A Level Drama, Theatre Studies and Performing Arts has expanded accordingly. Drama is also now firmly embedded in the National Curriculum where it is a requirement for students at Key Stages 3 and 4 to be given

> the opportunity to participate in a wide range of drama activities, including role-play, and in the performance of scripted and unscripted plays

as part of their work in Speaking and Listening, and to understand plays in terms of performance rather than simply as a form of literature.

Drama is not, then, a wilting subject, though there has been a shift in the thinking and practice of many teachers in recent years away from seeing drama's main purpose as a sophisticated and effective means of delivering other aspects of the curriculum, and towards regarding it as an art form in its own right, with its own corpus of knowledge and skills. This shift was recognised in the 1992 Arts Council document 'Drama in Schools', which posited that activity in drama could be seen as falling under three headings: Making Drama, Performing Drama, and Responding to Drama. These headings are very close to the model presented in the first edition of this book, which referred to Making, Performing, and Appreciating Plays. At that time some drama teachers baulked at the idea of making, performing and appreciating plays, perhaps assuming that the implication was to have students write scripts that would then be taken on to full-blown public performances which could be reviewed in a formal academic or journalistic manner. The shift that I perceive to have taken place in the last few years, though, is that many teachers would now say 'Why not?' to this. Certainly, the new GCSE and A Level syllabuses have put much more emphasis on the candidates' ability both to perform and to talk critically about their own work and that of others. However, I would still urge teachers to avoid taking too narrow a view of these terms.

Making plays involves a wide range of activities from research and discussion to improvisation. 'Performing' is a word that may be applied to many tasks in drama other than acting: designing and operating the technical aspects of the theatre, for example. The word 'plays' implies for me everything from extended role-plays and short improvisations in the classroom to the presentation of carefully rehearsed scripts. The new projects offered in this second edition attend closely to the demands of the new syllabuses, that students understand the processes involved in making and performing drama, and are able to talk and write about them in some detail.

The aim of this book is to offer a structured course that will enable students to gain a breadth and depth of knowledge, skills and understanding in drama. Its overriding principle is still that drama must be **about** something; that good drama is achieved when there is a close relationship between the conventions of the art form and a worthwhile content.

Many of the techniques and ideas used here to explore a given content may be quite familiar and may indeed have been used lower down the school. There is a debt to pay to many practitioners and commentators on drama in education. This book is concerned with applying those sophisticated and engaging methods to an education in drama. There is more than enough material here to satisfy any one of the new GCSE syllabuses. Five new projects have been added, and more attention has been paid to giving pupils an insight into the design and technical side of drama. Finally, in recognition of the demands of the new syllabuses, a new chapter is offered to give more guidance on producing written responses to drama.

As with the first edition, the book is directed at the students themselves, though at every stage the teacher is implicit as someone who will guide and evaluate the students and indeed carefully select which of the many ideas presented here would be most appropriate to offer their class.

Organisation

The book contains six chapters, the last one being solely concerned with advising students how to record their responses to their own practical investigations into drama and their responses to drama they have seen. Each of the first five chapters offers enough material to form the core of a term's work. These chapters are based on a wide range of resources, including extracts from scripts, gathered around a particular theme and exploring different key elements of the art form. Each chapter is appended by two projects which further develop the skills introduced in the chapter but might be used as units in their own right should the teacher see that as most appropriate for their students.

Although there is an assumption that most pupils taking GCSE Drama will have worked on the subject before, it is recognised that this may have involved them using drama as a method to explore other curriculum areas and not have been taught by specialists. Even so, through their previous experiences of drama, students will have been given an important foundation.

1 They will have recognised that drama involves co-operation and commitment in group situations, and the need to draw on their own experience and imagination.

Drama is concerned with personal and social development.

2 They will know that through drama they can explore their own and other people's ideas, attitudes and feelings. By playing roles outside their own life experience they can gain new insights into why people do what they do.

Drama is concerned with social and moral issues.

These aspects of drama are certainly not ignored in this book, but what is made explicit here is a third element of drama that some students may not have had the opportunity to consider explicitly before embarking on a GCSE course.

3 Drama is a highly developed form of communication. It is an art which draws on a wide range of skills and traditions. To understand drama requires an appreciation of both the craft and the context in which it is made and performed.

Drama demands a knowledge and understanding of how certain skills are used to communicate ideas to an audience.

The units within each chapter of this book, and indeed the order of the chapters themselves, are arranged so as to take account of the students' needs to progress and work in increasingly challenging ways. Each chapter contains a special assignment which may be used as part of the taught course or given to the students as an assessment task.

An Activity/Skills matrix at the back of the book is included to help you and the students identify how the different ideas for work relate to given areas of study. This will allow you to find alternative routes through the book and match what you are doing to the specific requirements of your syllabus.

Suitability for GCSE Drama

All of the GCSE syllabuses in England and

Wales have been scrutinised in the preparation of this book in order to ensure that the work caters for the Aims, Objectives and Assessment Structures of all of them.

The common elements of the GCSE syllabuses are the following.

IMPROVISATION Tasks are offered for spontaneous and prepared improvisations as well as whole-class role-plays. While most of these involve verbal language, others encourage students to explore communicating through movement and use of space. Some syllabuses now ask students to take a **realisation test**: Projects Two, Four and Six have been designed specifically to give students a grounding in how to go about such a test.

PRESENTATION All of the syllabuses offer opportunities for students either to 'realise' a piece of scripted drama or to take their own devised work on to performance. Indeed, this is a requirement in all but one GCSE option. Many of the tasks in this book will help students to identify appropriate styles and working methods for presenting drama.

TECHNICAL KNOWLEDGE Specialising in aspects of design is an option in most syllabuses. Acquiring a broad understanding of the technical side of drama in order to talk more effectively about how plays communicate should be expected of all students. Each chapter offers, variously, tasks on lighting, use of sound, set design, costume and make-up. The Special Assignment in Chapter Three focuses specifically on set design, lighting, sound and stage management.

REFLECTION A vital component of all the syllabuses is that students should be able to reflect on and evaluate their own work and that of others. Only by considering the effectiveness of the different elements of drama can students hope to improve their own ability to manipulate those elements. Reflection tasks appear throughout the book, and Chapter Six offers clear structured advice on how to record

responses in coursework and end-of-course examinations. Many syllabuses require students to keep a **working notebook**. Even where this isn't a requirement, many teachers would consider this to be good practice in that it raises the students' awareness of what they are doing and can help raise the profile of drama in the school as a serious subject.

Suitability beyond the GCSE

Students studying English Literature and Language at GCSE will also find many aspects of this book helpful. A number of short play extracts are included from a wide range of genres. Follow-up tasks to these extracts guide the students through the content and style of the piece and focus specifically on how the play works in performance. There is a balance between practical, discursive and written tasks in relation to the extracts which could be used as effectively for producing coursework assignments in English as in Drama.

The book's focus on the art of drama with its many references to different forms of theatre and the work of well-known practitioners makes it highly suitable as a foundation for the A Level Theatre Studies and Drama courses as well as a key text for AS Level Drama.

Some teachers have been very successful in using units from this book at Key Stage 3, having found the resources and practical ideas flexible enough to allow for adaptation across a wide age and ability range.

Inevitably no one book on drama can hope to cover every single aspect of the subject in the depth that some might require. However, ideas for further reading are offered at the end of each chapter. What I do hope is that you find this book at least a good starting point and, perhaps, a compendium which does in fact suit all of your needs in the teaching of GCSE Drama.

Introduction

People often describe things as being dramatic. 'All the world's a stage' they say, as if all the things that happen in it are deliberately planned, as they are in a stage play. But there is a difference between the 'dramas' that happen in the everyday world and drama which is deliberately created to understand and reflect that world. The type of drama you are studying starts with an idea or feeling. It then has to be shaped and moulded into something that others will understand.

Think of a cake. You will already have a clear idea of what cakes are all about, so if you were asked to go away and make one you'd know that you would need a number of ingredients and a recipe. Just having the ingredients on their own won't do. If you mix them together in the wrong order or wrong proportions, what you'll end up with won't be very cakey.

The process of making drama to communicate ideas and feelings to someone else, does not involve following just one particular recipe. It does involve a number of key ingredients, though. You need to be able to recognise the particular qualities of each ingredient so that you can select and mix them into a range of different dramas. There will be recipes for different occasions, if you like; each one distinctive and pleasing, rather than a gooey mish-mash of everything.

Like a cake, drama is a blend of **content** and **form**. The **content** of a drama is what is in it, what it's all about – its ingredients. The **form** is what makes it drama as opposed to anything else – its recipe.

Each chapter in this book presents a mixture of **content** and **form**. Each chapter looks at a particular subject and concentrates on particular skills. Of course, using those particular skills would not be the only way of exploring those subjects. By the end of the book you will have a sense of what makes good **content**, and the tools which are necessary to shape an appropriate **form**. At the end of this book you will find Activity charts listing those essential tools and showing you how you can learn to use each tool by concentrating on certain exercises.

The subject called drama

More people are exposed to the art form we call drama than any other. Just 50 years ago this may not have been true but now, with the worldwide spread of film and TV it certainly is. Of course, most people are probably totally unaware that they are engaged with something artistic. The fact is that when people are watching *Neighbours* or any other fictional story they are watching something which essentially has the same rules of **form** as *Hamlet*. The key to both *Neighbours* and *Hamlet* is that one group of people are telling another group a story by acting it out.

As students studying drama you would not reasonably expect to be simply sat in front of a TV screen for two years and just told to watch. Drama is an active subject involving finding, making and doing as well as reading, watching and analysing.

Studying drama involves you in three connected areas. You will learn how to **make plays**, **perform plays** and **respond to plays**.

MAKING PLAYS

researching	designing
discussing	questioning
writing	role-playing
improvising	selecting form
experimenting	creating
inventing	

PLAYS

PERFORMING PLAYS

reading	designing
rehearsing	adapting
developing characters	perfecting form
rewriting	using
lighting	

RESPONDING TO PLAYS

reading	discussing
watching	comparing
analysing	judging form
reviewing	evaluating

The diagram above is one person's suggestion for the activities which might go with each of these areas. It shows that it is often impossible to completely divide these three areas from each other.

Some of the words in the diagram may not appear to match what you do in drama. The sections below look at each one in more depth in order to explain this.

Making plays

Your starting point for actually making a play from scratch is most likely to come from one of two areas.

a There is a theme that you want to/have been asked to explore.

CHILDREN   CRIME   WAR
POLLUTION
CRUELTY TO ANIMALS

In this case you need to find some way of capturing and expressing your thoughts and feelings about it. You may have already found or been given a story line to use. Either way, you will need to find a **form** – a way of turning the starting point into something which an audience would call drama.

b It may be that you have already selected or been given a form to use such as mime or movement or a certain manner of speech etc. What you will then need to do is find a **content** – a story, perhaps – on which to use that form.

These look like fairly long tasks and indeed they may be the basis of one which will involve working as a group to discuss, research and write a piece of drama. This type of activity is sometimes called **prepared** or **polished improvisation**. The aim is to encourage a careful selection of form and content from an endless mass which may be available.

When you are asked to spontaneously **improvise** or join in a **role-play** involving the whole class, you are also making a play in one of the ways outlined here (though you may not have time to select so carefully). Perhaps the aim of the work is to capture your intuitive, instant thoughts and feelings about something. The process of uncovering those reactions is more important in this type of improvisation than shaping any finished product. In this kind of work you are 'making plays' and acting them out at the same time. Ideas and feelings can be generated which can then be inspected, weighed up and perhaps developed into a product at another time.

Making plays is an active thing – doing it is more important than talking about it. To develop your ability in this area you need to:

● **Experiment with ideas.** Don't be frightened to try out the first thought that comes into your head – it may be exactly the right one.
● **Trust your own feelings.** There is no ultimately 'right' answer or way of doing things. Don't allow yourself to be cramped by styles and ideas which you don't feel comfortable with.
● **Work around an idea.** Explore what other things it may suggest – one of these may be more interesting than your starting point. Look at what happened before or after an incident, or to someone on the sidelines of it, rather than just the incident itself.
● **Do more than you need.** Create too many ideas rather than too few. This way you at least have the opportunity to select the best things for further development rather than scratching around for padding.

Performing plays

Performing plays immediately suggests public performances, costume, glamour, the smell of the grease paint, LIGHTS, MUSIC

. . . Well it might involve all that, but in most cases it's simply an extension of the creative process of making plays. Your intention may still not be to actually perform a finished piece in front of an audience, but to move on from generating material to selecting and developing it.

Prepared or polished improvisations are going to link in with this type of activity and give you the chance to inspect and evaluate what you are doing. By trying out things more than once you will see which skills need to be adopted or developed.

You may need to see samples of how others have tackled the same problems in order to give you an idea of how else it might be done. Rehearsing and even presenting extracts from plays written by others need not be an end in itself, but a way of understanding what drama can or can't do.

Performing plays demands that you are **selective** and **decisive**. To develop your ability here you need to:

● **Work as a group.** Try out ideas on each other to see if they make sense. Listen to each other and don't reject ideas out of hand even if at first they sound crazy – these may be the ones most likely to stretch the drama into new and original areas.
● **Don't talk forever.** You won't know whether or not ideas will work until you've tried them out. Remember, you will need to select the ideas that work and reject the ones that don't. If this is to be the case then all ideas will need testing.
● **Rehearse.** Just because it doesn't come right first time don't give up. Maybe the material is alright but you haven't got to grips with it yet.
● **Revise.** Don't be frightened of making changes in the material to suit you. Rewriting to take account of your own situation is likely to make a piece much more successful.
● **Reflect.** Think about what you're doing, how you're doing it and why. If you don't keep reminding yourself of what you are

trying to get out of your work you'll never know when you've got it.

Responding to plays

Any audience, whether it's for *Neighbours* or *Hamlet*, actively tries to respond to what is going on. This response focuses on two different things.

Firstly, the audience tries to simply understand

- what is going on?
- who's who?
- what are they doing?
- to whom are they doing it and why?

Secondly, they judge how effective the techniques of the story-telling are:

- are they good actors?
- is the story being told clearly enough?
- is there sufficient tension?
- is it good to watch?

People don't need to study drama to know that some of the things they watch are done well and work and other things are done badly and don't work. What studying drama will help people do though is pinpoint *why* things work or not.

If things don't work for you it may be because you don't much care for the content. On the other hand it may be that the problem is something to do with the form.

Once you have understood what can or can't be done in drama, you will be more able to make any content you find interesting work for an audience. By mastering form, your ideas and feelings can be shared through the making and putting on of plays.

Responding to drama might involve reviewing plays or each other's work, reading and analysing scripts or still images, researching how certain conventions and styles came about and in what circumstances they have been used.

Understanding and responding to drama

also requires an understanding of audiences. They may be sitting formally, watching a play, or they may be the other people involved in a group improvisation. An audience receives the masses of images thrown out by the drama and untangles them into something it can make sense of.

How does an audience do that?

Does everyone come out with the same idea or feeling about what the drama means?

If not, is there some special ingredient which is added inside each individual spectator?

Finding answers to these questions will involve discussing responses, comparing what you felt before and after, noting what your expectations were and what the drama reminded you of. There are no pieces of drama designed to be watched by anyone, anytime, anywhere. Drama is not naturally good or bad, it is only judged to be so by an audience.

Responding to drama involves constantly asking yourselves and each other questions about the different drama experiences you have.

- When you experience a piece of drama just exactly what do you see and hear?
- What meaning do you give to what you see and hear?
- What is there about what you see and hear which is encouraging you to give it that meaning?
- Where are you, and who are you with, as you see and hear those things? What effect does this have on the meanings you are giving them?
- What old experiences can you compare each new one with?
- In what way are your feelings developing?

By understanding your own position as an audience better, you will become more able to judge not just **whether** something is a good drama, but **why** you think it is, and how you can use that knowledge in your future work.

Key to icons used throughout the text

 Practical work

 Reflection

 Improvisation

 Written Tasks

 Activities

 Understanding the text

 Producing the scene

 Further development

One

Starting from where you are

The process of playmaking

This chapter looks at how plays tell stories.
It explores the meaning of the word TEXT and introduces the ideas of FOCUS, FRAMING and STRUCTURE.
A lot of the practical work uses comics and photo stories to help you see how visual images are used to communicate a NARRATIVE.

All of the resource material is linked by the theme of childhood.

Everyone's a playwright

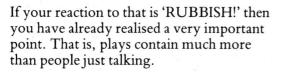

Writing plays must be really easy! After all, plays are only what people actually say. If you can talk yourself or listen to other people talking you must be able to write plays!

If your reaction to that is 'RUBBISH!' then you have already realised a very important point. That is, plays contain much more than people just talking.

So, if plays are not 'just' people talking, what are they?

As you work through the activities in this chapter, you will come to see that you already have the essential experience and ability to make plays of your own. You may already have been asked in creative writing work to 'write about what you know' or 'use your own experience'. The trouble is that it is often difficult to see anything particularly interesting about our own lives.

The practical work in this chapter will help you see how much potential there is in the common experience of childhood and growing up. It also shows how you can use that to start making plays.

 ## The Idea of 'Text'

You may be used to using the word 'text' to mean only written words. This book, for example, might be called a 'text' book as opposed to a picture book. Playmakers, however, know that there is a truth in the old saying that 'Every picture tells a story'. In drama the word 'text' can usefully describe everything that is seen and heard. In order to understand this important idea more fully, play the games below, then work through the activities on them.

BLOOD POTATO The group shut their eyes tight and the class teacher taps one person on the head. When she has done so she tells the group to start moving around carefully and quietly with their eyes shut tight. When players bump into each other they offer the pass word 'Potato'. However, the person who was tapped on the head will reply 'Blood Potato' – anyone receiving this reply dies an agonising and noisy death, opens their eyes and moves to the edge of the room. The aim of the 'Blood Potato' is, of course, to 'kill' everyone else by bumping into them. Variations might include 'Blood Christmas Pudding', 'Blood Easter Egg', 'Blood Chow Mein/ Lasagna etc' depending on the seasons or your taste!

GRANNY'S FOOTSTEPS One person (**A**) stands facing a wall at the end of the room. The rest of the group forms a line at the other end of the room and starts to slowly creep up on **A**. **A** may turn around at any time, and if he sees any of the group moving they are sent back to the start. If one of the group manages to get to **A** without being seen moving, that person takes his place.

> **WHAT'S THE TIME MR WOLF?** This is a variation on 'Granny's footsteps'. **A** stands facing a wall and the rest of the group starts creeping towards her slowly chanting 'What's the Time Mr Wolf', to which **A** replies 'One o'clock', 'Two o'clock' etc. The chanting goes on and the group get closer until, unexpectedly, **A** shouts 'DINNER TIME!', turns around and tries to catch one of the group who then replaces her as Mr Wolf.

Now work through these activities. Keep in mind the idea that you are exploring some of the basic ingredients of a play.

Games as text

1 A TV company has approached your school and asked for some help. They are recording a play and need to shoot some primary school children playing 'typical' games in the playground. Rather than take pot luck and simply record a real playground, they have asked your group to set up the scene so they can see what it might look like. As a whole class, make a list of as many 'kid's games' as you can.

2 Now imagine your room is the playground in a primary school, and you are the primary school children. Divide into smaller groups and set up some of the games on your list (use the games suggested above if you wish). Keep the improvisation going for at least five minutes without disturbing other people's games, and without adding any dialogue that isn't needed to play the game.

3 Discuss how well you think the scene will meet the TV company's purpose. Why do you think they chose not to simply go and record a real playground straight away? What might this say about the nature of plays?

4 Note down on a large sheet of paper all the ingredients that went into making the playground scene. Here are some examples.

- It involved people playing characters
- It contained some action
- It had a setting (the playground)

Display the list in a prominent position as you will need to refer to it later.

5 Go back into your small groups and discuss what the most exciting moment of your chosen game was. Play it again and freeze at the moment of greatest tension. For example, in 'What's the Time Mr Wolf?' it might be the moment Mr Wolf spins around and announces that it's 'Dinner Time'. In a play you might refer to this as the **climax**.

Songs as text

One key difference between 'real life' and life as it is shown in plays, is that in real life we never really know when the climax will be, or even if there is going to be one at all. In plays, the playmakers have already decided this. They arrange the text so as to keep the audience interested by building up to such moments.

6 The example below shows how one group of students used a children's song to create an unexpected and quite chilling scene. Working in pairs or small groups, remind yourselves of the sort of chants or songs you used to sing. Choose one as the basis for a scene. The only words spoken in the scene should be those in the song itself. You have to create images to show who the characters are and what they are up to.

> *(Three boys, lying down with chins in hands, looking very bored)*
>
> It's raining, it's pouring
> *(They look upwards, resentfully)*
> The old man is snoring
> *(As the next line is sung one of them clearly gets an idea and produces an axe)*
> He went to bed and BUMPED his head
> *(The other two cotton onto the idea. All three stand up, look up and grin evilly)*
> And couldn't get up in the morning.

Memories as a source for text

 By now you may be starting to see how the types of games and songs you used to play and sing can be a rich resource from which to make scenes. As a whole class, or in smaller groups, talk about your other childhood memories. You will find that once you start they will come flooding back, with each one reminding you of another.

- The day you lost your mummy at the shops
- Making dens in the woods
- Playing on the building site
- Getting into trouble with the neighbours
- Holiday disasters/adventures

7 Get into groups of three or four. Each member of the group selects just one memory and, in turns, places the other members of the group in a **tableau** of the clearest moment of the incident. A tableau is like a photograph of the 'climax' of the incident, but with real people 'frozen' in the picture. Don't join in the picture yourself but direct someone else to stand the way you think you stood in that incident. When you are satisfied with the picture, ask each actor to say what they think their character might be thinking about that situation. How do they feel about **you** as you are being played in the picture? How are they 'reading' the situation from their position? When each group member has directed a memory, discuss what problems you experienced in the exercise. Was it easy to see yourself from the outside?

8 Childhood memories can make effective poems as they tend to be very 'tight'. That is, the short text says a lot about the situation and people involved in it. Look at the following poem and use it as a basis for a scene in the same way as you did the children's songs. Alternatively, write a poem about the memory you used in the previous exercise, and develop that into a scene; or find one to use in an anthology. (A number of useful poetry anthologies are listed at the end of this chapter.) How are such scenes different from the original incident?

> Sometimes
> Dad would let me go into the loft with him.
> I'd be on a chair looking up
> He'd be astride the hole looking down.
> I'd reach up and grab his thick wrists
> He'd reach down and pull at my skinny arms.
>
> Dad said, "Only walk on the joists".
> I'd go for moon walks
> Grasping at the rafters
> Lurching across the crossbeams
> Longing to jump and disappear
> down through the plaster
> like a diver into murky depths.

Reflection

9 Think of some examples from films, plays or television which have used techniques like the ones above to produce a gripping or shocking climax.

What other devices are used to build tension? Examples might be the sudden 'freezing' of an image followed by a quick change of scene; or the use of background music which gradually builds up and is then suddenly cut.

In small groups, try to recall scenes from films and plays that you remember as being particularly effective. Discuss exactly what ingredients made them work so well.

10 How effective would your memories be as pieces of drama if they could be replayed *exactly* as they happened? For example, consider how long the original incident took. Would it be as exciting or tense for an onlooker as it was for you?

It's important to consider what an audience will read into a situation it witnesses. As playmakers you need to find ways not only of creating tension, but also showing the audience where that tension is coming from.

Visual Texts

When we look at pictures we respond in some way – even if it's just to dismiss it as unimportant and walk away. You have already seen how plays consist of a combination of what is seen and heard. In this section you will see more clearly how what you see can contain a meaning.

A picture is a 'text' which says something. If we want to make pictures affect other people in a particular way we need to understand **how** and **why** pictures affect people.

Look carefully at the picture below.

1 In pairs, talk about your initial feelings towards this picture. For example, which of the following statements would be true for you?

I like it

I don't like it

It reminds me of something

It reminds me of nothing

It makes me laugh/ cry/ feel angry

It doesn't do anything to me

Identifying your response to any 'text' is only the starting point for beginning to understand how the 'text' is working. What you need to do next is to 'deconstruct' it, that is, take it apart in order to identify each individual ingredient.

From *Worktown people: Photographs from Northern England 1937–38*

2 Answer the following questions about the photograph.

a How many people are in it?
b How are they dressed?
c Where are they standing?
d What are they doing?
e How many windows can you see?
f Are all the windows the same?
g List five other things that you can actually see in the photograph.

Separating what we actually see away from what we think we see is very difficult. It is tempting to say we see a factory, tyre marks, a wooden gate. However, we don't actually *know* that the building is a factory or that the marks are tyre marks.

3 Answer these questions, which are of a different nature.

a How old are the people in the picture?
b What sex are they?
c When was the photograph taken?
d What social class do the people come from?
e What is their relationship with each other?

Although you may not feel you can answer any of these precisely, use whatever evidence is available to arrive at a reasonable assumption.

If you used the caption above the photograph as evidence for your answers, you are doing no more or less than people do when they watch a play or film. You are assuming the words go with the pictures to create a particular meaning.

People 'read' texts in different ways. This allows us to constantly delight and surprise ourselves by seeing the world from a fresh viewpoint. An audience matches what it sees with its own past experiences and makes judgements on it accordingly.

4 Still working in pairs, write down on six separate pieces of paper, six people who you think may have very different reactions to this photograph. Fold the pieces of paper in half then swop them with another pair. Pick

one piece of paper each and improvise those two characters discussing the photograph as if it is being shown at an exhibition. Keep the improvisation going for just one minute, then refold the pieces of paper and pick another one each.

Improvise the conversations between four pairs of characters, then discuss

a why you think the characters reacted as they did to the picture
b how they seemed to react to each other.

Pictures as stories

If 'every picture tells a story' then clearly sequences of pictures can be used to do the same thing. Plays and films work in exactly this way.

5 Imagine that the photograph on p 5 was part of an exhibition called *Childhood: Pain and Wonder*. In pairs or small groups, position yourselves as if you are in one of the other photographs in the exhibition which show incidents of childhood. Write out an appropriate title on a piece of card and stand behind it. Each group takes a turn looking around the exhibition (don't take too long) and chooses one they are particularly interested in.

When each group has chosen someone else's picture to work on, discuss what there is in the chosen picture that gives you a clue as to what might have happened **before** it and **after** it. You have to create two other images, one which comes before your chosen picture, one which comes after it. After five minutes to prepare, each group presents a short sequence of photographs which will tell a story by showing a scene before the incident, the incident itself and after the incident.

6 In pairs, look carefully at the cartoons on the next two pages. As you can see, the speech balloons have been removed and the order has been deliberately jumbled up. Use whatever evidence you can find in the drawings to suggest

a the 'right' order (jot down the numbers on a piece of paper)
b the story that is being told.

Compare your decisions with another group.

Reflection

 7 In both tasks above, it is very likely that your group constructed stories in a different way to other members of the class. Did you have to guess the meaning of what you were looking at? Or did it appear to be immediately clear to you? If so, how do you account for the fact that others saw it differently?

There are no right answers to questions like these. They remind us that no matter how clearly we think we are putting a message across, others may think we are saying something quite different. Only by taking account of their interpretations can we hope to make our work clearer.

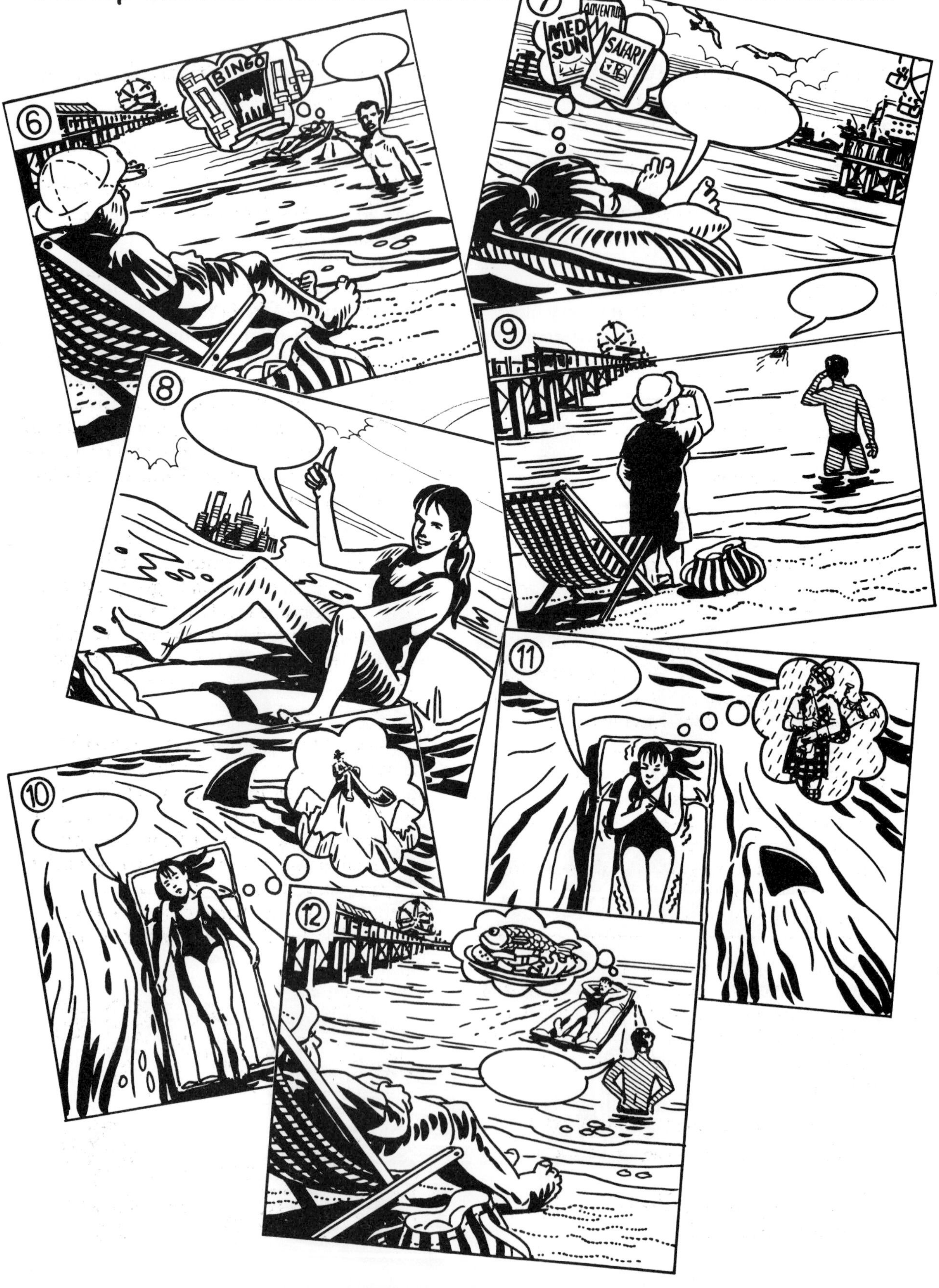
BINGO
MED SUN
SAFARI

C Treatments and Storyboards

Before launching into writing the dialogue for a play or film, the writer will often produce something called a **treatment**. Given that he will have a fairly clear idea in his mind about the basic theme he wishes to explore, the **treatment** shows how he will bring that alive. It will outline

a the plot
b the sort of characters involved.

In other words, it shows how the writer intends to **treat** his chosen theme.

Treating a story

Work through the following activities in sequence. They involve some writing but you may wish to try improvising bits of the story as you go along to see how well they will work.

1 In small groups, devise a very simple story involving no more than four characters. Write down the story in note form like the following example.

> Jane wakes up with a headache after a party the night before.
> She realises that she has slept too long and will be late for work.
> Just as she is getting dressed she sees, to her horror, a pair of man's feet sticking out from under the bed.

2 When you have written your story, set yourself the task of telling it in no more than 20 still pictures. Use your written notes as a guide but write out a more detailed sequence of pictures. Our example might go as follows:

1. Jane's hand reaching out for the alarm clock
2. Close-up of Jane holding her head.
3. Jane holding clock, hand to her mouth in despair.
4. Jane getting out of bed and pulling on dressing gown. In the background we see the feet.
5. Jane has noticed the feet and is screaming.

3 Imagine that your notes are going to be passed on to someone else who will make them into a film. What further details do you think they will need to get a clear idea of what the characters are like and how the plot develops? Write notes on character and plot for the film-maker.

Film-makers tend to take the idea of a treatment one stage further and make a **storyboard**. Before actually going out and spending money on real film, they will make simple drawings showing what will appear in each scene and from what angle they intend to see it. An example is shown on the next page.

4 Look at the notes you have made so far. Divide a sheet of paper into squares of approximately 50 mm × 50 mm (if you have an A4 sheet simply fold it into 16 rectangles) and draw sketches of the still pictures you described in your notes. Stick-figures will be fine, though you need to find a way of distinguishing one character from another. This is what the story about Jane might look like.

417o

Hitchcock cuts to a single crow behind Melanie perched on the jungle-jim. This is a scene that Melanie is not aware of, but the audience is.

417D

Camera moves in a little closer on Melanie and watches her smoke.

417E

Cut to scene behind Melanie. Now there are five crows . . . the audience gets worried.

417F

Back to Melanie, a little closer.

417G   5 MORE CROWS — TOTAL OF 10-

Cut back to the jungle-jim. Now there are ten crows. The audience is scared.

417H — HOLD FOR 20 OR 30 FEET.

Close-up of Melanie. The camera holds on her for twenty or thirty feet of film allowing the imagination of the audience to add more crows to the jungle-jim at the pace Hitchcock has established.

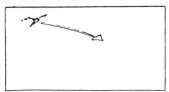

418

Cut to single crow in the sky.

420

Shot of crow flying over building.

421

Melanie watches the crow and turns to see . . .

422

Jungle-jim is now loaded with crows. The screen that was light and empty is now filled with black crows.

423 CAMERA WHIPS UP AS MELANIE LEAPS TO HER FEET

Close-up of Melanie as she leaps to her feet with shock showing on her face.

424

Closer in on the crows.

425

Tight close-up of Melanie, totally horrified.

426

Tight close-up on birds.

Focusing and framing

5 Look again at the storyboard opposite and, of course, your own. Each individual image is set in a **frame**. Imagine you are making a film from your own storyboard. In your groups, list five things that you want to appear in just one of the frames and a further five that **should** logically be somewhere near, yet you are choosing not to include. For example, in our story about Jane an audience must see:

a bed   the floor by the bed   an alarm clock

a hook on which is hung her dressing gown

a pair of shoes protruding from under the bed

What an audience will not necessarily see yet one can assume is there might include:

bedroom door   wardrobe

dressing table

Framing an image is as important on the stage as it is in films. A simple way of understanding how it works is as follows.

a Hold your arms out wide and look straight forward.
b Waggle your fingers.

Can you see them? If you have normal sight you will be aware of the movement of your fingers even though they span a whole 180° from the centre of your sight. This is called **peripheral vision**. We receive information about the world not only from what we look at directly, but also from what we see on the periphery (which is just as well, or even more of us would be run down by cars!)

c Now cup your hands around your eyes so you can only see straight forward.

That is what you see in a film because that is what a camera lens sees – limited, isn't it? The same process of selection works in theatre though perhaps not in such an obvious way.

Look at the 'Jane' storyboard and you will see that
- we are seeing the story as if we are in the same room as Jane
- although we can see her she cannot see us
- Jane is the character we are most interested in.

An audience will see Jane's story in a sequence of images which have been selected by the play/film-maker. The audience will be given the **frame**.

What is actually in the frame helps us to **focus** our attention, because it removes a great many other things that the writer or director don't feel are important to the theme they are dealing with. In the story above the focus is Jane's reactions.

6 Look carefully at your storyboard. What or who is the **focus** of each individual frame? Is this true of the whole story?

Write, discuss or improvise your story but try to make a different character the focus; tell it from their point of view. For example, what would the story be if we focused on how the person got under the bed? What would we need to put into each frame then?

By **focus** we refer to what the story is actually concentrating on, what it wishes to draw our attention to.

By **frame** we refer to the selection of things the audience is being shown.

D Selecting the Words

Plays are not simply reported conversations. What is seen has been carefully selected – it has a focus. An audience's attention is drawn to that focus by carefully placing it in a frame. This is not only true for what is seen, it is also true for what is heard.

 1 Look back at the jumbled cartoon frames on pages 7–8. Either look back at your notes on the 'correct' order in which they ought to appear, or if you haven't already done the question, tackle it now. In small groups, improvise the story following the sequence of actions. **Add** whatever you think the appropriate words should be. You will need to try this several times in order to make the improvisation flow. Once you are satisifed that the story is working, try to cut down on the number of words actually spoken so that only relatively few words will fit into each **frame**.

Conversations

Conversations in plays take place within a specific frame. Try out the following improvisations, to discover what type of conversations would take place within the frame suggested.

2 In pairs, improvise a conversation between two first-year pupils at the 'Big School' on their first day. They have both heard a number of things about the school and now are standing in the playground waiting to be told what to do next.

3 Stay in the same pair but imagine that you are two parents who have accompanied their children (the same children as in **2**) to the new school. You have seen them through the gate and are now watching, through the wire fence, to see what will happen to them next. You start chatting to your partner. Assume you don't know each other.

4 Still in the same pairs, imagine you are the older brother or sister of the two new children. What will you say as you stand in a classroom overlooking the playground with your best friend?

While such conversations might reveal something about the characters and the situation, the **focus** isn't immediately clear in any of them. If these were scenes in a play, what aspects of going to a new school would we want the audience to concentrate on?

5 Replay the three scenes above but at some point in the improvisation the school's most violent and renowned bully starts to approach the two new children (the bully does not actually need to appear in the scene). Make a mental note of what effect this has on the conversation as you improvise. Keep the improvisation going for two minutes then discuss the differences between it and the original one where there was no focus. Was it easier? More interesting? Were there possibilities for further scenes and the development of a story?

Decide on one thing that might have happened next and improvise the resulting conversation. For example, having hit one of the little kids, the bully is confronted by an angry parent. Keep the scene short.

6 The appearance of the bully should instantly focus the work on the problem of bullying in schools. Invent another particular incident which would shift the focus onto a different aspect of arriving at a new school. Improvise a scene again with its new focus and then invent two scenes which would follow it. Each scene need only be very short.

SPECIAL ASSIGNMENT

The practical work so far in this unit has been concerned with

> **treatments**
> **storyboards**
> **framing**
> **focus**

This special assignment will show you how you can use these ideas to create, rehearse and record a **photo story**.

On the next two pages you will see an example of how a photo story is written first as a script, and then 'realised' in pictures.

The example is an extract from a longer story especially prepared to show certain aspects of the typical photo story.

Look carefully at how each picture is framed.

Consider who the focus of the story is.

Look at the style being used for the characters' facial expressions, poses and words.

Would you agree that this is a 'typical' example of a photo story? Discuss your ideas with others in the class.

Now, as a whole class or in smaller groups:

a Devise a story on the theme of **childhood**.

b Write a **treatment** for the story which will show what aspects of childhood you intend to **focus** on.

c Draw a **storyboard** limiting yourself to 24 **frames**.

d Make notes on any important items that will appear in each frame.

e Write out what words will be printed on the frames as shown in the example.

f Take the photographs as outlined in the storyboard. Don't rush this task. Set up each frame carefully and, if possible, take a second picture after leaving a short interval. This will act as insurance in case one of the shots doesn't come out. The two shots will probably be slightly different; it's always useful to have a choice as one might be a little better than the other.

g Mount the developed photographs onto a sheet of card. Draw out speech balloons on white paper and either write neatly or type the dialogue and captions on before cutting them out and sticking them onto the photographs.

h Write a report on the project outlining the process you have been through and commenting on how effective you think your final photo story is.

Reflection

 What particular difficulties did you encounter in this project? Were they to do with

> Organisation   Materials   Storyline
> Time   Money?

If you could do the whole thing again, what changes would you make?

The Last Scene

FRAME ONE:	Stage Dressing Room. A few people are putting on stage make-up and costume etc. Dave's head is poking round the door.
CAPTION:	Curtain up in fifteen minutes.
DAVE:	Break a leg everyone. Just keep your minds on the job.
FRAME TWO:	Close-up of Katie looking glum.
CAPTION:	But that was easier said than done for Katie...
KATIE:	(thinks) It's OK for him - he doesn't have to kiss Nick in the last scene.
FRAME THREE:	Katie in the foreground having a last look over her lines. Nick and Lynn in the background holding each other affectionately.
KATIE:	(thinks) And to think how confident I was...
LYNN:	Good luck, Nick. Uncle Alan is a TV producer - I've told him to watch out for you.
FRAME FOUR:	Katie and Nick, outside a theatre, looking at a poster saying 'AUDITIONS - NEW FACES NEEDED'.
CAPTION:	"...six weeks ago."
NICK:	Come on, Katie, you're really good at acting.
KATIE:	But you've never been on stage.

FRAME FIVE: Nick and Katie looking sweetly at each other.

NICK: I'll be a Romeo to your Juliet. Besides, I want to keep an eye on you - I've heard about these backstage romances.

FRAME SIX: In rehearsal. Dave is directing Nick and Katie. They look very happy.

CAPTION: "Those first few rehearsals went so well..."

DAVE: That's great, Katie -just right. Now then, Nick, all you do to finish the play is kiss her.

NICK: My pleasure, boss!

FRAME SEVEN: Close-up of Lynn watching Nick and Katie kissing.

LYNN: Lucky girl. She's got the part I wanted and the boy. Maybe I should write my own private last scene...

FRAME EIGHT: Lynn and Nick in the foreground walking away from the stage. Dave and Katie behind: Katie looking after the departing Nick.

CAPTION: "...until Lynn started 'directing' Nick."

DAVE: You've got a good future ahead of you, Katie.

KATIE: Hmmm!

LYNN: Let me know if you want some help rehearsing that last bit, Nick!

NICK: Yeah, maybe I will!

STUDY EXTRACT ONE
Falstaff

If any theme can be treated in an infinite number of ways, we need to find ways of

a recognising clearly the ingredients of the theme (**deconstructing** it, perhaps)

b selecting those bits that interest us the most and seem to deserve further exploration.

This extract is from Robert Nye's novel *Falstaff*. Falstaff is a character in three of Shakespeare's plays. He is an unruly, overfed, comical and at times offensive man. The novel is written as if it is the diary of his thoughts in the last 100 days of his life. In this extract he is picking out his memories of childhood.

When I was a boy I plucked geese. It was like plucking the sky – a snow of snapt feathers everywhere. I played truant as well. Of course. Lord God! Who didn't? Who doesn't? And I whipped top. So hard and fast they must be still spinning – furious little rainbows in the corner of the granary. Nor did I escape being whipped myself. I liked dances and robins and candles and carols, and to hear minstrels tune their violas da gamba while the snow was falling outside from a night sky prickled with stars.

I made a paper boat with sails. My coat and shirts got soaking wet in a brook. My hat drifted away. For two miles I chased it. But it went into the sea.

I made a feather fly down the wind. I struck another feather in my belt, like a lawyer's quill. I set more feathers in a ring about my cap, making a crown. I was the emperor of grey-goose-feather country.

When I went to bed at night I pulled up patchwork covers to my chin and lay and listened to the stars falling into the waterbutt in our yard.

I rode on my father's boot.

I played at King Arthur and St George and the dragon and Gog and Albion and Robin Hood and all the English games. I played at marbles and Heads and Tails and Pinch Me and Follow the Leader.

I had a swing that my father made for me in the old barn, and I would swing and swing higher in the oaty air of summer, until the edge of Norfolk tilted and was gone, and I was over the thin line of green and out out out into the blue.

I was more like a monkey than a boy.

I used to sift mud from the Hundred River with a sieve. I was looking for gold.

And I had these many-coloured shells, brought to me inland by a sailor travelling home from Yarmouth, and I'd listen to the talk of the seven seas in them. The seas spoke of treasure and of dead men's bones.

I remember a day spent teaching grasses in my thumbs to hoot like an owl when I blew through them.

One hot afternoon I hid in an empty beehive to cool. Thieves came and took the heaviest beehive they could find, thinking to have the most honey. But their honey was me. I came out buzzing and they jumped the gate.

When I caught butterflies, I tied threads to them. Then, with the threads on my fingers, I would run through the meadows with a cloud of butterflies fluttering behind me.

I had a little oven of four tiles where I baked mud pies. And I liked to plunge my hand in the sand: making tunnels. And I told the time by a dandelion clock.

I flew a kite from a hill above the sea. It was like holding a plug plugged into the sky. The sky was trying to get away but my kite string held it.

I had a stick which I dressed with a scarlet trailing coat and it was my horse and I called him Roan Barbary.

My cap was my helmet when it was not my crown. Sometimes, when the girls from Runham came to the barn, I would take off my shirt and fight with the other boys, and we would hit each other with our caps, because the girls looked on. We played at Hide and Seek. I remember when I found little Margaret in the linen basket and climbed in with her in the dark.

1 Divide into small groups. Each member of the group should choose one idea from the extract that he or she thinks seems to have been a particularly important part of Falstaff's boyhood.

Having decided on a different one each, form them into a short sentence which begins 'Boyhood is . . .'. For example,

'Boyhood is making paper boats
falling into streams
chasing your cap'

Help each other to create a visual image for each chosen line. It may be a still image or involve some movement. The aim is to show clearly **what** Falstaff is remembering.

Find a way of linking the images together and presenting them.

2 Developing from the same technique, use your own ideas to create a presentation in which each line starts 'Girlhood is . . .'.

3 As a whole class discuss the different images that seem appropriate to 'Boyhood' as captured in the extract, and 'Girlhood' as you have seen it. Pool your ideas to make a presentation in which each line starts with 'Childhood is . . .'.

Improvisation

4 In pairs or small groups, choose any of the incidents which Falstaff remembers and use them as the basis of a scene to show what effect Falstaff had on other people in his childhood.

5 As Falstaff lies dying in his bed, the ghosts of characters from his childhood visit him. In groups, devise a scene illustrating what they might say and what his reaction would be. You may have seen or read a version of *A Christmas Carol* in which Scrooge is visited by the ghosts of Christmas Past, Present and Future. Each of them teaches Scrooge a little about himself. You could use this idea to help your own scene about Falstaff.

6 Imagine a female equivalent to the young Falstaff. Devise a scene which shows what the reaction of other people would have been to her. You may or may not choose to actually show the character in your scene.

Written tasks

7 Present any of the ideas for improvisations above as playscripts or use them as the basis for a short story.

8 Convert the extract into a treatment for a short film.

9 Write the last entry in Falstaff's diary before he dies.

F Structure

Making up stories for writing or improvisation at the drop of a hat is extremely difficult. Even when we have tapped a resource for ideas such as our own childhood and found a number of starting points, the problem often remains of how to **structure** the idea so that it can be communicated. To see what is meant by structure and how important it is, work through the following exercises.

1 ONE WORD STORIES Sit in a large circle. One person starts by saying the first word that comes into their head. The person on their right simply has to add another word which might follow in a story. Keep the story going for at least three rounds of the circle. Don't tell the person next to you what to say, just try to make the story make sense.

VARIATIONS on this game include

a telling one word stories in pairs
b allowing people to carry on for a couple of sentences – but they must finish half way through a sentence, so that the next person has to finish it off before adding their own ideas
c working in small groups and acting out the story as you are making it up.

After trying out one or more of these exercises discuss whether the story **made sense**, and whether it was **complete**.

2 THREE CHARACTERS As a whole class, decide on the types of characters typically found in fairy tales. Examples are

A King	A handsome Prince
A wicked witch	An orphan
A dragon	A goblin

and so on.

Write each one on a separate piece of paper and fold it (make sure there are at least the same number of characters as members of the class). Divide into groups of three and pick a piece of paper each. Give yourselves five minutes to devise and improvise a 'typical' fairy story using those three characters.

a In what way were they 'typical' fairy stories?
b What ingredients let them down as fairy stories?

3 INSTANT WRITING Work on your own.
a Take a sheet of paper and have a pen ready.
b Forget everything that you have read so far or done today and think instead of a bunch of bananas.
c You must remain completely silent for this exercise.
d After you have thought silently of bananas for two minutes the teacher will say GO!
e Fill the paper in front of you with dialogue. Stop either when you have filled the paper or after a maximum of 5 minutes.
f Do not write your name on the paper but simply put the number of characters which appear and hand in the papers.

Before moving on to using these scripts practically you may wish to discuss how easy or difficult you found this exercise, what sort of ideas came to you and whether or not you feel you have written a successful 'play'.

The common failing with stories generated in this way is that they tend to start full of promise and excitement but then fizzle away to nothing or drift into utter confusion and senselessness. The enjoyment created by them is short-lived as it becomes meaningless.

Structuring the ideas involves making the frame and focus clearer by selecting and ordering the images. If this is not achieved an audience will not understand what they are watching/listening to, and they will become bored. The following exercises provide an opportunity to see how you can structure your ideas.

4 Get into either pairs, threes or fours and collect one of the scripts produced in Task 3 (INSTANT WRITING). It must have the right number of parts for your group and should not have been written by anyone in your group. Attempt to act the script out **without** changing any of the words or stage directions.

a After a maximum of ten minutes' preparation time, share the work.

b Discuss the differences between what the writer imagined as she wrote and what the actors imagined as they tried to put it into practice. It is important to bear in mind that these were written and rehearsed ridiculously quickly. The purpose of this discussion **shouldn't** be to criticise the writing or interpretation.

c Get back into groups and add whatever you think is necessary to structure the piece so that it makes a clearer point. As far as possible try not to change the sense or atmosphere of the script.

STUDY EXTRACT TWO
Gentleman Jim

The extract printed on the next page comes from a book by the writer/artist Raymond Briggs. It tells the story of Jim Bloggs who has spent his whole working life as a lavatory attendant. Now middle-aged, he has come to realise that 'There's not much opportunity for self-advancement in toilets' and starts to scan the newspaper to see what else he might do. Look at the picture carefully, then answer the questions on it.

a Describe what Jim thinks life in the Commandos is like. What is it in the picture which shows this most clearly?

b Where do you suppose Jim has got his ideas from? Why do you think this?

c What other information is captured in the cartoon about Jim and his life?

d How does the artist distinguish between Jim's real life and his daydreams?

Practical work

1 In groups of no more than five, devise a way of structuring the images and words in the cartoon in a way that can be acted out. You will need to consider

a the order in which you speak the words

b a way of moving from reality to daydream then back again

c a way of focusing the audience's attention on key images.

You may add whatever movement and sound effects you wish, but try not to add too many more lines.

2 Invent another daydream for Jim in which he imagines what it would be like to have one of the other jobs advertised in the paper. Structure your scene so that it shows

a what he imagines the job to involve

b where he may have got that idea from

c how it would compare with an element of his life at the minute.

H STUDY EXTRACT THREE
Oh dear what can the matter be?

Oh dear what can the matter be? was devised by three women who wanted to help some teenage girls they were working with say something about how they saw their lives so far. The result illustrates that you don't have to look very far to find stories and themes which need commenting on.

The play is set, like *Gentleman Jim*, in a lavatory. This time, though, it is in a school where the girls are, for different reasons, skiving lessons. Each of them has a story to tell, an aspect of teenage life that is causing them some distress. In between conversations through which the girls get to know each other a little better, their individual stories are acted out by the others.

This extract is a complete episode in the play and tells one girl's personal story.

CHARACTERS

HELEN Quite a shy girl who has a bit of a reputation as a swot.

BARBARA A girl with a glamorous image to live up to. Outwardly confident but in fact not really happy with her image.

TRACEY Kind, honest and open – sometimes, particularly when she is with boys, she feels this to be a disadvantage.

HELEN I have to stay in at night because my mam works and I have to look after my little brother.
BARBARA What about your dad?
HELEN He's a taxi driver, he works at night too.
TRACEY Haven't you got a twin brother?
HELEN Yea, but he doesn't have to stay in.
TRACEY That's not fair.

HELEN Too right it's not. But me mam and dad say I have to do it, because he's a lad and wouldn't be able to look after kids. So he goes out every night and I have to stay in.
BARBARA You should put your foot down, tell your mum and dad that you've both got to share it.
HELEN I've tried, but me dad says he'd rather I stayed in the house anyway then he knows where I am. Oh it's hopeless. It's always been like that from the day we were born . . .

(HELEN becomes a narrator, TRACEY and BARBARA become the twins)

NARRATOR Once upon a time, Mr and Mrs Walton had baby twins, a pretty little girl called Helen and a handsome little boy called Tony. Helen was given a lovely pink bonnet, and Tony a nice blue helmet. Helen and Tony played nicely together.

(TONY and YOUNG HELEN play – TONY hits HELEN)

NARRATOR Tony, don't be so rough with Helen. Remember she's a little girl. There now Helen, don't cry. Now play together like nice children.
(They play again, YOUNG HELEN hits TONY)

NARRATOR Helen, that's very naughty, Little girls don't do things like that. Tony, sit up like a big boy, don't cry.
One day Tony was given a shiny red car and Helen was given a pretty dolly.

(They play for a while but watch each other)

YOUNG HELEN Can I play with your car?
TONY Can I play with your dolly?

(They swop and play happily)

NARRATOR Then they swopped their toys, silly billies, and mummy and daddy laughed. They told Helen and Tony that boys couldn't play with dollies and girls couldn't play with cars.
TONY But I liked playing with the dolly.
NARRATOR Don't be stupid, Tony, only softies play with dolls. You don't want to be a cissy do you?

YOUNG HELEN I want to help fix the car.

TONY Well you can't, you've got to do the dishes and then bake a nice cake for our tea.

YOUNG HELEN But I want to fix the car.

TONY Well you can't 'cos you're a girl and girls can't fix cars, only boys can.

YOUNG HELEN But boys can do dishes.

TONY No they can't 'cos dishes are soft and stupid and cissy, and boys don't do soft and stupid and cissy things, only girls do.

YOUNG HELEN Dishes aren't soft and stupid and cissy. You wouldn't like it if you had to eat off a dirty plate.

TONY I don't care, I can fix the car.

NARRATOR One day Tony and Helen were watching the television and *The Professionals* was on. When it was finished they played a great game.

TONY Bang Bang You're dead. Bang Bang Ow Ow I've been shot in the leg. Quick, Helen, come and help me.

YOUNG HELEN Be quiet, I'm playing at nurses.

TONY But I've been injured. You can come and nurse me.

YOUNG HELEN Oh, alright then. (*Examining him*) Hmmm, I'll have to give you a blood transfusion.

TONY A what?

YOUNG HELEN It's alright, it'll make you feel better. Hmmm, there's complications. I'm going to have to amputate.

TONY WHAT!

YOUNG HELEN Don't worry, it's a simple operation.

TONY Operation? You'd better get a doctor then.

YOUNG HELEN I am a doctor.

TONY No you're not, you're a nurse.

YOUNG HELEN I'm a doctor, I've just qualified.

TONY No you're not. You're a girl so you can only be a nurse.

YOUNG HELEN I can be a doctor.

TONY No you can't.

YOUNG HELEN Yes I can (No you can't/Yes I can etc)

NARRATOR Children, children, stop arguing.

YOUNG HELEN But he says I can't be a doctor.

NARRATOR What's wrong with being a nurse, Helen?

YOUNG HELEN Nothing, but I want to amputate his . . .

NARRATOR Well, be a good girl then and just be a nurse.

When they were older, mummy brought in a lovely surprise . . . a baby brother. Helen had practised putting nappies on her dolly so she was a great help to mummy. Daddy and Tony were pleased and they tried their best to keep out of mummy's, Helen's and the baby's way.

TONY And they all lived happily ever after.

HELEN Except me, 'cos I have to stay in every bloody night.

Understanding the text

1 Whose story is being told in this extract?

2 What specific aspect of growing up do you think the writers of this script are focusing on?

3 What reasons do Helen's mum and dad give to explain why they treat Helen and her twin brother differently?

4 Find three incidents in the story which illustrate how adults treat boys and girls differently as they grow up.

5 Find another three examples which seem to suggest that little girls are in some way inferior to little boys.

6 Why do you think Helen becomes the Narrator of the story rather than playing herself in it? What does this tell the audience about the story?

Producing the scene

7 This extract is similar in many ways to the *Gentleman Jim* one shown earlier in that the audience is taken from the real world into a different dimension and then brought back to earth with a bump (compare Helen's last line with the way Jim snaps out of his daydream). How could the actresses playing these parts use their voices and movement to make this switch into and out of the fantasy clearer?

8 What lighting or sound effects could be used which would also help the audience understand that the story isn't really happening?

9 Make a list of all the props that might be needed in order to play this scene. Discuss the advantages and disadvantages of actually using props and just miming them.

10 The scene attempts to show, through specific incidents, why Helen and her brother lead different lives as teenagers. Read through it again and imagine that it is to be retold as a photo story. Pick six key incidents and in groups of three devise a pose for each one. Think back to the work on visual images and make each pose clearly show how the children's lives are developing, their attitudes towards each other and their parents' attitude (as shown through the Narrator) towards them.

Improvisation

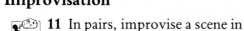

11 In pairs, improvise a scene in which Helen's mum and dad are talking about her. She has recently been questioning their decisions and demanding the same freedoms as her brother. How do you, her parents, feel about this and what explanations can you find for her behaviour and attitude?

12 What other expectations do you think adults have of children generally? Make a list of the ones which annoy you most and create a way of showing each one visually. Try to structure these images into a presentation which illustrates your annoyance. You may wish to add dialogue or a sequence of lines which fit the images.

13 In *Oh dear what can the matter be?* Barbara's story focuses on the pressures put on teenagers to be trendy and attractive.

Tracey's story recounts the embarrassments and disappointments of finding a boy/girlfriend. Using one of these themes as a focus, or finding another of your own, devise a scene which will show an audience the pressures of growing up as you see them.

Written tasks

14 Use the idea in Question 12 as the basis for a piece of script. Add stage directions which will clearly indicate what visual images you feel should be used with the lines. Look back at the photo story on pages 14–15 for more help with this.

15 Write out a script for either the whole or an extract from the scene you devised in Question 13. You may find it useful to give the script to another group to rehearse. You can then compare what you created with the meanings and interpretations that they find in it.

16 Imagine Helen and her twin brother have both been asked to write a short piece entitled *Childhood: the happiest days of your life?* Both Helen and Tony choose to write about the same incident. How would their pieces differ? Write the two pieces.

Reflection

17 The work in this chapter has focused on images of childhood. It's a common theme in books and films but what are your opinions about how children are depicted in fiction?

18 Neither *Gentleman Jim* nor *Oh dear what can the matter be?* tell a story in a straightforward way. Both jump through time and space to mix present reality with fantasy and memory. Can you think of other stories that work in this way? What are some of the advantages and disadvantages of structuring stories like this?

19 When you next watch a film or see a play, try to pay some attention not only to the story being told but also to the way it is being told. Consider which character it seems to be focusing on and ask why certain things are being picked out for special attention (the camera, for example, may keep dwelling on a particular object). Is the story told in the correct sequence or does it use flashbacks? How does it build tension?

Being aware of these techniques will not spoil the story – if anything, they will help you appreciate it more.

Further Reading

Plays

Gregory's Girl by Bill Forsyth and Andrew Bethell (Cambridge University Press).   This is an adaptation for the stage of the well-known comedy film about teenage love.
P'tang, Yang, Kipperbang by Jack Rosenthal (Longman).   A funny and charming play about a 1950s schoolboy infatuated with a classmate.
Blue Remembered Hills by Denis Potter (Faber).   A TV play which mixes nostalgia about childhood with a reminder about children's natural cruelty to each other. The play is unusual in that the children's parts are played by adults.
The Golden Pathway Annual by John Harding and John Burrows (Heinemann).   A very funny play with a sting in its tail about growing up through the 1960s.
Spring Awakening by Frank Wedekind (Methuen).   This is a challenging play that was denied public performance for many years because of its subject of sex and the adolescent.
Our Day Out by Willy Russell (Methuen).   A hugely successful TV play, since turned into a stage play with music, about a school outing in which the kids teach one of the teachers something about himself.
They Said You Were Too Young by Rony Robinson (Hodder & Stoughton).
A collection of plays about teenage life.
Stronger than Superman by Roy Kift (Ambert Lane Press).   A play about how a disabled boy is accepted.
Dirty Rascals by Leeds TIE in *6 Tie Programmes* edited by Christine Redington (Methuen).   This play explores the relationship between three young children from different racial backgrounds.

Poetry

Mind your own business, Wouldn't you like to know and *You tell me* by Michael Rosen (Puffin).   Collections of poems, generally written for and about children.
'Little Johnny's Confession' and 'Schoolboy' by Brian Patten in *The Mersey Sound* (Penguin).
Timothy Winters by Charles Causley (Penguin).

Fiction

The Destructors (in *Twenty-one Stories*) Graham Greene (Penguin)
The Go-between L.P. Hartley (Penguin)
No End to Yesterday Shelagh MacDonald (André Deutsch)
Bilgewater Jane Gardam (Hamish Hamilton)
Goldengrove Jill Paton Walsh (Macmillan)
The true story of Spit McPhee James Aldridge (Viking Kestrel)
I'll go my own way Mollie Hunter (Hamish Hamilton)
The Nature of the Beast Janni Howker (Julia MacRae)
Isaac Campion Janni Howker (Julia MacRae)
Joby Stan Barstow (Heinemann)
Buddy Nigel Hinton (Puffin)
Forever Judy Blume (Piccolo)
I'm the King of the Castle Susan Hill (Penguin)
Memory Margaret Mahy (Dent)
The Scarecrows Robert Westall (Puffin)
Northern Lights Philip Pullman (Point).

PROJECT ONE
Improvisation

This project explores what the activity called IMPROVISATION might include.

It shows how a number of techniques and resources can be used to generate practical drama work.
The work is concerned with IMAGINATION and CO-OPERATION. A guide is given on how to EVALUATE your own, and other people's, improvisations.

The theme of childhood is continued and developed.

Improvisation means making do with what is immediately to hand rather than using something prepared and planned. Most of your practical work in drama requires you to do this.

The final content and success of an **improvisation** depends on your ability to

- think quickly
- work together
- listen and watch carefully
- be open to the suggestions of others
- not **try** to be clever or funny
- above all, **accept** what your own imagination seems to tell you.

A good improviser tends to rely on his feelings and what seems to come naturally. There is often a temptation in improvisation work to try hard to be funny. Improvisations can of course be enormously entertaining but trying to use comedy can seriously limit the real use of improvisations as a way of exploring situations and characters. Being clever or funny may not feel right or be appropriate.

This Project focuses on some of the ways you can use improvisations to explore a wider subject. The ideas follow on from the theme of childhood and growing up in Chapter One.

A Generating Ideas

The most useful resources in any improvisation is your imagination.
Try the following ways of exercising your imagination to help you get used to accepting what it throws at you.

1 WORD ASSOCIATION Sit in a circle. One person says a word
CHILDREN
the person on their right must say the first thing that comes into their mind as a result of hearing the first word
KIDS
the next person adds a word
GOATS
and so on. Don't worry if you think your idea won't make sense to other people – the important thing is to **accept** what you thought of.

2 BRAINSTORM Working as a whole group, try to list all the things that come into your mind using the same word as a starting point, eg
CHILDREN
might produce a list which includes
NAPPIES   TEDDY
FIRST DAY AT SCHOOL
PLAYING   PARTIES

3 THE MAGIC OBJECT Sitting in a circle, one person starts by holding up an object, for example, a large child's crayon, and says what else it might be.
It's a heel from a high heeled shoe
She passes it to the next person who declares that it is actually something quite different and so on.
It's a unicorn's horn
It's a fang from a sabre tooth tiger
It's a telegraph pole from Lilliput
Keep it going for at least two rounds trying to be as fast as possible.

Other resources

Absolutely anything can be used to start an improvisation. Be on the lookout for things which strike you as odd/funny/remarkable/sad/suspicious.

Look, for example, at these things in newspapers.

ADVERTISEMENTS   OBITUARIES
WEDDING NOTICES   LETTERS
SPORTS REPORTS
PERSONAL COLUMN

Sunday magazines often have useful and interesting photographs.

Watch television programmes that you wouldn't normally watch.

Read books, comics and magazines that you wouldn't normally touch.

Talk to people about aspects of their lives that you don't see.

4 Look at these headlines, for example. In small groups choose one of them and with no more than ten minutes' preparation time, re-enact the story that led to the headline being written.

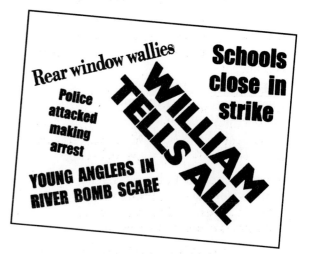

Games themselves are not improvisations but playing them can
● exercise your imagination
● help you work with the rest of the group.

More importantly they can be used to start improvisations by using the same actions in a different situation. For example, try to develop these ideas.

> **5** THE KEEPER OF THE KEYS One person shuts her eyes and sits on a chair in the middle of a circle. Underneath the chair is a bunch of keys. Other players take it in turns to try to steal the keys without being caught by the keeper.

Where might this game be set? A castle, a prison, a bank?

Who are the people in the scene? A giant and some children whom he intends to have for breakfast, a guard and some prisoners of war, a security guard and some robbers?

How might the group plan the theft? What happens next?

6 Working in small groups, choose another common game and use it as the basis for an improvisation simply by deciding where it is taking place and adopting appropriate characters to fit the situation.

Recording ideas (evidencing)

If something strikes you as being interesting, even if you can't really say why, make a note of it or, if it's a picture/story etc, keep it safe.

When you are working on improvisations, record those ideas or scenes which worked well. You may wish to develop them later or compare them with other ideas and scenes to find out why they were successful.

Sometimes it can be useful to record your personal feelings and thoughts about the work in progress. This technique is sometimes called **evidencing**.

Keeping a **working notebook** of the way your skills and personal response to drama are developing will help you in the preparation of coursework and in writing exam answers.

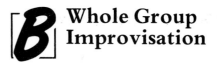

B Whole Group Improvisation

Working as a whole group can help build a good atmosphere and allow you to mix and work together more freely. A great many ideas can be both generated and shared. The dangers are that just a few people take over the work or the improvisations become so riotous and noisy that they lose their focus and therefore their value. Try to involve everyone and avoid turning every improvisation into some kind of argument. Use the following techniques as starters.

1 Tag improvisation The whole group stands in a circle. Using one of the ideas from the brainstorming session (p 26) one person (**A**) enters and starts acting by saying a line which will make it as clear as possible who they are and what the situation is.

> *'I've lost my mummy!'*
> *'Happy Birthday to me, Happy Birthday to me . . .'*

A second person (**B**) enters and joins the improvisation.

As soon as either of them say or do something which reminds you of some other situation say 'Freeze!' You may then enter the circle and 'tag' **A** who leaves the playing area. You must then restart the improvisation in *your* situation, by saying a new line which makes it clear to **B** what the new situation is.

Try to keep this going until everyone in the group has had at least one turn in the middle. Try not to leave people in the middle for more than one minute. This will stop the improvisations drying up.

2 Switch the emotion This can use the same organisation as 'tag improvisation' but in this case each new player should deliberately try to change the emotional feel of the work. So, if the first pair are involved in some kind of celebration where there is a feeling of happiness, the situation should change, after the 'tag', to one in which the people are confused or frightened or angry.

There is a temptation to overact in order to make the emotional change clear. Try to find other ways of showing the emotions. For example, you could show anger by smouldering quietly and saying through clenched teeth

'When I see people doing that, it makes me really angry!'

3 Props and costumes Place a box of props or costumes or both in the middle of the circle. Three volunteers grab an item each from the box, look at it and what the others have and start to improvise a scene in which the items play an important part. As with the 'tag', it's important to try to find a way of letting the others know immediately what sort of character you are and what you might be doing in the situation. After a maximum of two minutes the improvisation is stopped, the three players put their items back and choose someone from the circle to replace them.

4 Snowball The aim of this is to end up with everyone involved in the same scene. Instead of tagging people so that there are always just two people in the centre, after 'freeze' is called the new player joins the first two. This player then starts an improvisation with three people in it. After the next 'freeze' there will be four players and so on. You may choose to make it more difficult, though perhaps more interesting, by deciding to keep all the improvisations on one focus. For example, an exploration of the theme of children could produce

- a scene between a mum and a child at the school gate
- three children making a secret den
- one child being bullied by three bigger ones
- a class of reluctant children faced with a super-keen gym teacher.

5 One in – all in Like the 'snowball', the aim is to get everyone involved, only this

time the scene doesn't actually change though different people find a reason to butt in. For example:

A little boy is throwing stones. A second player enters and tells him off. The boy's mother arrives . . .

Try not to end up in a massive argument, but to find ways of giving new players a chance to explain why they've entered the scene and what they feel about the developing situation.

6 Role-play Whole-group role-play can be an extremely interesting and productive way of working. To make it work well, you must want it to work; in other words, you must be committed to it. It also demands that you are sensitive to each other. Listen carefully to what people say, watch what they do and try to accept the roles they are creating. One way of starting is to decide on a situation in which everyone could be involved from the start. The aim is both to develop a sense of character and to explore what the character might feel and do in the situation. For example, imagine that the room is a reception centre for young refugees. Choose one of these roles.

- A refugee who does not know what has happened to his parents.
- An adult who has travelled with the refugees.
- A volunteer in the reception centre.
- A newspaper reporter. (And so on)

Spend a few minutes on your own thinking about your chosen character. Write on a piece of paper what your character is feeling as they enter the reception centre (this is an example of *evidencing*).

Only start talking/mixing with others when you feel like it, letting the character and situation develop at its own pace rather than trying to make something exciting happen.

After playing the situation for at least ten minutes (this sort of work needs plenty of time to develop), discuss as a group how well it worked. Did people manage to stay in role? Did the situation feel real or was it too obviously dramatic?

7 Hot-seating Hot-seating is an effective way of getting to know what a character is like and why they have done something. The work involves actors being asked questions and answering in role as if they were an actual character. This might mean that they choose not to answer certain questions. Hot-seating can usefully develop a scene. For example, as a whole class, hot-seat one of the newspaper reporters from the role-play in Task 6. Try to find out how she feels about this job, which requires her to take pictures of and report on people in distressed situations. What other incidents has she reported on? What made her want the job? Has she ever been faced with a situation she found difficult to cope with? What was it?

Hot-seating with attitude! Hot-seating can be usefully developed by asking questions from a particular perspective. So, for example, one person might ask the reporter this question:

> *'I've worked with refugees for many years and have to say that I found your report on the centre very unhelpful. Why did you make it all sound so sensational?'*

The answer the reporter would give to this person would make an interesting contrast to the reply she may give to this question:

> *'I've been running this newspaper for years. Our sales are pathetic. There's rarely any news around here, so tell me: how are you going to cover this refugee stuff?'*

 Pairs Work

An advantage of working in pairs is that you are likely to be more actively involved in practical work for more of the time than when in a larger group. There is often a temptation to work with the same partner all the time, though. Avoid this – working with a wide range of people will give you more ideas whereas the same partner can become predictable. Below are a number of exercises which will help you develop your improvisation skills.

1 Instant stories Working in pairs, one person starts to tell a story but stops after only a few sentences leaving the partner to carry on:

> *'One day, a little boy called Sidney woke up very excited. It was his birthday! Leaping out of bed he ran down stairs and to his delight he saw . . .'*

> *'. . . that his mum had cooked him a bacon sandwich for his birthday breakfast. Yummy! His favourite! Just as he was about to bite into it he heard . . .'*

Don't try to force your partner into telling the story your way but try to stop in the middle of sentences which allow a number of possible developments.

Another way of doing this is to start a simple story by making a statement and acting it out.

> *'I was walking down the street one day . . .'*

Your partner must add something and it must start with the words 'And then . . .' For example:

> *'. . . and then I saw my best friend so I waved to her and started to cross the road . . .*
>
> *. . . and then a truck hit me and sent me flying . . .*
>
> *. . . and then I discovered I was having this weird out-of-body experience . . .'*

The story will probably become more and more bizarre, but a lot of fun to act out!

2 Mime Imagine that the two of you are sorting stuff out for a jumble sale. In turns, take an imaginary item from an imaginary sack and mime what you might do with it. As soon as you know what your partner is miming, take the object off them and show in your mime that you have understood what it is. Then mime a new object of your own. Being imaginary, the sack can, of course, contain absolutely anything!

3 Telephone calls Place two chairs back-to-back. The aim of this improvisation is to make you use words only. Sitting back-to-back, you won't be able to see the reaction of the other person. Use the brainstorm chart from p 26 to get an idea for starting.

For example:

- Parent **A** rings up Parent **B** and asks them to come and collect their child from a birthday party . . . there's been a bit of a problem!
- A young child answers the telephone and doesn't really understand what the person on the other end wants.

Because you can't see each other, telephone conversations can be used to explore sensitive situations with less risk of laughing.

- A doctor telephones a parent about the results of a test on their child.
- One young teenager calls somebody they really like to ask them out. They've never done this before.

Accepting and blocking

Improvisations can fall flat on their face if one of the players is offering ideas and the other one is rejecting them or **blocking**. For example:

A *Excuse me, your secretary rang me about Sara. I came as quickly as I could to pick her up. Where is she?*
B *I haven't got a secretary. You must be in the wrong place.*
This makes it very hard for **A** to continue.

4 Try, in pairs, to start as many scenes as you can in five minutes in which **B accepts** the idea. Play the scene for a few lines to get an idea of how it could develop, stop, and start a new one:

A *Excuse me, your secretary rang me about Sarah, I came as quickly as I could to pick her up. Where is she?*
B *Thank you. She's just down here but I'm afraid the news isn't very good.*
A *Will she be all right? What happened?*
B *She's got quite a nasty bump. We'll have to keep an eye on her . . . STOP*

Sometimes blocking can actually be useful in developing the scene along an unexpected line. Notice, though, how **B** has to offer something else to keep the scene going, if she wants to block.

A *Excuse me, your secretary rang me about Sarah. I came as quickly as I could to pick her up. Where is she?*
B *I'm sorry. You must be in the wrong place. Can I help in any way?*
A *It's my daughter — she's had an accident. Isn't this the hospital?*
B *No madam, this is a garage but we do repairs if that's any help.*

5 Start as many scenes as possible in five minutes in which **B** seems to block **A** but doesn't, in fact, stop the scene from developing.

Small Groups

Many of the tasks suggested for the whole group or pairs could be tackled in small groups.

Here are some ideas which show how small groups could work to explore and develop an idea further. They relate to the role-play in Unit B, Task 6 (p 28), so you will need to remind yourself of that scene.

1 The family album If the refugees had a family photo album, what sort of pictures would be in it which might tell the volunteer centre workers something about the lives they have left behind them? In small groups, make a tableau as if you are in such a photograph. Where is it taken? Who is in it? What are they like? Hold the tableau for a count of three then bring the characters to life.

2 Explanation The group devises a scene which shows how the young refugee came to be separated from his parents.

3 Split brief This involves two small groups working together but each group having a different purpose. For example:

GROUP A You are the volunteers who have been looking after these young refugees. Decide on what you think should happen to them.

GROUP B You are government officials who know that the refugees are continuing to arrive at the centre. Decide what you think should happen.

After five minutes working separately, improvise the scene where **GROUP B** visit the centre.

4 Exploration The group devises a scene from the refugee's future.

 # Evaluation

Evaluation of your work is important so that you

a understand the situation or subject you have been exploring
b get better at using improvisations to understand situations.

Discussing what you thought of each other's work can be extremely helpful. Other people often notice things that you don't.

Writing evaluations can be a particularly useful way of making your thoughts about your own work clearer.

In either case, before starting to evaluate your work you must decide _what_ you are evaluating and _why_. Do you want to
a concentrate on the content of the work?
b concentrate on making the drama better?

1 Evaluating content Whether you are thinking back on a piece of your own work, or considering a piece you have seen someone else perform, asking the following questions will help you evaluate the **content**.

What was the work about?
What happened? Where was it set? What characters were shown?
How interested were you in the subject being explored?
How did the work make you feel? Angry? Sad? Amused?
Did the work make you think something new about the subject being explored? Can you say what exactly?
Was the storyline or situation very predictable or unexpected in some way?
What attitudes did the characters in the work have? Why did they behave in the way they did and say the things they said?
In what ways were the characters the same as or different from you? What would you have done or said in the same situation?
Did the work raise any issues, for example

was the situation fair? Does the work seem to have a clear message?

2 Evaluating form When you watch other people improvising, you will immediately start to evaluate how well they are using the form of drama. Ask yourself the following questions.

How easy is it to hear what is being said?
Can you see everything clearly?
Are the actors aware of an audience?
How well are they using the space? Are they moving effectively?
Are they staying in character? Are they concentrating?
Do they know what they are doing or are they badly organised?
Is the story being told in a clear, structured way? Is it imaginative? Is it focused?
Are conventions being set up and maintained – for example, if one character mimes going through a door at a particular point, do all the other characters do the same thing?

Criticising other people's work in this way will help them to improve only if
● criticism is actually asked for
● it is given positively and sympathetically
● it is relevant and appropriate (miming a door accurately may not be very important to the scene as a whole).

Get used to asking yourself these questions about each piece of work **you** do – you should try to satisfy your own standards before anyone else's.

You will find more advice on how to write up submissions for coursework in Chapter Six.

Structuring a presentation

This project looks at the different types of writing that can be used as the basis for a DRAMATIC PRESENTATION and introduces the idea of NOTATION as a way of recording work as it progresses. The technique of MAPPING is introduced as a way of helping create a coherent and dramatically interesting STRUCTURE.

What Makes Writing Dramatic?

In Chapter One you began to explore how plays involve much more than just putting on stage what people say in their everyday lives. Most plays do tend to have a good deal of **dialogue** in them but there are other forms of speech that can be dramatically very interesting and help an audience gain new insights into what is going on in the play. In this project you will see how most types of writing or speech can be used in a dramatic context. Using a variety of forms will make your own work more varied and interesting.

Study Extract

Anansi

Anansi is a character from African mythology. He is a trickster rather like Coyote in North American tales or perhaps Puck in *A Midsummer Night's Dream*. Anansi is a sort of half-man half-spider who survives through his cunning. Playwright Alistair Campbell re-tells some of the traditional stories of Anansi in his play about the slave trade. Through the course of the play the Girl finds where her own strength lies by listening to the stories and coming to understand what she may have to do in order to survive the ordeal of being taken into slavery.

```
CHARACTERS
BOY
CAPTAIN
GIRL
SAILOR
```

The good ship *Hope*. West African coast. 1791

The Cabin

Listen. . . hear the last sounds of a ship preparing for the Atlantic voyage. The BOY *is seated at a desk, reading and writing. His father, the* CAPTAIN, *consults ledgers and maps.*

BOY Father, why do I have to study when everyone else is up on deck?

CAPTAIN Silence, boy, and look to your books.

BOY But Father, I still don't see how all these people on the shore can be cargo.

CAPTAIN Books or no books you have a lot to learn on this voyage. Look to it and do not bother me with damn fool questions.

BOY But who are the people on the shore, Father?

CAPTAIN You are on a serious trading venture whilst you are on my ship, and as the ship's boy you'll address me as Captain, especially in front of the ratings. You'll learn all about the cargo and such soon enough.

BOY They looked just like people to me. But they were tied together. They looked frightened. Why. . .?

CAPTAIN (*cutting him off*) I do not have to give you explanations. I am your father.

BOY I thought you said your name was Captain.

CAPTAIN (*hits him*) You young pup! Have that for your cheek. And there's worse waiting for you when you get down below.

On Deck

Look . . . a GIRL *is waiting to be taken below. She is terrified. She stands, tied to several others. She calls out to deckhands as they pass. But they don't understand her language. They don't look at her or slow down.*

GIRL Where are we going? Are we going to die? What is this place, with all the people tied together and so much crying and fear? And why has the world come to an end? Blue, blue nothingness. Water, waves and more water. The water reaches up and touches the sky. Where is my mother? Where did all the pale men come from? Why don't you answer me?

SAILOR Come along my beauty. Less jabber and down the hatch with you. I don't know! At least a bale of cotton doesn't chatter in some heathen tongue, and whatever it is you're blathering about you'll have to get yourself down this hatch. Can't throw you and damage the goods, eh? Move!

He bundles her down the hatch.

The Cabin

BOY (*reading*) Yesterday we put in to the West African coast for the last time before the long haul to the Indies. I was looking forward to this trip with Father: I really was. I thought we'd be away for a few months, and I knew we'd be coming back to Bristol with Rum and Coffee. I did not think to be so puzzled. No answers come to my questions. Who were those people on the shore? Herded together like cattle. Some of them were crying and falling down with fear. Some were whipped and beaten. One old woman was standing stiff and proud, with her hands tied, waiting her turn to be loaded aboard. She looked so calm as if she'd done it all before and didn't care. But she can't have, can she? They brought them down river from far away upstream, and she can't have seen the sea, even, until just then. She caught my eye but I turned away. She reminded me of Grandmama.

Dear Diary, you're my only friend on this ship. There's one Sailor who teaches me knots and talks to me. I shall tell you all my secret thoughts if Father gives me the chance from time to time.

The Hold

It is almost completely dark, but look . . . The outline of hundreds of people packed together in rows on the floor, lying on narrow shelves that line the walls. Some are tied back to back to an upright beam. One of them is the GIRL. *A little light filters down from a crack in the roof. Behind her is the dim outline of someone tied to the other side of the beam. We will hear but never see this person.*

GIRL I remember the river, carrying me further and further away from my mother on its great brown back. They tied us together. I don't know why.
They threw us into a huge canoe, bigger than the biggest war canoe of our tribe, and I didn't know why.
The jungle slid past. Two green walls of giant trees. We lay in the bottom of the boat, tied together like goats waiting for the knife, and I didn't know why.
Now all I see are people tied together, chained together, crushed together in the dark. It's so dark, Mama, like the big hut with no windows where the tribe stores the grain. Everyone is lying in filth and sickness and fear. Please, please come and hold me, Mama. Tell me this isn't true.

WOMAN What's true is true. Don't fight it. You're alive and it's true. It's true.

GIRL Who are you? I can feel your warmth but I can't see you.

WOMAN I am who I am, and you are who you are. No amount of fear and darkness can change that truth. Hold on to it! Hold on!

The Cabin

CAPTAIN Dictation.

BOY Yes, Captain.

CAPTAIN Our last port of call on the African coast. Only three slaves of the last batch of forty have died on the six-day river passage. May God be thanked for it. We have branded and documented and all slaves are now insured against death on route to the Indies.

They are to be exercised daily in the hope that fresh air will reduce disease. One cup of maize porridge per slave per day should ensure that stores are sufficient for the voyage.
That'll be all.

BOY Yes, Captain.

Understanding the text

1 Look at this list of different types of writing. Try to match these up to the script of *Anansi*.

dialogue   monologue   soliloquy (one person speaking their thoughts aloud) diary   journal   caption   stage direction narration

2 Look at the very first line:

The good ship *Hope*. West African coast. 1791

What is the purpose of putting this line into the play script? Do you think that an audience will need to know this at the start of the play or is it just for those reading the play? If you decided to give the audience this information, how would you do it? By showing it on a projected slide? Having it written on a board next to the stage? What other options would there be?

If you decided not to use this caption, how could you make it clear to the audience where and when the play is set?

3 Look at the first stage direction again. Would you just use this to tell you, as actors, what you are doing, or could it also be used as a part of the scene in some way? What would be the advantages and disadvantages of actually having someone speak this direction aloud?

Look at the other stage directions. How could speaking some of these aloud save you from having to use a complicated set and lots of lighting and sound effects?

4 The extract is quite short yet nevertheless contains five different scenes. How possible would it be to change the scenery for each one? How else could you signal to the audience that the scene had changed if you decided to play this piece on a fairly empty stage?

5 In this script the Girl is speaking English. What would tell an audience that she is not actually speaking the same language as the Sailors? In pairs, play out the second scene and experiment with ways of physically showing that the Girl and the Sailor do not actually understand each other.

6 The extract contains four monologues – that is, characters speaking aloud but in a way that isn't a conversation. Compare these monologues and talk about

- who is actually being spoken to
- what information each monologue gives the audience
- in what way this type of speech isn't like 'real life'.

Written tasks

7 In this extract we see the Boy writing his diary and also the ship's log, and we also hear what he is writing. Make a list of other types of speech that could be used to give an audience information apart from dialogue.

8 Simply putting two types of speech against each other can produce quite a good dramatic effect. Select one idea from column A and one from column B below. In pairs,

work out a way of putting the two types of speech together so that, when they are presented on stage, the ultimate effect will be either comical or perhaps rather tragic.

A	B
A radio news bulletin warns the public that a psychopath has escaped from gaol.	An old person is telephoning the police to complain about his noisy neighbour.
Someone is reading aloud an article from a newspaper about falling standards in school.	Someone is dictating a letter of resignation from an important job.
Someone is writing in their diary about a person in their class whom they can't stand.	A teenager is praying for good luck in his exams.
A child is talking to a toy about what she wants for Christmas.	Someone is writing a love letter to a person they have liked for ages yet never had the courage to tell.

Mapping a Presentation

It would be rare to find a playwright who could just sit down and write a play by starting at the beginning and carrying on to the end. The process of finding an idea and developing it into a piece of drama is usually a bit more chaotic than that. You will probably have already found out that sometimes what you end up with is miles away from where you thought you'd be when you started. New ideas bubble up while old ones fade away, or you realise that in order for one thing to make sense you really need to add something new.

Just as a musical score is the **notation** that musicians use to guide their performance, so we could say that a play script is the notation used by actors, directors and designers to guide their production of a play. They may not always stick to it rigidly but it's the foundation on which they build their own interpretation.

When you are devising your own plays it is enormously helpful to **notate** what you are doing. In this way, you will not forget what you have already done and you will be able, ultimately, to use your notes to structure the play in a way that will make sense and be dramatically interesting.

1 Look at the pictures below. You may not think that any of them are particularly inspiring but, in groups, decide on one which you like the look of. Jot done the reasons for your choice. Note down anything the picture reminds you of and what sort of feelings it provokes.

2 Adopt the poses shown in the photograph as accurately as you can. If there are more people in your group than in the picture, use them as directors to make sure your image is accurate. Talk about what it felt like to be actually in this kind of physical position wearing these facial expressions. Jot down what new ideas this exercise gave you.

3 Imagine that this picture is the central one of three. Make a still image of the other two pictures. One will show what occurred immediately before the photograph was taken. The other will show the next significant moment. This could be immediately after or you may decide that it happened a week, or even years after. You may decide to involve new characters in these new images.

Write down stage directions for these two new images in a way that would help another group understand what they had to do to make them. Your directions could be highly detailed and say exactly where each actor had to stand:

> *A man sits on a chair, his head in his hands. A woman stands behind his left shoulder turned slightly away from him. The fingers of her right hand are on her cheek. A teenage boy and his younger sister stand in front of the man and to his right. They are holding hands. One of the boy's hands is stretching out to the man.*

Alternatively you could focus on the nature and atmosphere of the scene:

> *A small, poorly furnished flat. A brother and sister are imploring their father. He sits, unable to talk to them or even look at them. Behind him the mother is turning away to hide her tears from them. It is a moment of grief.*

It is up to you exactly how you write these stage directions but you must be satisfied that, if they were followed by another group, the image would capture what you wanted to say.

Now make each pose in order 1, 2, 3. What you have effectively done is created a basic storyline.

4 Make the original pose again and on the count of three bring it to life. Improvise for about 30 seconds. Make notes on what sort of things people said or did in the improvisation – it doesn't have to be written out exactly like a play script but should be detailed enough so that you could repeat the scene in the future.

Each character in the picture should now write a short monologue based on the story you have developed so far. This might take the form of a letter or diary written after the event or perhaps you can imagine a character stepping out of the picture and talking directly to the audience:

> *'Yes, I remember that day at the railway station so well. Of course, I didn't realise then that the events of that day would have such a big effect on my life but I do remember feeling that what was happening was unfair and that I couldn't just stand by and watch . . .'*

5 Thinking about the characters you now have, can you imagine any new situations that would involve just two of them talking together? Jot down your ideas then try to improvise these duologues. Again, after you have improvised them, make a note of anything you said that would be worth using again.

6 Look once more at the photograph you started with. Give it a short title and then use the letters of the title as the basis of a piece of writing which sums up the story you have created. For example:

> ***W**ithout friends or family*
> ***A**ll alone in a hostile world, trying to*
> ***R**emember what childhood should be like.*
>
> ***C**oming one day upon a place she thought was*
> ***H**ome.*
> ***I**t seemed that even there no one cared if she*
> ***L**ived or*
> ***D**ied.*

Experiment with how the whole of your group could use this as a piece of **choral**

speech. Perhaps all of you could say it together or maybe split the lines between you. Think about how you want to stand or move when you are speaking these lines.

You now have quite a lot of material to use as a basis for a play. The next task is to structure the different scenes and develop a way of linking them together. One way of doing this is to create a map that will show what the running order of the scenes is and how the images and lines spoken in one relate to others. It can be effective to start a play at the end of the story and use flashbacks to show how the characters have got to the situation. Breaking up the story by having characters step out of the action to comment from a personal perspective on what is happening is another interesting option.

Look at this example of how one group mapped out their presentation, then try the technique with your own material.

Looking at this map you would probably agree that there still seem to be some holes in the storyline, or the possibility of tying some things more closely together. The complexity of your map will obviously depend on how much time you have available. The main thing is that you should be able to follow it and use it to see where you still need to develop links. Notice how, in this map, the group decided to invent a scene which just involved movement and soundscaping. You might also consider how song could be incorporated into your play to give variety and make a particular point.

Reflection

7 Write up your reflections on this project. Say whether or not you think it is a good way of working and why. Were you surprised at how much you could get out of one picture? Perhaps you got stuck at some point – can you say why this was?

8 Collect a few photographs for yourself which you think might make a good starting point for a drama. Either include them in your working notebook and say what made you choose them, or simply discuss them with other members of your group to see if they can also see the pictures' potential.

War Child

1 Still image of people at train station.

2 Abraham steps out. Tells audience about how the day affected his life.

3 Two soldiers talk about clearing out the local population.

4 Abraham and his sister ask their parents why they must go to the station.

5 Soldier writes to his wife expressing horror at what the army is doing.

6 Abraham and sister on train. Where are they going?

7 Mother prays for her children's well-being.

8 Soldiers enter and arrest her.

9 Movement/sound sequence to show air raid.

10 Soldier and Abraham talk about sister's death.

11 Soldiers retreating. They have lost.

12 Abraham walks alone. Comes across bombed house. Tries to talk to passers-by but they don't listen.

13 Choral speech/movement sequence using title.

Keep the home fires burning

Characterisation

Plays must be about **something** and usually they are about **someone**. This chapter investigates how dramatic CHARACTERS are created. It shows how RESEARCH and INTERVIEWING can provide the basis for a character. The activities use historical resources and extracts from plays to look at how ROLES can be adopted and maintained.

All the resource materials in the chapter focus on the theme of women in the war.

Brainstorming: What Is the Home Front?

The subject of war is a very common one in plays, films and books.

1 Just to get your minds tuned into the subject, get into groups of four or five and note down everything that comes into your mind in response to the word 'war'. Do not take more than five minutes.

Bombs   Soldiers

FIGHTING

Heroes   Death

FEAR   Macho

Nazis

Refugees   KILL

2 As a whole class play 'word association'. One person starts by simply saying something that they think of in relation to the word 'war'. The person on their right says a word that is related to the previous word but must also fit in with the general theme:

NAM . . . RAMBO . . . GUN . . .
FIGHTER . . . PLANE . . . TARGET . . .
etc

It would be useful to either tape record this or find a volunteer to jot down all the words the class comes up with.

3 Take a close look at the ideas recorded in Tasks 1 and 2. How many of the ideas were to do with the active, fighting side of war and how many to do with what life was like for civilians? What does this suggest? Discuss, either as a whole class or in smaller groups, where you have got your ideas about war from.

4 There seem to be hundreds of books and films which focus on the action part of war – the 'front line'. Rather less is available about the lives of those who stayed at home and tried to keep life as normal as possible on the 'Home Front'.

What do you think might be the reasons for this?

Those who have lived through a war, whether they were fighting or waiting at home, have a great many memories associated with the experience. These memories, which may have seemed quite routine at the time, can be used to create interesting characters and make new dramas. Most of the work in this chapter will focus on the Second World War. Ask almost anyone old enough to remember 'their' war and you will very likely find plenty of information on which to base your own work.

5 Try to uncover what else you and your group know about the Second World War. Start with these questions.

- How did it end?
- When did it start?
- Who was it between?

Some of the answers may have already been mentioned in 1 and 2 above.

6 List all the ways you can think of in which war might affect people on the 'Home Front'. In what obvious ways would their lives be different? What new things would they have to get used to?

Fact Finding

Look at the following facts and figures about the Second World War.

On the 1st September 1939, 827,000 unaccompanied children; 524,000 mothers with children under the age of 5; 51,300 pregnant women; and 7,000 blind and crippled people were moved from their homes in Britain's major cities to country towns and villages.

By November of the following year 68% had returned home and refused to go away again.

By May 1940, 5½ million women were being employed in civilian occupations. Many more were in the voluntary services. However, many of them wanted to resign. To prevent this, military law was extended, so that they were obliged to either stay on in their jobs or face imprisonment.

Women at work on bomber production lines were on duty from 8am to midnight seven days a week with no bank holidays.

The average wage for a woman in engineering was £3.10s. The average for a man was £7.

By 1944, approximately 80,000 deserters were on the streets of Britain. The crime rates for theft, violent crime and vandalism rose dramatically.

Cases of venereal disease went up 63% amongst women and 113% amongst men.

Due to emergency reservoirs being built and blackout restrictions being enforced, many more children were drowned or run over during the war than the peacetime average.

In 1945 when the war ended, 25,000 divorce petitions were filed (2½ times the number registered in 1939). 70% were on grounds of adultery.

During the six years of the war (1939–45) air raid sirens were sounded, on average, once every 36 hours.

Analysis

Try to answer these questions yourself, then discuss your answers in pairs or small groups to see how other members of the group responded to them.

1 Are there any facts here which had never occurred to you before? Which ones do you find most surprising? Can you say why?

2 Which of the above facts do you think might have had the greatest effect on families?

3 If you were an ordinary person living in Britain during the war which of these facts do you suppose you would have known about and which ones not? Why do you think this?

4 If people had known about all of these facts at the time, which ones do you suppose would have bothered them most?

Improvisation

5 In pairs, imagine that you are living during the war. Some of the facts printed on p 42 have just appeared in a national newspaper. **A** is a reporter from that paper sent to interview an ordinary person, **B**, about his or her reactions to these facts. Keep the interview going for just two minutes, then swap over. Use the improvisations to show how and why different people might have reacted to different facts.

6 Improvise a scene in which some of the information given on p 42 is actually seen to be affecting the lives of the characters involved. Here are some examples of what might be possible.

a A policeman calls at a house with some bad news about the child that lives there.
b It is pay day on a production line on which men and women are working alongside each other.
c Your work is in some way ruining your life. You decide to resign but the manager informs you that you can't.

Reflection

7 Split into pairs. Tell each other five ways in which the character that you played in Task 6 is clearly different from you in reality. When you have done this, describe, *in the way you think that character would*, your feelings about the incident in which you were involved.

Further Investigation: What the posters didn't tell you!

The war put new demands on people in many ways. They had to learn new skills and routines and the way they spent their time was often vastly different from what they had previously been used to. With the need for everyone to 'lend a hand' for the war effort the Government tried to change people's image of themselves and the situation.

A great many posters like the one on the next page were designed to encourage people to get involved in war work. Women who had previously been housewives went to work in factories, and town girls who had never seen the country enlisted in the 'Land Army'.

Such a drastic change in lifestyle caused many people to become confused and sometimes quite desperate. The Government tried to tackle the problem through using 'propaganda', that is, devices such as films and posters which would actively change the way people thought and felt.

Analysis

1 Look carefully at the poster on the next page, which was designed to encourage people to give up their free time to help out on farms. What impression does it give of country life?

How do you think the poster would be attractive to

a soldiers?
b girls who had left the towns to work in the Land Army?

2 Compare the bright and cheerful image of the poster with this account from a girl who went to work on a farm.

'When the last sheaves were lifted, the men used sticks, forks and dogs to kill as many rats as possible. I tried to get out of the way but the farmer said to me, "I'll hold the sack while you put the dead rats in." I had to pick up the rats by the tails and count them as they went in – forty-two of them.'

How do the lives of the girl on the poster and the girl who wrote this account seem different? What does this seem to suggest about the nature of the propaganda?

Practical work

3 Imagine the extract in Task 2 has come from a letter that the girl is writing to a friend in a town who is thinking of joining the Land Army. In small groups, imagine that you are all working on the same farm. Discuss, in role, what other things you are finding different about life in the country. Use this discussion to
a compose a similar letter home or
b construct a scene that illustrates some of the incidents which the characters might mention in such a letter. Make it clear what their attitudes are to their new life.

4 Improvise the scene in which the girl goes home to visit her own town. She meets a group of her friends and realises that her experiences in the country have changed her. Try to show what changes in her character have taken place and what the reactions of her friends to them are.

Girls from the towns may have been attracted into the Land Army by the fresh air and healthy life of the country as shown on the posters. In the same way, country girls, or women whose lives had been completely domestic, may have been excited by the idea of taking a more direct role in the war effort and experiencing life in a lively town. Look at the poster on the next page.

5 What does this poster suggest about
a life in the factories?
b the role of women in the war?
How is the poster different from 'Victory Harvest' in what it says about
a women?
b war?
Discuss how you think the posters achieve their different messages.

6 Devise your own poster which will encourage girls to either
a join the land army and go to work in the country
b join the armed forces (women weren't allowed to fight, so imagine what jobs they could be given)
c go to work in a factory doing vital war work.

7 In addition to making posters, the Government also made short films for propaganda. Choose one of the ideas from Task 6 and in small groups devise and present a scene which would be appropriate for such a film.

Reflection

8 In what way do the characters shown in your propaganda posters or scenes seem different from those you played in Tasks 3 and 4 above? In small groups, discuss what you think makes a 'believable' character.

9 Consider the way you made the 'film' in Task 7. How appropriate was your use of language and style of acting? In what ways did it capture the right period and atmosphere?

Finding a Focus: Women at War

Although women were kept away from the actual fighting, many of them took on dangerous or unpleasant duties. Some women were stationed on searchlight and watch duties, while others ferried new aircraft from the factories to the aerodromes.

For the woman who had been brought up to believe that her place was in the home looking after her husband and children, the experience of war might have caused conflict not only with her image of herself, but within the family too. While Government was keen to get women working for the war effort, the attitude of the men who had also grown up believing that the woman's place was in the home may not have changed so readily.

Look at the advertisement on the next page.

Analysis

1 What is Mrs X's attitude to
a the war?
b her husband?

2 What does Mr X expect of his wife? How does she seem to feel about this?

3 What is the purpose of this advert?

4 Why do you think the advert uses characters rather than simply announcing that Mrs Peek's Puddings are worth buying?

5 Do you think these characters are 'believable'? Give reasons for your answer.

6 Read this account from a woman ambulance driver.

'A warden brought in a basket and said, "You're to have these." Well, we asked what it was and he took the paper off and it was all fingers and toes.
"The hospital won't take it because it's not a casualty and the mortuary won't take it because it's not a corpse. So it's yours to do what you like with." Well, talk about red tape! The basket was there for two days. Eventually an ambulance driver buried it on the common.'

In what ways does this woman's attitude seem different from Mr X's? What do you think this woman ambulance driver's reaction to the advert might be?

Practical work

7 Using the advert as a script, act out the scenes depicted as if the advert was being shown on television. What sort of voices and characters do you think would fit best? Is it possible to portray this seriously or does it simply become laughable?

8 In pairs, improvise a scene in which a woman warden comes home after having dropped off the basket full of fingers and toes at the hospital. Her husband enters and says, 'Cold dinner, again!'

9 In small groups, devise a scene which will be used to advertise some household product. Like the *Mrs Peek's Puddings* advert, yours will also have a wartime setting and show certain types of characters discovering how this product will make their war a bit easier. After a short time for preparation present your scene to the rest of the group.

10 Having watched the scenes from Task 9, your group should imagine that you are characters who are particularly insulted by one of the adverts. Devise another short scene which illustrates why.

You may find these poster images unattractive and unlikely to appeal; and the advert may seem silly to you. However, both may have been quite effective at the time.

What sort of things do you think make your reactions different now to those of people 50 years ago?

CAN A WARDEN BE A GOOD WIFE?

Mrs. X discovers how!

COLD DINNER AGAIN!

I'VE BEEN ON DUTY ALL DAY. I REALLY HADN'T TIME TO COOK A MEAL

OH DEAR I'LL HAVE TO RESIGN FROM THE WARDENS POST I JUST CAN'T GET JIM A HOT MEAL AT NIGHT

NONSENSE! YOU MUST MEET MRS PEEK

WHO IS MRS PEEK?

INSIDE EVERY MRS. PEEKS PUDDING TIN IS A DELICIOUS

COMPLETELY MADE PUDDING, MORE THAN ENOUGH FOR 3 PEOPLE

ALL YOU DO IS POP THE TIN IN A SAUCEPAN, LEAVE IT TO BOIL FOR ONE HOUR. RESULT — A PIPING HOT...

TEMPTING PUDDING!

MRS. PEEKS PUDDINGS ARE MADE FROM THE FINEST INGREDIENTS INCLUDING REAL FRUIT

NEXT MORNING

AND A MRS. PEEKS PUDDING PLEASE

Save the situation, and the ration coupons, too, with a Mrs. Peek's Pudding! READY MADE for you by the famous house of Peek Frean, from old family recipes. Perfectly sweet, no extra sugar needed.

Mrs Peek's PUDDINGS

6 *kinds: Xmas, Light Fruit, Dark Fruit, Date, Ginger, Sultana* . . .   1/-

DARLING WHAT A FINE HOT PUDDING I GUESS YOU'VE RESIGNED YOUR JOB

NO I HAVEN'T I'M STILL HELPING MY COUNTRY AND MRS. PEEK IS LOOKING AFTER YOUR DINNER

Made by PEEK FREAN & CO. LTD. · MAKERS OF FAMOUS BISCUITS

STUDY EXTRACT ONE
'When the Lights Go On Again'

People often deny being able to write good stories or being in any way artistic, yet they can retell tales from their own lives in a lively and entertaining way. Read this extract from an interview with a school cleaner.

> So this big Yankie says to me, 'Come with me for a little walk, honey, an' I'll give you something for trusting me.' So I says to my friend Sheila, 'Look, you follow on behind an' if you hear me scream, give me another ten minutes then come running!'
>
> Anyway, we gets down to the furthest bench on the platform an' he starts to slowly unzip his flying jacket. 'Well, sweetheart,' he said, 'I told you I'd give you something for trusting me so.' And he pulled out the biggest box of chocolates I'd seen in years!'

1 In pairs take it in turns to read out the extract above and see if you can find ways of bringing the story to life by using suitable tones of voice and accents. Comment on each other's performance with the aim of making it more 'believable'.

2 When people tell a story they often embellish it by adding extra little details. They may use pauses to deliberately make the tale sound more interesting, exciting and important than perhaps it was when it really happened. In pairs, experiment with ways of telling the story in this extract so that it becomes a rather 'tall tale'.

When people tell stories like this they often report speech in a direct way, that is, they try to say the actual words that were said when the incident originally happened. Often they even try to put on the voices of the people in the story. Getting people to tell such stories can provide a rich resource for making drama. The work in this unit will show you how you might go about collecting and using such original material.

When the Lights Go On Again is a play that was devised by a group of GCSE students from a number of interviews with people living near the school. This 'original data' was supported by wider research from books, records and films. The group became particularly interested in the role of women in the war and chose to focus on

a what sort of roles women actually had
b what the reactions of the men at the time were.

The following scene was constructed by matching actual material recorded during the war with a number of stories provided by the school cleaner.

CHARACTERS

ANNOUNCER Because the play was a series of unrelated episodes rather than one single story, it was necessary to have some sort of narrator to link the scenes together. A taped voice could have been used but in order to keep the atmosphere of the 'Home Front' the links were made by an announcer who stood at an old-fashioned microphone wearing a variety of period costumes and using a number of different voices. He was a kind of one-man radio show!

WOMEN (ONE, TWO AND THREE)
The three women are all quite young, perhaps in their late teens or early twenties. Joining up would have been quite exciting at first but by now they have all become rather bored by the routines.

SERGEANT Working with women isn't what he joined the army for, particularly when they are as cheeky as these three. He is rather a stereotype of a pig-headed army man who believes in following orders without question.

Scene Seven: WOMEN AT WAR

The Official **ANNOUNCER** *appears in a spotlight and speaks in a jovial 'BBC type' voice.*

ANNOUNCER Mr Churchill was at first adamant that women should not be involved directly with military operations. But after seeing the work of the ATS girls at a Richmond air gunnery station, he has clearly been forced to reconsider. The girls' message is loud and clear: 'Think again Mr Churchill!'

The stage falls into blackness.

VOICE ONE What's time then?
VOICE TWO 'Bout right I 'spect.
VOICE THREE Stick 'im on then.

A powerful spotlight beams out into the auditorium and slowly sweeps from one side to the other. Having almost reached the side it suddenly jumps back a short way as if 'double taking'.

ONE 'Ere! Look at they!
TWO 'Oo is it?
ONE Can't see. Arms an' legs all over there is!
THREE Don't even look like they noticed. *(pause then laughter)* Oh aye, they 'ave!
TWO It's that Daisy Stacey. *(shouts)* No good 'iding your face – we seen you!
ONE 'Oo's the fella?
TWO Looks like some Yankie.
THREE Off they goes look. Come on then, let's 'ave this light 'round.

Silence

TWO Sea's comin' up rough.
ONE It's that wind. Goes right through you.
TWO Wouldn't like to be out in that.
ONE Two minutes all you got.
THREE Eh?
ONE Out there in th' Atlantic. Water's so cold you're dead in two minutes.
TWO Boys on 'The Hood' didn' get that long mostly.
THREE Horrible way to go I reckon. All that cold. Bad enough 'ere.
TWO It's me 'ands that gets me. Don't know 'ow we're 'spected to keep this thing still – weighs a ton. What we s'posed to be looking for anyhow?
ONE Jerry subs I reckon.
TWO Bloody daft they come up 'ere!
THREE They say one did last year. 'Spect he turned back sharpish once he'd seen the place. *(pause)* Gor! It's cold. Got two pair me Dad's long johns on over me own woolly knickers an' I'm still perished.
ONE Ought to give us a Yankie each to keep us warm.
TWO Like you 'ad las' night eh? We heard.
ONE Oh, did you now?
TWO You go on! We knows what you been up to.
THREE I don't!
TWO Walking off into the sunset with her Gary Cooper she was.
ONE His name's Leroy.
THREE Never mind 'is daft name, you going to tell me what you been doing with him?
ONE Well, me an' Sheila went down The Kings Arms last night and there's all them Yankies there from Shirehampton. Well, I gotta be home at nine so I had a couple a drinks and when I says I gotta go this bloke Leroy says 'e'll give me something if I lets 'im walk me to the station. Aye aye, I thought, I bet you will! So I says to Sheila, 'Look, you follow on behind an' if you hear me scream, give me another ten minutes then come running!'
Anyway, we gets down to the furthest bench on the platform an' he starts to slowly unzip his flying jacket.
'Well, sweetheart,' he said. 'I told you I'd give you something for trusting me so.' And he pulled out the biggest box of chocolates I seen in years! You should've seen the faces on the train.
THREE You seein' 'im again then?
ONE No. The chocolates was stale.
SERGEANT Get that bloody light moving!
TWO Oh crikes! 'Ere come 'Itler's granddad!
SERGEANT You're not 'ere to talk. Alertness is what we need, alertness. Be prepared for the unexpected. Stop Jerry creeping up in 'is submarines.

THREE Be easier if we had a fire going.

SERGEANT A fire! A fire! Don't be stupid, girl! Light a fire, Jerry'll be able to see his way clear here.

ONE 'Ow can 'e see a blinkin' fire from a submarine?

SERGEANT Not from a submarine – from an aeroplane.

TWO But an aeroplane'll see this flamin' spotlight anyhow!

SERGEANT (*Confidently, not realising the stupidity of it*) Not if you turn it off girl.

ONE If we're gonna turn it off we might as well all go home and stay warm in bed.

SERGEANT Just do as you're told, will you? Alertness. That's what we need, alertness. Now, just swing the lamp round a bit so's I can see me way past the boating lake.

ONE No submarines in there.

SERGEANT Mind your cheek or you'll be on a charge. (*Exit*)

ONE Silly old bugger.

TWO Where is 'e?

THREE Just by the lake.

TWO Turn the light off.

THREE What?

TWO Turn the light out a sec.

(*The light goes out. There is a loud splash followed by muffled swearing*).

TWO Sorry, Sergeant. 'Course, if we had a fire you could come and dry out up 'ere!

Spotlight on **ANNOUNCER** *dressed as comedian Max Miller*.

ANNOUNCER 'Ere. 'Ere's a funny thing, now this is a funny thing! When I joined the army – this'll surprise you – I joined the ATS and one morning I got all the girls on the parade ground and I said, 'Strip for gym,' I said, 'I'll be back in a minute.' Anyway, I came back and there's one of them standing there with all her clothes on. I said, 'I thought I told you to strip for gym.' She said, 'I should think so – I want to see him first!'

Soundtrack: Arthur Askey singing 'Kiss me Goodnight Sergeant Major'

Understanding the text

3 What factual material is there in this extract which tells you something about the war?

4 Look back to the way the story about the chocolates was orginally recorded in an interview (p 49) and compare it with the way it is used in the script extract. What differences can you see in
a the details of the story?
b the actual way it is told?
Why do you think these changes have been made?

5 What role are the girls playing in the extract? What is the attitude of their Sergeant towards them playing this role?

6 What is their attitude towards
a their role?
b the Sergeant?

7 What is the attitude of the comedian Max Miller towards girls in the services as it is presented here?

Practical work

8 No details are given as to what sort of characters the girls in the scene have, except through what they actually say (because of the lighting effect the audience would only be able to see them as figures in the darkness). How would you imagine them to be? Choose just one of the three and make notes on your impression of her. Consider a range of details such as age, looks, background as well as characteristics such as wit, opinions, habits and so on.

9 Find two other members of the class who have chosen the other two girls to focus their comments on. As a group of three, pick a short section of the script – 12 lines or so – and work on how the characteristics you have imagined could be used to bring that section to life.

10 In the same group, invent a new scene in which either
a the girls are talking about another incident involving their social lives, or
b they get into trouble with the Sergeant.

Reflection

11 How successful do you think you have been in maintaining the characters presented in the extract in your own improvisations? For example, the writing of the extract indicates that the women all talk with some sort of accent. Have you kept this going?

12 To what extent do you feel you have invented convincing characters rather than stereotyped ones?

SPECIAL ASSIGNMENT

Who do you know that might be able to provide you with some stories about life during the war? As a whole class, or in a group of your own choice, try to list as many people as you can who might talk to you about their memories. It is worth your while to remember that everyone has a story to tell and sometimes the most unlikely people come up with the best ones. Your task in this Special Assignment is to get them to start talking in order to collect some original data on which to base your own drama work.

You need to learn how to ask the right sort of question to get the ball rolling, so that one memory sparks off another. 'Open' questions are ones designed to let the person answering do most of the work because they give them more scope. So, instead of saying
  'Was it hard to live on rations?'
to which the answer might simply be
  'Yes'
try something like
  'Rationing is difficult for us to imagine now. How did you manage?'

Write down five questions that you think would produce interesting answers from people who have lived through the war. Check that they are written in the 'open' style so that they demand a full answer rather than one or two words.

Before going out and talking to the public it will be useful to try out your questions by setting up an improvisation in the classroom/studio. This is a 'split brief' improvisation like the one on p 31.

Take five or six members of your class to act as interviewers while the rest of the class set up a scene in the day room of an old people's club. On this particular day a group of students from the local school have been invited to talk to the members about their experiences in the war. Some might be quite looking forward to chatting, others might not be too keen to drag up too much of the past. Others may feel they have nothing to remember that will be useful. The interviewers' job is to gather as many stories as possible by making the old people feel that their stories are useful.

As the interviews go on, try to pick up on details as in this example.

OLD PERSON 'Of course, we all had to carry gas masks around.'
INTERVIEWER 'All the time or were there times when you couldn't be bothered?'
OLD PERSON 'Certainly. You try and dance romantically while you've got a something the size of a lunch box hanging round your neck!'

This exercise will help you see what sort of things might arise in a real interview. After keeping the improvisation going for perhaps 20 minutes, discuss what sort of dramatic possibilities there are in the material. Use the extract from *When the Lights Go On Again* as a model. Of course, in a real interview, things you know nothing about can come up (gas masks for example). Such things can be followed up after the interview by further documentary research.

The key is to be receptive and find out as much as you can.

If you are using a tape recorder, try it out first in the laboratory or the classroom or studio. You'll kick yourself if you discover too late that you were holding the microphone too far away and your interview sounds as if it's coming through a thick fog!

Turning research into drama

 Make a list of all the other ways in which you could record and collect original information about life on the 'Home Front'. Divide up the list, assigning specific research tasks to individuals or small groups.

As the stories begin to come in, improvise them and keep a record of how you have turned them into action.

Write out each piece of interesting information or story on a separate piece of paper. This will allow you to juggle them around to see how they might be linked together.

(Three different ones were used in the extract above. There was a searchlight based on the sea front and a submarine had been spotted in the Bristol Channel where the play was set. However, the woman who told the chocolates story was nothing to do with these pieces of information.)

This project may provide enough material and enthusiasm to create a whole play. However, it would be equally useful just to create a number of short scenes which use genuine stories to *bring characters to life convincingly*.

F Creating a Character

A valuable resource for both practical drama and written work is original photographs. Like so much source material, though, photographs need a certain amount of 'processing' before they can be used for a story or piece of drama.

Look at the photograph below. The only 'hard facts' we have are the women's names and that they are in uniform. With a little imagination, though, we could use this to create an infinite number of stories and situations.

Practical investigation

1 On your own or in pairs, devise a form that girls wanting to join the forces would have to fill in. Such a form would obviously ask for the applicant's name, age and address, but what other information do you think they would have to give?

In pairs, improvise a scene in which a recruitment officer is interviewing one of the girls. Decide which branch of the forces the girl wishes to enter. She may have a specific idea of what sort of job she wishes to do. If not, what sort of things might the recruitment officer be able to suggest? The officer has the application form but now needs to gather further details about the girl's attitude and 'suitability' for a position in the forces.

2 The girl on the right of the photograph is unnamed, yet in the top left-hand corner it says 'With love to all from Betty'. What might you assume from this?

3 Look at the girl called Lily. As a whole class sit in a circle. In turn each person contributes one small detail about Lily. Some of the information might be apparent from the photo:

> She is in the forces.
> She has a friend called Betty.

Invent other details which will help build an idea of her as a person.

> She has two brothers.
> Both are in the forces.
> She likes life in the forces.
> Her boyfriend disapproves of her new role . . .

Hot-seating

4 From the information you have just created you could try to bring this character to life further by 'hot-seating' her. Either as a whole group or, if you prefer, in groups of five or six, sit a member of the group in the gap of a horseshoe of chairs. Start by asking Lily some simple questions about herself so that she can get used to this difficult situation:

> *So, you're Lily, aren't you?*
> *How many brothers have you got?*
> *Have you got a boyfriend?*
> *What's his attitude to you being in the forces?*

From a straightforward opening you can see in the example above how you can start to find out about Lily as an individual. What are her attitudes to things? How does she see other people's attitudes to them?

An important rule in useful hot-seating is that anything the person being hot-seated says should be taken as being true. They may also refuse to answer if they feel that the question asked is too personal.

5 From the information you now have about Lily list some situations in which you would like to see her.

> *Lily tells her parents she has joined up.*
> *Lily sees her first corpse.*
> *Lily goes out with her boyfriend after a day in which she has done some unpleasant work / made her first really important decisions / been promoted.*

Record these ideas on a piece of paper as they come up. In suitably sized groups, produce an improvisation around a number of different situations. Each group must try to stay true to what you have agreed Lily is like as a character.

6 Having tried out some ideas through improvisation, work on your own or in pairs and write a script or story in which the character of Lily features.

G Maintaining a Role

Having created a character, how can an actor 'maintain' it? That is, how can the actor stay consistent and convincing through a number of different scenes and exchanges? The work in this unit should help you develop this difficult skill.

The picture below shows a document which everyone in the war would have known. It outlines the limitations on the buying of food, clothing and many other items which we tend to take for granted. It might be possible for you to find a genuine example of a ration book. It would certainly be worth asking anyone you interview about what rationing involved.

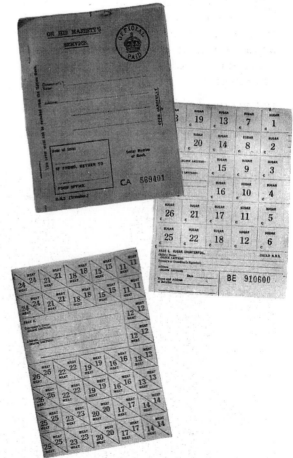

Improvisation

1 Rationing certainly involved long queues for items in short supply. Look at the picture below. Imagine that you are one of the people standing in such a queue. The shop you are queueing at is a general store. Decide what it is, precisely, that you are hoping to get today. As a whole class, form a queue waiting for the doors to open and start to improvise the sort of conversations which might have taken place. Try to keep the improvisation going for five minutes by inventing information as in these examples.

I hear they've got some new stock coming in this morning.
These flippin' kids around me ankles are driving me mad.
Oh no! It's starting to rain and I haven't got a brolly!

Be aware that each new contact or conversation you have will tell you something about
a your character
b the characters in the queue around you.
Make a mental note of how your character seems to be developing and what his or her attitudes are to the other characters in the queue and the situation in general.

2 After five minutes stop the improvisation and discuss the following questions:
a What was your impression of the other people in the queue?
b What sort of character were you trying to develop?
c Did you feel that each other's characters were convincing? Try to identify what worked and what didn't.
d What sort of things seemed to tell you most about the characters you used?

Deepening the characters

Real people have a 'three-dimensional' quality. Their characters seem to be made up of

a what they say about themselves
b what they say about other people and things
c what other people say about them
d what they actually do.

Very often these different factors conflict. Is the person who openly claims to be very modest seen like that by other people? When people insult others don't we sometimes feel that they might actually be jealous of them or unnecessarily unsympathetic?

On top of what people say, we have to consider that what they really think might be rather different. People who come across as being very confident and lively sometimes admit, in quiet conversations, to feeling lonely and unsure of themselves. For an acted character to be convincing, an audience has to see some depth in the character. Their actions and attitudes shouldn't be totally predictable. Instead, they should be able to change depending on the situation and what other characters are present. Try out the following improvisations, which aim to make a character feel more authentic and 'three-dimensional'.

3 Get into groups of three.
a **A** and **B** meet in a queue, **A** has a large family to feed and has recently been offered some goods on the 'black market'. The two of them discuss whether or not the offer should be taken. A decision is reached.
b **A** leaves the scene but is replaced by **C**. **B** tells **C** about **A**'s decision and the two of them discuss it.
c **B** leaves the scene as **A** returns. **A** and **C** only know each other slightly. How does their conversation go on?
Stop the improvisation and discuss what you have learned about each of the characters. Try to pinpoint how you learned this.

4 Choose a frozen picture (a **tableau**) from each of the three scenes you have just played. Remind yourselves of what was actually being said at this point. Then add, in a different tone of voice, what the characters are thinking. For example:

THAT'S IT, MRS FOTHERGILL, SOCK IT TO THEM!

WEAR THAT HAT AND THEY'LL ALL DIE LAUGHING!

Using a tableau in this way can allow you to create some interesting drama work. The technique is rather like the cartoon 'think' bubbles and can also be detected in those moments in some plays when the actors talk directly to the audience (these are often called **asides**).

5 In small groups, improvise a scene in which a soldier, home on leave, is telling his family about his exploits in the army. After each line actually spoken add an **aside** which would tell an audience either what the speaker is really thinking or what the attitude of one of the listeners is.

SOLDIER Aye, it's a hard life alright!
WIFE (*aside*) I bet he's down the pub every night!
SON Have you killed any Germans?
WIFE (*aside*) He wouldn't kill a spider he found in the bath last year if I remember rightly!
SOLDIER Loads, son. Loads. An' all big 'uns.
SOLDIER (*aside*) How can I tell him I haven't even seen a German?

Another way of developing a sense of character is to describe the world from their point of view. Simply by changing the way you say or write things, you can launch yourself into a new world belonging to a fictional character.

6 Look at the picture below. It shows women marching in protest against the lack of nursery provision, which stopped them going out and getting war work. Describe the scene but instead of saying, or writing, 'They are walking up a hill,' say it as if you are there – 'We are walking up a hill.' Get into small groups and, talking in the first person like this, create as much detail as you can about who and where you are.

7 The picture of women marching might be usefully developed into a sequence of tableaux. The women are clearly on their way somewhere. In groups, organise a series of still pictures which eventually show
- where they are going
- what happens when they get there.

For each individual tableau add any key lines that you think might be spoken at that moment or thoughts which could be spoken as 'asides'. The aim is to present a clear picture of what sort of characters are on this march and why.

Reflection

 8 Ask yourself the following questions about your work on character so far.

- Were you able to invent things to say in your role?
- Did you change the way you spoke? Did you feel this was convincing or did it sound terribly false?
- Did you change the way you moved?
- Did you manage to accept other people in their roles or did their acting make you lose concentration?
- What sort of things do you think might have helped make your character more convincing in other people's eyes?

STUDY EXTRACT TWO
Killed: July 16th 1916

Killed: July 16th 1916 is based on a true story from the First World War. It raises a number of issues about life on the 'Home Front', and particularly the role and situation of women there. We are going to use it to discover how characters can be developed by using a script. The story concerns a soldier, Billy Dean, who was tried for cowardice and sentenced by court martial to death by firing squad. The play cuts from the last night of Billy's life which he spends in a hut in France to a munitions factory in England where his wife is working on the night shift making bullets.

CHARACTERS

MAY A young wife whose husband Billy is at the front in France.

ELSIE A close friend friend of May's. Her husband was a friend of Billy's. He has already been killed in the war leaving Elsie to look after two young children.

Lights up on May in the munitions factory.

MAY (*writing*) July 16th, 7 o'clock.

She reads through her letter while putting on her hat.

My darling Billy, hoping you are well as I am. I thought I'd start this little note now and try and get it finished in me breaks. I'm doing a night shift tonight.

ELSIE *enters. She hangs up her shawl and starts to put on her overall.*

ELSIE Not another letter. That poor boy must be up to his ears in them by now, the number you send.

MAY (*still writing*) He likes them. Oh my God, is it time?

ELSIE Mmmm.

MAY Right, I'll have to finish this later now.

They start work.

Oh my God, Elsie, I'm that tired. I hardly got any sleep today. Bloomin' kids were out in the street playing tin-tan-alley man at the tops of their voices.

ELSIE Mother was trying to keep my lot quiet. Fat chance.

MAY Is she looking after them tonight? Is she?

ELSIE No, George.

MAY Oh eh, he's getting his feet under the mat isn't he? Be móving in next!

ELSIE Don't be so wet. He's very good with them. The boys love him, especially Sammy. Thinks the world of him. Makes him into a real hero.

MAY Oh. It'll be a shame when he has to go. Has he had his call-up papers yet?

ELSIE Yes, they came last week.

MAY Charlie Harris had his last week and he's got to go on Monday and he's got a hacking cough. Me dad says they'll be taking them with wooden legs next.

ELSIE They're taking anything now. And he's married, Charlie Harris. It's hitting families hard now they're forcing men to go.

MAY Aye, well, they need them. They need all the men they can get.

ELSIE I remember when this factory was full of men. Now look at it. Three left. That's why they've got us here. 'Cos there aren't any men left. We're filling up dead men's places here.

MAY Don't be so morbid. They're not all dead.

ELSIE Did you see that man in the pub the other night? Sitting over in the corner. His hand was shaking so he couldn't hold his beer glass. He looked dreadful. Shell shock, that's what they're calling it. He'd no control. His nerves were all shot to pieces. He'll never work again that feller.

MAY I know, poor man. My God, these bullets. D'you know, I dream about them?

ELSIE Do you? So do I.

MAY Yeah.

ELSIE I'm packing bullets in me sleep now.

MAY D'you know, Elsie, no kidding, the other day I woke up and I was saying. 'More bullets, more bullets, more bullets.'

ELSIE *laughs.*

ELSIE I wonder how many we've made since we've been working here.
MAY (*unthoughtfully*) Thousands.

They continue to work.

So, when's George going then?
ELSIE He won't be going.
MAY Why, is something wrong with him?
ELSIE No, there's nothing wrong with him.
MAY Well, why isn't he going, then?
ELSIE He says he's not going. He sent back his papers. He's refusing to go. He says nobody's got the right to make his decisions for him.
MAY Well, it's the same for everybody else.
ELSIE He says nobody's got the right to tell him to kill men he doesn't want to kill, if it's against his conscience.
MAY Oh, he's a conchie then.
ELSIE That's what they call them.
MAY Don't you mind?

ELSIE He's a good man, May.
MAY People will say he's a coward.
ELSIE Well, people can say what they like.

Lights fade.

Understanding the text

 1 How would you describe the relationship between Elsie and May at the start of this scene?

2 How do you think their relationship changes as the scene develops? Where in the extract would you say these changes took place?

3 What reasons seem to lie behind the changes in attitude of Elsie and May to each other?

4 List what you have found out about Elsie's home life from this scene.

5 Who is George?

6 What do you think Elsie means when she says, 'We're filling dead men's places here'?

Recreating the character

7 Try 'hot-seating' Elsie and May by taking two people from your group to play their parts. Seat them at opposite ends of the room and go to interview them both on
- who they are
- their attitude to their job
- their attitude to each other
- their hopes and fears for the future.

8 Improvise the scene in the pub which Elsie refers to. She talks of a man in the corner who has come back from the war. In your improvisation try to show different people's attitudes towards him. Include the following people and any others you can think of.
- Men who have not been fighting.
- A couple of soldiers home on leave.
- The women whose husbands are at the front.

Maintaining the character

9 As Elsie is on night shift in the factory she probably doesn't see much of her children. In small groups, improvise the scene when Elsie arrives home in the morning just as the children are going to school. What is the relationship between them like?

10 In pairs, improvise the next scene in which the women meet. Do Elsie and May make up? If so, how? Or does the relationship continue to be strained? If so, what happens to make it dramatically interesting?

11 There is often a temptation when telling a story or making a play to tie things up at the end so that everything makes sense. You may feel that real life isn't actually like this. People often do things which are unexpected and seem out of character. It is this individuality and unpredictability that makes life both interesting and frustrating.

Develop an improvisation or story from this scene which shows how the characters' lives change as a result of their wartime experience in the munitions factory.

STUDY EXTRACT THREE
Touched

For the six years of the Second World War many women had to look after themselves in a way they had never done before. Just as it must have been hard for women to get used to their new roles and responsibilities, it must have been hard for them to go back to their old way of life when the war ended. Women who had good jobs and had learned to cope on their own were expected to revert to being housewives for men who, sometimes, came home very different from the ones who had gone away.

Women weren't the only ones on the 'Home Front' of course. The particular pressures some of the men might have faced are also worth investigating – consider George in _Killed_, or Johnny in this extract from _Touched_.

Touched is a play all about life on the 'Home Front'. This is what playwright Stephen Lowe says about it.

> I was not born until the Second World War had been over for two years. I was part of the post-war boom, the 'babies boom', bred out of joy, relief, accident or simply the resumption of old habits. And I grew up with the usual pulp of heroic war films, and comics, only much later challenged by a purge of anti-war literature. While I therefore gained a fairly graphic picture of the life of the soldier, it occurred to me, one fine day while talking with my mother, that I had hardly any picture of the world of those who stayed at home – those whose different battles had been fought in the landscape I had grown up in. I knew nothing, really, about the sacrifice and suffering of the women who only a few years later were to pick me up and put me down, and place pennies in my hand. Pennies I had never thought to return.
>
> As I listened more closely to the tale of my mother and her friends, the background to this play about three sisters began to grow . . .

This extract comes from near the start of the play. It is VE night – the Prime Minister has announced earlier in the day that the Germans have surrendered. (Fighting is still going on in other places around the world.) People have come onto the streets and spontaneous celebrations start. Church bells ring for the first time in six years. The scene is set in the backyard of a terraced house in Nottingham. The play centres on the character of Sandra.

CHARACTERS

SANDRA Something of a mystery to her family. She often seems to be in a dream world. Some might say she is a romantic; others think that she's a bit 'touched' ie mad.

PAULINE Sandra's niece.

JOHNNY At seventeen, Johnny isn't yet old enough to be called up though due to his epilepsy he probably won't be anyway. He is fond of Sandra who, unlike many of the other women, doesn't tease him.

Slow spot up on an eight-year-old child, **PAULINE.** *She wears a pinned-up 'tunic' of the Union Jack, with a pillow stuffed under it, an old suit jacket, and a black saucepan on her head. She smokes a mock cigar, and holds a card with '1st' on it.*

ANNOUNCER He's wearing his boiler suit, the famous boiler suit he has made so wonderful, and he's putting on his black hat, nobody can say that it goes with the boiler suit but you heard what a cheer it raised from the crowd. And he stands in the floodlight and he's giving his Victory sign, with all his might from the floodlit balcony.

PAULINE *makes a victory sign, and giggles. She slowly begins to revolve, almost dancing in a tired fashion.*

CHURCHILL This is your Victory. Victory of the Cause of Freedom in every land. In all our long history we have never seen a greater day than this. Everyone, every man and woman, has done their bit, everyone has

tried, none have scrimped, in the long years and the dangers, or the fierce attack of the enemy, have in no way weakened the unbending resolve of the British nation. God Bless you ALL!

ANNOUNCER And now, listen. The band is playing Land of Hope and Glory, and the crowd is singing, and this suddenly has become a very moving moment. For Mr Churchill is singing, and he is conducting the singing of the song. Will you listen, please?

Sudden silence.

PAULINE (*softly*) Land of Hope and Glory Mother of the Free . . . (*pause*) God who made thee might . . . er . . . Make thee . . .

She can remember no more. She's very tired. Slow fade.

Scene Two

The scene as before. Night. The curtains of **SANDRA'S** *house have been taken down, and the dark yards are now lit in elongated patches by the light from hers and the houses opposite. Occasionally the sound and colours of fireworks illuminate the stage. Sounds of party from* **JOAN'S** *house. At the edge of hearing, Glen Miller's version of 'Don't Fence Me In',* **SANDRA** *leaves* **JOAN'S** *house and enters her own. She appears on her step.*

SANDRA Pauline, Pauline! Where are you?

She crosses down-stage to the darkened lavatory.

Anyone in there?

Silence. She listens.

Pauline, are you in there?
PAULINE (*off*) Yes, Auntie Sandra.
SANDRA What are you doing?
PAULINE (*off*) Listening to the music.
SANDRA Come on. You're s'posed to be tucked up in bed. Out. No mucking about.

PAULINE *comes out.*

SANDRA Well, you do look a sorry sight, and no mistake.

PAULINE Can I go to the party?

SANDRA You've had your party for today. You can hardly stand up you're that tired. Anyhow, it's not a proper party. No jelly, or ought. Not too keen on it meself.

PAULINE I put me party dress back on.

SANDRA So I see.

PAULINE I won.

SANDRA Your mam's ever so proud. She's telling everybody about you.

PAULINE Is she?

SANDRA Well, if you don't fancy bed, come keep me company a bit, eh? What have you got up here – kittens?

She removes the pillow padding.

Sit on that, it'll take the cold off your bum.

They sit in the dark.

PAULINE What you doing?

SANDRA Lighting a fag.

PAULINE Light mine as well. (*Holds up cigar.*)

SANDRA You save that one. Special.

PAULINE Do you think me mam'll let me have a pet now?

SANDRA She might. You never know.

PAULINE Are you going to have a pet?

SANDRA I'm going to have more than a pet. I'm going to have hundreds of animals. Lots of cows and sheep.

PAULINE Round here?

SANDRA No, not round here. I'm going to join one of them Wagon Trains, and go out West. And soon I'll be sitting up on high, with a pretty little bonnet on, and my dress all swelled out with petticoats bouncing across the Prairies. Jess by my side, a quiet, strong man, a man a woman could be proud of.

PAULINE Where's Uncle Albert?

SANDRA Do you remember your Uncle Albert?

PAULINE Not really.

SANDRA Remember your Dad?

PAULINE Oh yes. Don't like him.

SANDRA Why not?

PAULINE Rows all the time.

SANDRA Be different now.

PAULINE Where will you live?

SANDRA Just keep going 'til we come to the end of the rainbow.

PAULINE What rainbow?

SANDRA An't they told you the story about the rainbow at Sunday School?

PAULINE Don't remember.

SANDRA Oh, it's a smashing story . . . You see. God once thought men were so wicked that he'd start all over again, so he flooded the world and everybody got drowned. Everybody except Noah, who he had let in on it, and Noah put his family and loads of animals all in a big boat and they rode the storm out, and to show Noah that he wouldn't wipe men out again, he gave him a sign which was the rainbow. The rainbow is made by the sun coming out whilst it's still raining, you see. And you get all these colours like the fireworks, and you know everything's going to get better and the rain isn't going on for much longer, and then you follow that rainbow, and when you get to the end you find a pot of gold, and that's the promised land; California. And me and Jess will build this big house there, and have a huge family, and lots of animals, and work hard, and sing songs, and you can come and spend your holidays with us.

Another flare illuminates her face – the child is asleep. She puts out her cigarette. JOHNNY *coughs.*

SANDRA Who's that?

JOHNNY (*stepping into the light*) Me. Johnny.

SANDRA You shoun't go sneaking up on folk like that.

JOHNNY I was trying not to make you jump. That's why I coughed. Only I walk light, I'm not very heavy.

SANDRA I'm a bit nervy, that's all. Were just telling the kid a story.

JOHNNY Yes.

SANDRA What you up to then?

JOHNNY I wondered if Betty were here.

SANDRA She weren't in the party when I was there.

JOHNNY Lost her up the arboretum. It's floodlit up there.

SANDRA I saw they'd done Slab Square.

JOHNNY And the castle. Just like the back of the fag packets. Would you care for a cigarette?

SANDRA You've bought some, have you?

JOHNNY Ye', I did.

SANDRA Pop in. Have a look. She might have turned up.

JOHNNY Might. Here you are.

SANDRA I've just put one out, duck.

JOHNNY Can treat yourself a bit now.

SANDRA Go on then. Don't wake little un up, though.

He lights her cigarette, and begins to walk around.

JOHNNY Much warmer now, in't it?

SANDRA Ye'.

JOHNNY Do you think she'll be all right?

SANDRA She's got a head on her shoulders. She'll come to no harm tonight.

JOHNNY I don't mind. I just keep her company, make sure she's all right.

SANDRA Not a lot of mates left for you to knock around with, is there?

JOHNNY Get used to it.

SANDRA Do you still get your . . . you still have your fits, do you?

JOHNNY Nought like I used to. I woun't be surprised if it disappeared completely. Mr Fowler who runs the warehouse says when we get a proper health system, they'll set me up in no time, and I'll be out there wi' the lads, gi'in' it the Japs.

SANDRA (*pauses*) Good.

JOHNNY Where did they find Mr Downes?

SANDRA One of them camps near Rangoon, somewhere.

JOHNNY Be home soon, then, will he?

SANDRA Telegram said they were sending him to Australia for six months. To recuperate. Doing that with all the POWs. I don't know that they won't send him back in the fight again. You never know what they'll do.

A really incandescent, iridescent firework.

JOHNNY They must be shooting them off the castle.

SANDRA The last time I remember the sky lit up like this, was '41 Summer. When they hit us. I was coming out of the house, with Jimmy, to get down the Anderson, just coming out the back door here, and he starts laughing. He'd be what, two, and we stood on this step and looked up at that sky. It don't seem real after all that waiting for 'em, more like a film. 'Course it didn't have any meaning to Jimmy not at his age, but it didn't have a lot for me. It was just a fantastic night sky with these long white beams and flares of all colours, reds, blues, greens; the whole place lit up. Like a giant bonfire. Fires. Like tonight. And he was killing himself laughing, and reaching out to catch the flares, like night butterflies. Funny that he were safer then wi' all the lights and bombs, than in the blackout.

JOHNNY Mr Fowler says there'll be an election soon. Get our people in this go. Labour Party. I'm going to canvas round here. For Mr Harrison, I think. They need people like me, he said.

SANDRA Me arm's gone dead. I'd better get her up to my bed, 'fore she catches her death.

JOHNNY Here. (*He laboriously picks the child up.*)

SANDRA Don't drop her, for Christ's sake. Here. Give her me.

JOHNNY You shouldn't be carrying her.

SANDRA Why ever not?

JOHNNY Well, you are a woman.

SANDRA (*smiles*) Out the road.

She enters the house with PAULINE. JOHNNY *stands outside, watching the flares. He pretends to machine-gun an aeroplane.*

Understanding the text

1 One way of approaching a new text is simply to make some 'informed guesses' about it. Look at these questions and try, by picking out actual lines from the script, to make a judgement on them.

a Who is Betty?
b What is her relationship to Sandra?
c What is her opinion of Johnny?
d Who is Mr Downes and what do you think might have happened to him?
e Who was Jimmy?
f Why does Johnny change the subject after Sandra's line, 'Funny, that he were safer then wi' all the lights and bombs than in the blackout'?
g Why does Sandra smile after Johnny's line, 'Well, you are a woman'?

2 Some of the themes of a play are open to wider interpretation. There are rarely 'right' answers but you can use the script and combine it with both your imagination and what you know about life on the 'Home Front' to make up your own opinions. These are just some of the questions you could ask yourself.

a What are Sandra's hopes for the future?
b Do you think they are realistic?
c What sort of life has Johnny had through the war?

3 What will be the audience's attitude to Pauline when they see her twirling in the spotlight as Churchill's voice is played over the loudspeakers?

Producing the scenes

4 In groups of three, look at the lines in which Sandra tells Pauline the story and Johnny enters. Rehearse the scene in order to show clearly
a Sandra's attitude to Pauline
b Sandra's attitude to Johnny
c Sandra's own hopes and fears at this moment.

Pay careful attention to tone of voice and position on stage in order to show these attitudes.

5 Sketch or describe a set for this scene that would say something about Sandra's character and lifestyle.

6 List the lighting effects mentioned in the scene. Draw a plan view of the set and show where you would position the lights to achieve these effects. State what type of lights you would use, and what colours. (See the Special Assignment in Chapter Three for guidance.)

Practical improvisation work

7 In small groups, invent some characters who have mixed feelings about the war ending. To start off with, just let them express two simple contrasting feelings, as in these examples.

THE YOUNG WIFE My husband will be home soon . . . I shall have to tell him about my affair with the American.
THE UNFIT MAN My mates will come back . . . and they'll all be talking about the action which I haven't seen.
THE FACTORY WOMAN There'll be no more raids on this factory. . . . but I'll probably lose this job now anyway.

This format can be developed into an interesting piece of theatre simply by positioning the speakers carefully and perhaps putting an action to each line spoken. You might choose to finish the piece by finding one idea that is common to all the characters.

8 It is VE (Victory in Europe) night. A group of people are talking about their great plans for the future. Devise a scene in which the audience both hears what those plans are and gets a sense of whether or not the characters really believe they may come true. (A development could be made here by adopting the 'aside' technique explained earlier.)

Daily Mail

FOR KING AND EMPIRE

TUESDAY, MAY 8, 1945

NO. 15,290 — ONE PENNY

I SMELL PINEAPPLE

TUESday FIELD-DAY

3-POWER ANNOUNCEMENT TO-DAY; BUT BRITAIN KNEW LAST NIGHT

VE-DAY—IT'S ALL OVER

All quiet till 9 p.m.—then the London crowds went mad in the West End

By Day ↑
↓ By Night

THE Face of Victory—by day and by night—Broadways in and around Piccadilly circus were jammed nearly solid yesterday afternoon by crowds waiting to hear VE-Day announced. Then they decided not to wait—they began to celebrate. These Daily Mail pictures give you a vivid impression of the great crowds—of the—above by day; in the left, by night. Other scenes—Pages THREE and FOUR.

PM put off the big speech
UNTIL TO-DAY
By WILSON BROADBENT, Diplomatic Correspondent

GERMANY surrendered unconditionally to the Allies yesterday. But there will be no official announcement of victory until 1 p.m. to-day—officially described as VE-Day—when Mr. Churchill will give the news to the world.

CZECHS TOLD TO 'SMASH GERMANS'

TARAKAN NEARLY CUT IN TWO

U.S. made it VE-Day all the same
Work walk-out
From DON IDDON, Daily Mail Correspondent

THIS was VE-Day in the U.S.—official or not.

Jammed roads

SYMBOL, of the mood of London. lamp-post, wears a flag above the this man, at the top of a crowds—Daily Mail picture.

The war still goes on here—
PRAGUE BOMBED AS SS SHOOT CZECH CIVILIANS

GERMAN bombs are falling on Prague for the first time as the war in Europe enters its last hours. In defiance of surrender orders, German forces in Czecho-Slovakia are fighting on. They are venting their last spite on the Czechs, shooting them down ruthlessly in the streets of the capital.

'Evil Hitler'

Pilsen kisses

THE WEATHER

Beacon chain begun by Piccadilly's bonfires
By GUY RAMSEY

LONDON, dead from six until nine, suddenly broke into victory life last night. Suddenly, spontaneously, deliriously. The people of London, denied VE-Day officially, held their own jubilation. "VE-Day may be to-morrow," they said, "but the war is over to-night." Bonfires blazed from Piccadilly to Wapping.

The sky once lit by the glare of the blitz shone red with the Victory glow. The last trains departed from the West End unregarded. The pent-up spirits of war-time, burst out, and by 11 o'clock the capital was ablaze with enthusiasm.

Processions formed up out of nowhere, disintegrating for no reason, to re-form somewhere else. Waving flags, marching in step, with linked arms or half-embraced, the people strode down the great thoroughfares—Piccadilly, Regent-street, the Mall, to the portals of Buckingham Palace.

They marched and counter-marched so as not to get too far from the centre. And from them, in harmony and discord, rose song. The songs of the last war, the songs of a century ago. "Roll out the Barrel" and "Tipperary"; "Tifla Moor" and "Loch Lomond"; "Bless em All" and "Pack Up Your Troubles."

ROCKETS AND SONGS

Rockets—found no-one knew where, set-off by no one knows whom—streaked into the sky, exploding not in death but a burst of scarlet fire. A pile of straw filled with thunder-flashes salvaged from some military dump spurted and exploded near Leicester-square.

SCHACHT SAVED BY 'FIFTH'
Niemoller, too
Daily Mail Special Correspondent

GOEBBELS' BODY IN A SHELTER

GOEBBELS, the German Propaganda Minister, his wife, and five children have been found dead in Berlin.

MONTY MEETS ROKOSSOVSKY
4 toasts at lunch

Home by searchlight

ARRESTED POLES MAY BE TRIED BY LUBLIN

LUBLIN radio said yesterday

Victory lunch

Continued in Back Page, Col. 6

9 In the play *Killed* the audience becomes aware of an irony in that while Billy is waiting to be shot, his wife is making bullets. In a scene in *Touched*, a group of women are seen working in a factory which makes condoms for the soldiers abroad; some of them are married to soldiers abroad! Invent a scene in which someone on the 'Home Front' is placed in a situation that makes them do something which in normal circumstances would seem unacceptable to them.

Written tasks

10 Imagine a group of people standing on a hilltop watching fireworks launched in celebration of the end of the war. As they watch fleeting memories occur to them about things that have happened in the war. Write them down in a short and sharp way. They don't necessarily have to lead on from one another. The object is to simply find and tie down as many ideas as possible that might lead on to further development, like these examples.

a *Remember that first siren? How scared we all were?*
b *Those dreadful gas masks, I don't even know where mine is now.*
c *The day Harry went away in that brand new uniform . . .*

11 Try to write a dialogue in which one short memory sparks off another and a story begins to develop through the conversation.

a *The night Aunty Flo was in the lav when the siren went . . .*
b *She came running out with her drawers round her ankles . . .*
c *Laughed so loud, didn't hear the bombs at first . . .*

12 By choosing just a very few words and arranging them carefully your dialogue might start to look like a poem.

Dank, dark shelters.
Got used to them.
And the blackout.
'Put the light out'
The voice in the dark.
You didn't argue . . .

Working in small groups, try to write a sequence like this. How could this be effectively staged in order to create an atmosphere of people lost in their own memories? After trying it out yourselves practically, insert a series of stage directions into the script which would help another group of actors recreate that atmosphere.

13 Stories and plays often benefit from having an ending which allows the audience to go away thinking that there is more to come for the characters they have met. Rather than ending scenes with 'Right then, let's all go down the pub (*exit*)' or stories that end 'then they all went home and had tea,' it can be better to stop on something less final.

That's it then.
All bar the shouting.
Look at that sky.
Yes, tomorrow will be a lovely day . . .

Write the last sequence of lines for a scene set on VE night and add any stage directions or suggestions for lighting or sound effects which might produce an effective ending.

14 Design either a set for this new scene or suggest a lighting plot that would help create an appropriate atmosphere. Explain, in note form, what effect you want and how your designs will achieve it.

Reflection

15 This chapter has focused on **characterisation**. Imagine you are a well-known and experienced actor who has been asked by some young students to give some advice on building and maintaining characters. Jot down in your working notebook what you would consider to be five important tips for them to remember.

Further Reading

Plays

The Accrington Pals by Peter Whelan (Methuen). A powerful play about life in a Lancashire town during the First World War. Many of the town's men were killed on the same day during the battle of the Somme.

Andorra by Max Frisch (Methuen). Set in a fictitious country which is occupied by an enemy army. The play is a harrowing account of what happens to people who live under constant threat.

Ghetto by Joshua Sobol (Nick Hern Books). The extraordinary story of how the Jews in a Polish Ghetto managed to keep their theatre company going throughout the Nazi occupation.

Fear and Misery of the Third Reich by Bertolt Brecht (Methuen). A series of very short playlets which combine to give a rich and varied picture of Germany under Hitler.

Oh! What A Lovely War by Charles Chilton and the Theatre Workshop (Methuen). This musical play tells the story of the First World War through a series of short, often comic, scenes and well-known songs from the period.

Schweyk in the Second World War by Bertolt Brecht (Methuen). The story of a very reluctant recruit in Hitler's army, which focuses on the way people deny responsibility for the things that happen in the world.

Plenty by David Hare (Faber). How do women who are trained and used in exciting and dangerous wartime operations cope with quiet, domestic life once the war is over? This play is about a resistance fighter who can't stop fighting.

The Imitation Game by Ian McEwan (Penguin). Focuses on an ATS girl who, while working for military intelligence, accidentally gets to know too much.

Salonika by Louise Page (Methuen). When a woman goes to Greece for her holiday she is surprised to encounter the ghost of her grandfather who died there in the First World War.

Evacuees by Jack Rosenthal (Faber). Two Jewish boys from Manchester are sent away to safety only to find their foster mother far too fond of them.

No Man's Land by Paul Swift (Thomas Nelson). Maggie Bell goes from working as a housemaid to arms factory worker and finds herself fighting a system that discriminates against women, as well as fighting the First World War.

Fiction

A Long Way to Go Majorie Darke (Puffin)
Goodnight Mr Tom Michele Magorian (Puffin)
The Summer of My German Soldier Bette Greene (Puffin)
Carrie's War Nina Bawden (Puffin)
Dawn of Fear Susan Cooper (Puffin)
The Dolphin Crossing Jill Paton Walsh (Puffin)
Fireweed Jill Paton Walsh (Puffin)
Maus Art Spiegler (Penguin)
After the Dancing Days Margaret Rostkowski (Heineman)
Strange Meeting Susan Hill (Penguin)
Evacuee Gabriel Allington (Walker)
The Machine Gunners Robert Westall (Puffin)
Fathom Five Robert Westall (Puffin)
The Silver Sword Ian Serrailer (Puffin)
The Edge of War Dorothy Horgan (OUP)
War Games by Michael Foreman (Puffin)
Rose Blanch by Roberto Innocenti (Cape)

Non-fiction

Bombers and Mash Raynes Minns (Virago)
No Time to Wave Goodbye Ben Wicks (Bloomsbury)
What Greater Glory B W Caws and R F Watts (Blackie)
Living Through the Blitz Tom Harrison (Penguin)
The People's War Angus Calder (Panther)
We'll Meet Again Robert Kee (Dent)
The Home Front 1939–45 Marion Yass (Wayland)
The Day they took the Children Ben Wicks (Bloomsbury)
Evacuees by Andy Kempe & Rick Holroyd (Hodder & Stoughton)

Relationships and conflict

A What Makes a Character/69
B Study Extract – *Master Harold . . . and the Boys*/71

This project further develops the skill of CHARACTERISATION by looking at DRAMATIC RELATIONSHIPS.

The work involves ANALYSING a PLAYSCRIPT. It illustrates how characters can communicate the message of a play and will help you PLAN your own improvisations.

What Makes a Character?

What do you think makes characters the way they are?

- Their biological make-up – the way they look, for example?
- Their parents?
- Their education?
- The area they come from?
- The general society in which they live?

The truth in most cases is probably a combination of all of these. But what if just one of these factors becomes, for some reason, particularly important in the way that person mixes with other people?

Consider, for example, the dramatic possibilities of the following.

- A person who has been born with enormous physical deformity (you may have seen the film *The Elephant Man*) into a society which allows 'freaks' to be displayed in circuses.

- A person who has been extremely spoiled by their parents in an area where other children have little.

- A person who has been to an exclusive public school and is transferred to a very average comprehensive.

- A person who has a strong regional or cultural accent (Cockney, Scouse, Jamaican, Bangladeshi and so on) whose job involves talking to people unused to the accent.

- A person who has strong political or religious beliefs who lives in a country where such beliefs are banned.

1 In small groups, choose one of the situations above and improvise a scene which illustrates
a how the person (we'll call them the *Subject*) reacts to those around him or her
b how other people react to them.

2 Watch each other's scenes and discuss what you thought they suggested about

a the character of the *Subject* (Were they tough enough to cope? Did they resent their situation or the way they were treated? What were their expectations of others?)
b the nature of the society in which they were placed (Was it tolerant of people who were different? Was it helpful? Obstructive? Cruel?)

3 In small groups again, devise a second scene in which the *Subject* finds they have a *Friend* in the new situation. Your scene should show this friendship demonstrated in some way. For example, the *Friend* intervenes when they see the *Subject* being bullied, or explains how to do something which everyone else seems to be able to do but the *Subject* can't.

Dramatic relationships

In Task 1 above, the drama focused on the relationship between a character and the situation they were in. In Task 3, the focus began to change more to the character's relationship with another character.

Relationships between characters serve an important function in drama. The more clearly they are drawn, the more clearly an audience can understand both the individual characters and the general situation they are in. One way of making a relationship clear is to show it when it is being threatened. Just how much will it stand before breaking?

4 In small groups, develop a scene which follows on from the one in Task 3. In the new scene it becomes clear that most of the people in the situation resent the *Friend* being close to the *Subject*. They put pressure on the *Friend* to leave the *Subject* alone. Will the relationship between the *Friend* and the *Subject* be able to stand up to this?

5 Share these scenes with the rest of the class and discuss the following points.

a What sort of pressures do relationships sometimes have to face?
b What do these pressures suggest about those who apply them?
c What effect do these pressures have on the relationship between the *Subject* and the *Friend*?
d What does your answer to **c** suggest about the characters and their relationship?

The closer a relationship is, the more there is at stake when it is threatened. For example, in most cases people would do more to protect their family and closest friends than they would to protect strangers. The way these relationships are seen to react to pressure tells an audience a great deal and can, in fact, be the central theme of a piece of drama.

B STUDY EXTRACT
Master Harold . . . and the Boys

Athol Fugard is a South African actor, director and playwright. Until quite recently his country had strict apartheid laws which discriminated against the black population. Fugard was a stern critic of these laws and often fell foul of the government because of the way he made his views public and wrote plays which exposed the unfairness of the system.

The extract that follows comes from *Master Harold . . . and the Boys*. The play takes place in a café in South Africa in 1950. Harold, or Hally as he is called, is the son of a rich and powerful local white man. Hally is about 17 years old. Although Harold's father is the most important person around, he is also a notorious drunk. He has clearly not been a good father to Harold, or a good husband to his wife, or a good boss to his workers. Now, at the end of the play, the old man is dying and Harold will soon take over his business which includes the café. Willie and Sam are two black South Africans who run the bar. They are both older than Hally and he treats them as friends and equals rather than servants. His relationship with Sam is particularly close. Hally relates with affection how Sam made him a kite and showed him how to fly it when he was a small boy.

Despite their friendship, Harold is a member of the white 'master race' and Willie and Sam are black workers. How close can such a relationship ever really be? When Harold is made to feel small and insecure by the news that his father is home from the hospital where he is being treated for alcoholism, he reacts by attempting to display his racial superiority at the expense of that friendship.

CHARACTERS

HAROLD A white seventeen-year-old South African. The son of the café's owner. Hally, as he is known to those close to him, is an open and friendly young man but not really sure of himself. His attitude towards his father is ambivalent – that is, he loves him because he is his father but doesn't always like what he is or how he acts.

SAM He is at one level a friend to Hally, at another just one of his workers. However, in this extract we can see that there may be an even deeper sort of tie between them.

WILLIE Like Sam, he is a black worker and friend of Hally's. He isn't as old as Sam and his relationship with Hally isn't as close.

SAM Let's finish up.

HALLY Don't turn your back on me! I haven't finished talking.

He grabs **SAM** *by the arm and tries to make him turn around.* **SAM** *reacts with a flash of anger.*

SAM Don't do that, Hally! (*Facing the boy*) All right, I'm listening. Well? What do you want to say to me?

HALLY (*Pause as* **HALLY** *looks for something to say*) To begin with, why don't you also start calling me Master Harold, like Willie.

SAM Do you mean that?

HALLY Why the hell do you think I said it?

SAM And if I don't?

HALLY You might just lose your job.

SAM (*Quietly and very carefully*) If you make me say it once, I'll never call you anything else again.

HALLY So? (*The boy confronts the man*) Is that meant to be a threat?

SAM Just telling you what will happen if you make me do that. You must decide what it means to you.

HALLY Well, I have. It's good news. Because that is exactly what Master Harold wants from now on. Think of it as a little lesson in respect, Sam, that's long overdue, and I hope you remember it as well as you do your geography. I can tell you now that somebody who will be glad to hear I've finally given it to you will be my Dad. Yes! He agrees with my Mom. He's always going on about it as well. 'You must teach the boys to show you more respect, my son.'

SAM So now you can stop complaining about going home. Everybody is going to be happy tonight.

HALLY That's perfectly correct. You see, you mustn't get the wrong idea about me and my Dad, Sam. We also have our good times together. Some bloody good laughs. He's got a marvellous sense of humour. Want to know what our favourite joke is? He gives out a big groan, you see, and says: 'It's not fair, is it, Hally?' Then I have to ask: 'What, chum?' And then he says: 'A nigger's arse' . . . and we both have a good laugh.

The men stare at him with disbelief.

What's the matter, Willie? Don't you catch the joke? You always were a bit slow on the uptake. It's what is called a pun. You see, fair means both light in colour and to be just and decent. (*He turns to* **SAM**) I thought *you* would catch it, Sam.

SAM Oh ja, I catch it all right.

HALLY But it doesn't appeal to your sense of humour?

SAM Do you really laugh?

HALLY Of course.

SAM To please him? Make him feel good?

HALLY No, for heaven's sake! I laugh because I think it's a bloody good joke.

SAM You're really trying hard to be ugly, aren't you? And why drag poor old Willie into it? He's done nothing to you except show you the respect you want so badly. That's also not being fair, you know . . . and *I* mean just or decent.

WILLIE It's all right, Sam. Leave it now.

SAM It's me you're after. You should just have said 'Sam's arse' . . . because that's the one you're trying to kick. Anyway, how do you know it's not fair? You've never seen it.

Do you want to? (*He drops his trousers and underpants and presents his backside for* **HALLY'S** *inspection*) Have a good look. A real Basuto arse . . . which is about as nigger as they can come. Satisfied? (*Trousers up*) Now you can make your Dad even happier when you go home tonight. Tell him I showed you my arse and he is quite right. It's not fair. And if it will give him an even better laugh next time, I'll also let *him* have a look. Come, Willie, let's finish up and go.

SAM *and* **WILLIE** *start to tidy up the tea room.* **HALLY** *doesn't move. He waits for a moment when* **SAM** *passes him.*

HALLY (*Quietly*) Sam . . .

SAM *stops and looks expectantly at the boy.* **HALLY** *spits in his face. A long and heartfelt groan from* **WILLIE**. *For a few seconds* **SAM** *doesn't move.*

SAM (*Taking out a handkerchief and wiping his face*) It's all right, Willie.
(*To* **HALLY**) Ja, well, you've done it . . . Master Harold. Yes, I'll start calling you that from now on. It won't be difficult anymore. You've hurt yourself, Master Harold, I saw it coming. I warned you, but you wouldn't listen. You've just hurt yourself *bad*. And you're a coward, Master Harold. The face you should be spitting in is your father's . . . but you used mine, because you think you're safe inside your fair skin . . . and this time I don't mean just or decent. (*Pause, then moving violently towards* **HALLY**) Should I hit him, Willie?

WILLIE (*Stopping* **SAM**) No, Boet Sam.

SAM I don't want to help! I want to hurt him.

WILLIE You also hurt yourself.

SAM And if he had done it to you, Willie?

WILLIE Me? Spit at me like I was a dog? (*A thought that had not occurred to him before. He looks at* **HALLY**) Ja. Then I want to hit him. I want to hit him hard!

A dangerous few seconds as the men stand staring at the boy. **WILLIE** *turns away, shaking his head.*

But maybe all I do is go cry at the back. He's

little boy, Boet Sam. Little *white* boy. Long trousers now, but he's still little boy.

SAM (*His violence ebbing away into defeat as quickly as it flooded*) You're right. So go on, then: groan again, Willie. You do it better than me. (*To* **HALLY**) You don't know all of what you've done . . . Master Harold. It's not just that you've made me feel dirtier than I've ever been in my life . . . I mean, how do I wash off yours and your father's filth? . . . I've also failed. A long time ago I promised myself I was going to try and do something, but you've just shown me . . . Master Harold . . . that I've failed. (*Pause*) I've got a memory of a little white boy when he was still wearing short trousers and a black man, but they're not flying a kite. It was the old Jubilee days, after dinner one night. I was in my room. You came in and just stood against the wall, looking down at the ground, and only after I'd asked you what you wanted, what was wrong, I don't know how many times, did you speak and even then so softly I almost didn't hear you. 'Sam, please help me to go and fetch my Dad.' Remember? He was dead drunk on the floor of the Central Hotel Bar. They'd phoned for your Mom, but you were the only one at home. And do you remember how we did it? You went in first by yourself to ask permission for me to go into the bar. Then I loaded him onto my back like a baby and carried him back to the boarding house with you following behind carrying his crutches. (*Shaking his head as he remembers*) A crowded Main Street with all the people watching a little white boy following his drunk father on a nigger's back! I felt for that little boy . . . Master Harold. I felt for him. After that we still had to clean him up, remember? He'd messed in his trousers, so we had to clean him up and get him into bed.

HALLY (*Great pain*) I love him, Sam.

SAM I know you do.

Understanding the text

 1 In this scene, Hally is trying to show his authority over Willie and Sam. Divide a piece of paper into two columns and mark one 'Hally' and the other 'The Boys'. What sort of things give Hally authority over the boys? Note them down on your paper. Are there any ways though in which the boys – particularly Sam – have some authority over Hally? Compare the two lists and discuss, in small groups, what they suggest about

a the characters in the scene
b their relationship with each other
c South African society at the time.

2 Why do you think Sam says

'If you make me say it once, I'll never call you anything else again'?

Why does Sam think that it is an effective threat?

3 Look at the way the word 'boy' is used throughout the scene. For example, is there a difference between what it implies in the stage direction

The boy confronts the man.

and when Hally reports his mother saying

'You must teach the boys to show you more respect'?

What do we learn about Hally's relationship with Willie and Sam, and his parents' relationship with them, through the way the word 'boy' is used?

4 What is the effect of Hally explaining the joke he has with his father on the relationship between him and Sam?

5 Sam suggests that Hally only laughs to please his father. Why do you suppose Hally wants to please his father in this way?

6 When Sam threatens to hit Hally, Willie suggests that he will hurt himself also. What do you think he means by this?

Producing the scene

7 Look at the lines at the beginning of the extract, down to the stage direction *'The men stare at him . . .'*. In pairs replay the lines a number of times over, concentrating on the effect that changing the pace will have at the end of each sentence. For example, try it with

- Sam talking slowly and patiently and Hally snapping
- Sam shouting and Hally talking calmly
- both of them shouting
- both of them being calm
- moving from calm to shouting/shouting to calm.

Which combination seems to best show that the relationship between them is at a turning point?

8 Look at Hally's speech in which he tells the joke. In groups of three, act this out but, before starting, decide on where the characters should stand in relation to one another. Should Hally talk directly to them, or face away from them, or change at certain moments (which ones)?

Having experimented with various positions, freeze in what you feel to be the most appropriate position for the stage direction

The men stare at him with disbelief

Share your ideas with the rest of the class and discuss what effect different solutions have on an audience.

9 In contrast to this speech look at Sam's retelling of the story of Hally's drunken father. In threes again, experiment to see how you could position the actors to show

- that their relationship has broken down forever
- that Sam feels sorry for Hally
- that Sam feels distrust and anger towards the whites
- that the two of them want to be friends but can't because of the political situation
- that the three men 'make up' but, inside, they know things will never be the same again.

Further development

 10 In line 18 Sam has warned Hally that if Hally insists on being called 'Master Harold' he will never call him anything again. He tells Hally 'You must decide what it means to you'. In pairs, improvise a scene in which one person is faced with a choice between keeping a friendship or gaining something else. Decide
a what it is they stand to gain
b why they can't have this thing as well as friendship.

11 As a whole class consider other social rules or conditions which could affect personal relationships. Record your ideas. In small groups, choose one and create a chart like the one shown on the next page to see what scenes might be created from just one issue. (You may wish to add other possible scenes to this chart.)

12 Improvise or write a script for one of the scenes outlined on your chart.

13 Write a **treatment** for a play which traces the course of a relationship. The scenes described in the treatment will show

a how the relationship came about
b how the characters grew closer
c why the relationship was threatened
d how the characters reacted to that pressure
e whether or not the relationship withstood the pressure.

Reflection

14 Can you think of any films, plays or television dramas which seem to have focused on a personal relationship in order to say something about a society more generally? Write a review of one which you enjoyed, describing briefly what the story was and then discussing how the relationship was developed and used to reflect the society.

15 How would you judge an actor's ability to play a character? In the Evaluation section in Project One I suggested that drama work can be evaluated by considering its **content** and **form**. To judge somebody's playing of a character (including, of course, your own work), you will need to consider

● how well are they communicating in the actor/audience situation (volume and clarity of voice, use of space and movement)?
● what is the purpose of this character in the play (what is their attitude, what sort of person are they, what effect does their personality have on other people, including the audience)?

Choose just one character from a TV series or film with which you are familiar. Jot down some notes about

● how well the actor playing the part acts in your opinion (you must, of course say *why* you think what you do)
● what the purpose of that character seems to be in the series/film.

Employer/Employee

A boss of a small firm is very fair to all her employees, regardless of their race. Other bosses in her Trade Association resent this and are unwilling to support her plans for extending the business.

Scene: The morning after a Trade Association meeting, an employee asks the Boss for a rise to pay for his child's operation.

RACIAL DISCRIMINATION

Activist/Pacifist

Two close friends witness a police squad savagely victimise a group protesting against police brutality. One of the witnesses has a sister beaten up in the incident.

Scene: After the incident, one of the witnesses wants to lodge a formal complaint. The other is not so keen.

Parent/Child

A parent feels strongly about racial discrimination and has spoken out publicly. This results in the child being bullied at school.

Scene: The child comes home having been beaten up.

Boy/Girl

A boy and girl from different racial backgrounds have been going out together. Both sets of parents have forbidden them to see each other again.

Scene: They tell each other what their parents have said and decide what to do next.

Building a play around characters

This project offers a structured way of generating dramatic material around the life of one character. It uses a variety of DRAMATIC WRITING and suggests how PROXEMICS and FLASHBACK may be used to create a vivid CHARACTER PORTRAIT. The work also raises awareness of how objects can be used to SYMBOLISE a character.

Some plays rely heavily on their storyline, others on a particular issue. This project will show you how you might build up a play around one central character. A storyline will emerge and no doubt what you create will also throw up a number of issues but the main thing is to build a character that feels very real.

The exercises below will lead you to create a play about an old coal miner. But once you have worked through this structure you will see how the same techniques could be applied to all sorts of different characters of your own choosing.

Finding the Essence

There is a form of poetry that comes originally from Japan called 'haiku'. The purpose of these very short poems is to capture an emotion or attitude by focusing on one strong image. Although there are very few words in haiku poetry they seem to conjure up a strong visual image which means a lot more than it actually shows. In this they are rather like a shot from a film that only fills the screen for a few seconds but tells the audience a great deal about the characters and the situation.

1 Read this haiku very carefully a number of times. Imagine that it refers to a certain man. As a group, jot down other words and phrases of your own that would fit the man you have in mind.

Deep within the stream
the huge fish lies motionless
facing the current.

2 Place an ordinary classroom chair in the centre of the room. You will also need to place a scarf over the back of the chair and rest a walking stick up against it. On the seat of the chair you will need to place a lump of coal that someone has started to carve. (Carving coal is quite a popular hobby in some mining areas, and the character in this drama was a coal miner. It's a good idea for this exercise to coat the coal in PVA to stop it making your hands dirty!)

Now, sitting in a circle around the chair, imagine that it isn't an ordinary classroom chair but one that belongs to the character you have started to create. For the time being, call the character 'Dad'. Consider what the scarf, stick and coal also tell you about Dad.

Take it in turns to add a detail about what the chair actually looks like. For example:

It has big, bulky arms.
It looks quite old. The fabric is faded.
The legs are short and stumpy. They are wood and look a bit like paws.

The more detail you give at this stage the better. The aim is that you should all be able to build a very clear mental picture of this chair.

3 Use the ideas generated above to write a piece of choral speech. It could start something like this:

Here is Dad's chair
With its big, bulky arms.
The fabric is faded now
But its claw-like feet still clutch the floor . . .

4 Now you know about Dad's chair – but what does Dad look like? How would he sit in the chair? Get some volunteers to show how Dad would sit when he is reading, or watching the television, dozing or carving coal. Actively direct the volunteers so that you are all happy that the image is 'just right'.

You've now created the real essence of Dad, that is, those very particular things that make him different from anyone else. From this, you should be able to add some details of Dad's physical features: What does his face look like? What sort of clothes does he tend to wear? How well built is he?

B The Character in Context

Drama is about people. By watching the lives of others unfold on stage we can gain a new insight into our own beliefs, attitudes and feelings. Perhaps this is even more true when you make and perform your drama as you reshape things that you already know or have seen in your own life and look at them from a new angle, through the eyes, as it were, of somebody other than yourself.

The fact is that people do not see the world in the same way. It can be a surprise to discover that someone you think is wonderful is viewed by others very differently. Good dramatic characters, like real people, are 'three-dimensional'. Unlike a drawing or photograph which can only be looked at head-on, we can look at dramatic characters from a number of different viewpoints. We can obviously do this physically but more interestingly we can get different perspectives on their personality. One way of doing this is to hear what other people say about them.

1 Dad has a wife and four children, one of whom (I will call him Jack but you can call him or her whatever you like!) left home some time ago. He or she is still alive but never makes contact. Dad prefers not to speak about this one. You must decide whether the remaining family live together or close by or whatever. Give them names and ages. It would be useful to display these on a board or piece of card.

Now read this haiku and think how it might relate to Dad.

A night train passes:
pictures of the dead are trembling
on the mantelpiece.

2 Give Dad a name. Agree on a name that somehow seems to fit the character you have created so far, and decide how old he is.

Now place four chairs around Dad's chair. Use plenty of space. On these chairs should sit volunteers who will, for the time being, play Dad's wife and the three remaining children. The rest of the class should hot-seat these characters. You need to find out two things through your questioning:

a What are they like? What do they do? Where do they live? etc.

b What is their relationship to Dad? How does he treat them and what do they think of him?

It may be that you find out through this process a bit about why Dad never talks about Jack, or why he has a walking stick.

As a class, share what you have found out about this family. Don't worry if there are contradictions: Mum might describe Dad as a kind and sensitive man yet one of his children might think he is uncaring and too strict. These contradictions can make the character of Dad seem all the more real. What you will need to iron out is factual details. So, for example, if Mum has said that Dad is a retired coal miner and one of the children has said he is a bus conductor you will need to decide which one you want to go with.

Record your ideas on another piece of card, then work in four groups, one for each member of the family. Devise a monologue for that character that could be used to tell an audience how the character fits in with Dad's life.

The back-story

We are the people we are today because of what happened to us yesterday. Our attitudes and beliefs and the way we treat others have been shaped by past experiences. To create and play a dramatic character effectively can depend on thinking about what has made them the person they now seem to be. One way of doing that is to give them a 'back-story'; a personal history of moments that have affected them in some important way.

3 Imagine that Dad has, for many years, kept a scrapbook. He keeps it very private. In it one might find newspaper cuttings about him or his family, perhaps school reports, invitations to special events, cards and letters from people he wants to remember.

Work on your own and create something that would be found in Dad's scrapbook.

4 You will know that the way you stand is full of meaning. Deliberately turning your back on another person will tell them exactly what you think of them, as will cuddling up close!

Position yourself somewhere around Dad's chair. If your scrapbook item is something Dad is very proud of you might choose to face the chair and stand quite close to it. If it is something that lies deep in Dad's heart or mind you may choose to stand at some distance behind the chair. Using the space in this way is called **proxemics**. The very way you position yourself will give an extra meaning to the items you have written when you read them aloud.

Take it in turns to read your scrapbook item aloud from your chosen position. When you are listening to other people, look also at how they have positioned themselves. Discuss how the use of space added meaning to what was said.

Home learning → Proxemics

Building Dramatic Tension

So far you have done a lot of work to make Dad feel like a real character, but just showing the way real characters walk and talk on a stage isn't tremendously interesting: some sort of situation needs to be created so that we can see how they react to it. A tension needs to be introduced so that the audience isn't sure what will happen next or how the situation will affect the characters. So let's make something happen in Dad's life . . .

1 Here is another haiku that relates to a specific incident in Dad's story:

After the snowfall
deep in the pine forest
the sound of an axe.

The incident that the haiku refers to is this:

One day Dad learns that the local coal pit is to be closed down. He decides to protest by going to the mine, somehow getting down to the bottom of the shaft and disabling the winding gear. He sends a message up to the surface saying that he will not come out until the decision to close the mine is reversed.

Discuss how Dad's action fits in with the three haiku you have read so far.

2 Place one volunteer on Dad's chair with Dad's scarf around their neck and the stick and coal in their hands.

Imagine that a number of people go to the mine and try to speak with Dad by the pit's telephone. What sort of people would go? Newspaper reporters? His family? Union officials? The mine managers? Old friends? Of course, one person who wouldn't turn up at the pit would be Jack.

Take it in turns to speak with Dad as if you are one of these people. What will you say to Dad through the telephone? What will his reply be?

Make some kind of record of those conversations which you felt were particularly effective in that they gave the character of Dad more depth.

3 Imagine that after several days at the bottom of the mine shaft Dad's telephone goes silent. The people at the surface launch a rescue, believing him to have fallen ill. Sure enough, when he is brought to the surface it is clear that he is.

As he lies in bed at death's door, Dad's wife and three children remember incidents from the past. Work in four groups – one for each character – and devise a short flashback scene to show a moment in that character's life in which Dad was very important. One of you will need to play Dad and another the person having the memory. Others in the group can be anybody else you decide should be in the scene. When you show your scenes to each other, make it clear who is playing Dad by giving them the scarf and stick.

Heightening the tension

Having done all this work to grab an audience's attention and made them concerned for what happens to Dad and his family, it wouldn't make sense dramatically to let them off the hook. As playwrights and performers you have tremendous power to make an audience watch as you peel away more layers of your characters' lives by putting them in increasingly challenging situations. This doesn't necessarily imply making dramas that are full of hectic action. On the contrary, the most profound moments of tension in drama can be when the silence is interrupted by one small incident . . .

4 *Into the blinding sun
the funeral procession's
glaring headlights.*

Today is the day of Dad's funeral. He has died as a result of his protest in the mine.

Four volunteers play the family members. They should make a line as if by the front door of the house. One by one the rest of the group should enter as people who have attended the funeral. Who are they, and what will they say to the family? Improvise the scene.

5 There is one last guest. What happens when Jack appears, perhaps saying the opening line:

'Hello, Mum. I'm sorry I'm a bit late. I've been tied up with something else. . .'?

Carry the scene on until someone says or does something that you feel would make a really strong ending. At this point just shout STOP! What reaction would there be if Jack at some point picked up the lump of coal? Would this lead to some kind of ending? Whoever stops the scene will need to explain why they felt that would be a dramatic place to stop. Discuss other possible ways of ending this scene.

The End?

Finding the best 'stop point' for a scene can be difficult but it's essential if your drama work is going to be crisp and effective. It is helpful to think of how films and television dramas cut from one scene to the next. Think in particular of how each episode of a soap opera tends to leave the audience in suspense and waiting for the next episode.

1 Although you found a 'stop point' for the scene in which Jack returns, do you think this would make a good end to the whole play?

Jot down a list of at least three more scenes that you think it might be worth improvising following Jack's return. Consider which one of these would make a strong ending to a play about Dad. Show your chosen scene and explain why you have selected it as a suitable ending.

Reflection

2 Take another long look at Dad's chair with its scarf, stick and coal. Working on your own, create a very short piece of writing like the haiku used already which sums up Dad's story.

3 Talk about

a how 'real' you think your **character portrait** of Dad was even though the character was played by a number of different people in the group
b the way in which the scarf, stick and coal came to symbolise the character
c how the haiku came to represent Dad even though they were not, in fact, originally written for this purpose
d what feelings the drama personally generated for you
e what sort of issues the story of Dad brought up.
Make a personal record in your working notebook of this devising process and your response to it.

Further development

Through this structure you will have generated a good deal of material which would have great potential as the basis of a short play about Dad. For example:

the choral speech about Dad's chair
the four monologues from his family
memories captured in his scrapbook
telephone conversations with him while he is protesting
his family's memories played in flashback
the scene at his funeral
your own final comments.

You may add to this the haiku printed here.

In Project Two you will find advice on how these different scenes can be 'mapped out' to create a performance (p 39). If you were to re-shape your material to make it suitable for performance, what new scenes would you want to add? Could you think of any songs which would add something if they were used in the structure?

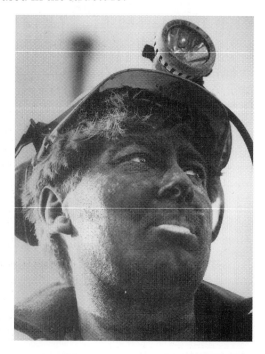

Three

Signs of the times

Dramatic style

STUDY UNITS

This chapter tries to show what the difference is between *real life* and *life as it is shown in plays*.

It looks at what gives a piece of drama its STYLE, and introduces the terms MELODRAMA, NATURALISM and REALISM.
The relationship the AUDIENCE has with the drama is considered.
The practical tasks develop your ability to create TENSION for them, particularly through the use of DESIGN and LIGHTING.

The popular theme of crime and punishment links all the work together.

Drama and the Dramatic

All the world's a stage,
And all the men and women merely players.

. . . or so Shakespeare famously wrote! But is there a difference between the dramas people experience in their own lives and the drama they watch on a stage?

The following short extract comes from a play called *Rosencrantz and Guildenstern are Dead* by Tom Stoppard. The characters Rosencrantz and Guildenstern appear in Shakespeare's play *Hamlet* in which they have been employed to spy on Hamlet. However, like an audience that has turned up after the play has started, neither of them really know what's going on. In Tom Stoppard's play, Rosencrantz and Guildenstern start to question just how much they are in control of their own lives. It's almost as if they are starting to suspect that they aren't 'real' people at all but just two of Shakespeare's inventions! In this scene they have met a group of travelling actors and watched them rehearse a particularly gory and rather overdone piece of drama. This leads them into questioning the differences between 'real' life and life as shown on stage.

CHARACTERS

PLAYER An ageing, very experienced actor. He knows what audiences like and how to give it to them. He has a clear understanding of how drama works and the difference between real life and acted life.

ROSENCRANTZ A gullible, almost childlike man who tends to believe everything he sees and hears though often without really understanding it.

GUILDENSTERN Tries to work things out logically, but doesn't really understand any better than his friend Rosencrantz.

PLAYER (*to* GUIL) Are you familiar with this play?

GUIL No.

PLAYER A slaughterhouse – eight corpses all told. It brings out the best in us.

GUIL (*tense, progressively rattled during the whole mime and commentary*) You! – What do *you* know about *death*?

PLAYER It's what the actors do best. They have to exploit whatever talent is given to them, and their talent is dying. They can die heroically, comically, ironically, slowly, suddenly, disgustingly, charmingly, or from a great height. My own talent is more general. I extract significance from melodrama, a significance which it does not in fact contain; but occasionally, from out of this matter, there escapes a thin beam of light that, seen at the right angle, can crack the shell of mortality.

ROS Is that all they can do – die?

PLAYER No, no – they kill beautifully. In fact some of them kill even better than they die. The rest die better than they kill. They're a team.

ROS Which ones are which?

PLAYER There's not much in it.

GUIL (*fear, derision*) Actors! The mechanics of cheap melodrama! That isn't *death*! (*more quietly*) You scream and choke and sink to your knees, but it doesn't bring death home to anyone – it doesn't catch them unawares and start the whisper in their skulls that says – 'One day you are going to die'. (*He straightens up*) You die so many times; how can you expect them to believe in your death?

PLAYER On the contrary, it's the only kind they do believe. They're conditioned to it. I had an actor once who was condemned to hang for stealing a sheep – or a lamb, I forget which – so I got permission to have him hanged in the middle of a play – had to change the plot a bit but I thought it would be effective, you know – and you wouldn't believe it, he just *wasn't* convincing! It was possible to suspend one's disbelief – and what with the audience jeering and throwing peanuts, the whole thing was a *disaster*! –

he did nothing but cry all the time – right out of character – just stood there and cried . . . Never again.

Audiences know what to expect, and that is all they are prepared to believe in.

Understanding the text

 1 What do you think this extract seems to suggest the differences are between 'real' life and life as acted on stage?

2 What is Guildenstern's opinion of actors and their ability to portray real life?

3 What is the Player's attitude towards
a audiences
b death?

4 What do you think the Player means when he says that he extracts 'significance from melodrama'? Do you think that drama as seen on a stage can help us understand the real world even though it is actually make-believe? Is this because of the drama itself or our interpretation of it? Consider the Player's words when he suggests that it is 'a significance which it does not in fact contain.'

5 What do you think the Player means when he says that audiences are 'conditioned' into believing in what they see on stage? Do you agree? To what extent do you 'believe' in the dramas you watch on stage or TV?

6 Would you agree that when an audience watches a drama, it knows 'what to expect'?

7 In groups of three, rehearse this short scene, taking into account the notes on the characters above. How can you show the differences between them through use of voice, gesture and facial expression?

 ## Audience Expectations

The Player in *Rosencrantz and Guildenstern are Dead* claims that he once had a man really hanged in a play. The picture and the passage below give some idea of what a public hanging might have been like. Look at both then answer the questions on them.

Some jail sites lent themselves admirably to this (ie public hangings). In September 1849 John Gleeson, a murderer of some note, was hanged outside Kirkdale Jail in Liverpool, before a gathering estimated at 100,000 strong, many of whom had been brought by special trains. 'All the vacant ground in front of the prison and spreading down to the canal presented much the same appearance with respect to numbers as Aintree or Epsom on the Cup or Derby day.' And it was not merely in numbers that these turnouts resembled race meetings, for like any other open air festivity, executions were marked by high spirits and hearty appetites. Sellers of fried fish, hot pies, fruit and ginger beer commonly drove a humming trade, as did hawkers of mournful ballads and fake condemned-cell confessions – known in the business as 'lamentations'.

Understanding the text

 1 What do you learn from the picture and passage about the public's attitude towards hanging?

2 In small groups discuss what you think the public reaction would be today towards such an event.

3 In what way do you think a public hanging could be described as 'dramatic'? Consider, for example:

a the relationship of the audience to the action
b any specific roles played out during the action
c the mood of the crowd
d the build-up of tension as the moment approaches.
e the possibility of a last-minute reprieve.

4 In what ways is a public hanging different from a drama? Consider

a who is making the action take place
b what the purpose of the action is
c what will happen after the hanging to the characters involved.

Crowds going to a public execution presumably had a fair idea of what to expect when they got there. It is hard to imagine 100,000 people turning up unless they thought they were going to get something in return for their effort! What they no doubt expected to see was something 'dramatic'. What do you expect from a drama? Answer the following questions in order to get a clearer picture.

 5 What do members of your group expect to get out of watching something

a at the theatre?
b at the cinema?
c on television?

Do they have different expectations of each one? If so, how and why are they different? Discuss these questions in small groups, then report back to the rest of the class in order to draw some general conclusions.

6 What films, plays and television programmes are most popular with people in your group/year? Draw up a Top Ten list for each category (you could include plays that you have read as well as seen). What 'types' of each appear to be most popular – Horror? Comedy? Romance? Crime? Thrillers? Fantasy? Others?

7 Repeat these investigations with both an older and a younger age group and compare the different results.

8 Discuss and in some way record the conclusions you draw from these findings. Look particularly at the popularity of dramas (this includes films and television shows of course) which deal with **crime** and **punishment**.

Look at the posters on the next two pages. One is advertising a play called the *Red Barn* which appeared, according to the poster, in 1830 (you will see that it was presented as the main part of a double bill). The other poster is of a film from the early 1960s. Work through the exercises on each. As you do so, try to consider how far audience expectations might affect the drama and how far the drama is actually changing audience expectations.

 9 In what ways do the posters actually tell the audiences what to expect?

10 What information is used or what promises are made, in order to try to draw in the crowds?

11 Read the *Red Barn* poster again very carefully. What does it actually tell you about the plot of the play? It suggests that 'Everyone must be aware of the Incidents on which the Piece is founded', so what do you suppose the audience might expect to get from going to watch it?

12 Using the details given on the poster, set out the plot as a **treatment**.

THEATRE, LINCOLN.

BY DESIRE OF

G. E. WELBY, Esq. M.P. & C. FURNOR, Esq.

THE STEWARDS OF THE STUFF BALL.

On WEDNESDAY Evening, OCTOBER 27th, 1830,

Will be presented, the celebrated drama of

Sweethearts and Wives.

Admiral Franklin, ... Mr. SHIELD.	Charles Franklin, ... Mr. SIMMS.
Sandford, ... Mr. CULLENFORD	Curtis, ... Mr. HODGSON.
Billy Lackaday, ... Mr. GURNER.	
Mrs. Bell, ... Mrs. DANBY.	Susan, ... Mrs. GURNER.
Eugenia, ... Mrs. W. ROBERTSON.	Laura, ... Miss STEWART SMITH.

A COMIC SONG ...... by ...... Mr. HODGSON.

With (for the **LAST TIME,**) the new Tragic Melo Drama, in 4 Acts, founded on Fact, called the

RED BARN;

OR, THE PROPHETIC DREAM.

THE MUSIC SELECTED AND ARRANGED BY MR. STANNARD

WITH NEW SCENERY PAINTED FOR THE OCCASION BY MR. SIMMS.

Mr. ROBERTSON is induced to bring forward this piece, not only from the unprecedented success it has been received with at the various Theâtres in the Kingdom, but as a moral lesson, that Murder, however for the time concealed, will speak with most miraculous organ. Every one must be aware of the Incidents on which the Piece is founded, but the Dramatist has avoided the real names of the parties, still blending all the principal Incidents, with an effect at once awful and instructive.

Cordel, a young Farmer, ... Mr. HAMILTON.
Mr. Delamere, a Magistrate, ... Mr. BRUNTON.
Wilton, a Gipsy Confederate of Cordel, ... Mr. TALBOT.
Marlin, a labouring Farmer in the vale of years, ... Mr. STYLES.
Robin, a Factotum to Chatteral, ... Mr. SIMMS.
Peter Christopher Chatteral, a Barber, Beadle, &c. .... Mr. GURNER.
Nell Hatfield, a Gipsy, .. Mrs. W. ROBERTSON. Anna Hatfield, her daughter, .. Mrs. GURNER.
Dame Marlin, ... Mrs. DANBY. Mrs Cordel, ... Mrs. HAMILTON.
Maria Marlin, ... Miss STEWART SMITH.

A Brief Sketch of the Incidents:
CORDEL for his numerous Crimes receives the CURSE of the GIPSY CHIEF.
CORDEL'S FIRST MEETING WITH MARIA MARLIN.

His promise to marry her—The anguish of old Marlin and his Dame at parting with her—His proposition to meet her at the RED BARN disguised in Man's Apparel—Her joy at the thoughts of Marriage.

AWFUL MEETING AT THE RED BARN,
WHERE THE DEED IS PERPETRATED.

THE APPEARANCE OF MARIA TO HER MOTHER IN A DREAM.

The Interior of the Barn where the Body is discovered.

CORDEL's Marriage in London.—His living in splendour when the GIPSY's CURSE is fulfilled.
CORDEL'S APPREHENSION AND CONFESSION,
And the appearance of the Shade of Maria Marlin in Cordel's Dream, which produces the denouement.

Among the minor Incidents to give effect to the serious part of the Melo-drama, some Comic Parts are introduced which must set gravity at defiance.

13 Think of any films you know that were so popular, a sequel was made. In small groups, discuss what techniques the sequel used to maintain the interest generated in the first film.

14 In small groups, imagine that you are the team who first presented the *Red Barn* in 1830. It has been so successful that you now plan to produce a sequel to it. What problems are you going to face in trying to draw in the crowds for this new play? What do you think they will expect? Write out a brief treatment and improvise a tantalising trailer for *Red Barn 2*.

15 What do you think an audience going to see *Les Maitresses de Dracula* were expecting as a result of seeing this poster?

16 Compare the style of the two posters. Look at

a what is written
b style of writing
c amount of writing
d visual impact.

What do your comparisons suggest about the audiences for each and the societies in which they lived? Do you think there are, in fact, any similarities?

A dramatic incident is one which generates excitement and emotional response in those involved or watching. The Hillsborough disaster, the Dunblane tragedy, a public hanging – all of these are dramatic incidents. Drama is deliberate retelling of the story surrounding a dramatic incident (which may be entirely fictitious). One thing that is required to make drama successfully is an understanding of what sort of things an audience sees as being dramatic – what does it expect?

 Harnessing Tension

In a dramatic incident, there is a tension which comes from not knowing.

- Not knowing when something will happen
- Not knowing where something will happen
- Not knowing who it will happen to
- Not knowing why it is happening
- Not knowing what it will mean to you.

It is this tension that results in some kind of excitement or emotional response. (Sometimes the tension arises because we do, in fact, know precisely what is going to happen yet are unable to prevent it. A wit once said that 'when a man knows he is to be hanged in a fortnight, it concentrates his mind wonderfully!' Can you think of any other examples in which tension is generated through knowing?)

1 Discuss, in groups, any recent news item which you would describe as a 'dramatic incident'. What was tense about the situation? Have any crimes been extensively reported recently? What were they? Why do you think they were reported when so many aren't? Record your ideas as you may need them later.

In Chapter One, on p 3 a game called 'What's the time Mr Wolf?' was explained. It is a good example of how people can deliberately create a dramatic incident for themselves. Creating and controlling tension is a key ingredient in the making of drama.

The crowds who turned up to a public hanging knew that either the man would be hanged or, perhaps more excitingly, a last-minute reprieve would save him as he stood with the noose around his neck. They presumably wanted to feel some kind of tension which didn't directly affect them, but which had some significance for their own lives. Perhaps it was simply that they wanted to be reminded that villains get punished, good men go free. Of course, this might not actually be true, but that might not matter if the audience wanted to believe that was what they were seeing.

The improvisations that follow show how, by concentrating on one particular type of tension, different types of drama arise.

Tension created by time and space

2 Do this in pairs, **A** and **B**. **A** is the person condemned to die on the scaffold. **B** directs **A** on how to walk up the steps and approach the noose. Try out this scene at various speeds. Don't use any lines but add, if you wish, any other ways you can think of to heighten the tension of this short scene.

3 Form into groups of six or so and repeat the above scene with one person playing the condemned man, one the executioner and the rest the crowd. How can you use the space between the crowd and the man to heighten tension? Try, for example, starting the scene with a large space between them. At a certain moment, the crowd could surge forward to close the space. What would be the best moment to do this? What might trigger this reaction in the crowd?

4 As a whole class, work on other ways you can heighten the tension by controlling the timing of the scene. At what point, for example, would you bring in a messenger carrying a reprieve? Could you bring in somebody whom the crowd would think is such a messenger – but in fact isn't?

Tension created by characters

5 In small groups, imagine you are part of a much larger crowd at a public hanging (such as in Task 4). The two lists in the diagram suggest who the condemned man might be, and who you might be. Pick one from each list and improvise your actions/reactions to the execution.

The
Condemned
Man is

A famous
nobleman
A petty thief
A notorious
highwayman
A poor
poacher
A child
murderer

You are

nobles
parents
thieves
labourers
servants

6 Choose another pair from these lists but add one detail to each which you think would heighten the tension in the scene as in this example.

| A nobleman famous for his cruelty | The parents of the servant he killed |

7 In pairs, improvise a conversation between two members of the crowd who have just gone along for the entertainment. As the condemned man (just imagine his presence in this scene rather than actually having someone act him) walks up the steps one onlooker realises that he/she knows him. How do they know him? Would they want this known?

Tension created by situation

8 In groups of six improvise the conversation in the crowd again. It is believed that the condemned man had an accomplice who is still at large. One of you is that accomplice.

9 As a whole class re-run the scene outside the gaol again (see Task 4). This time though, imagine that the man has been condemned for poaching from a wealthy landowner in order to feed his family. Some of you may know him, some of you may also have poached for the same reason, some of you are wealthy landowners. Improvise the scene freely at first then decide how you might change it to

a make the audience sympathise with the condemned man
b feel an active hatred for landowners
c see the hanging as a justifiable warning for thieves and poachers
d be excited by the whole event.

Don't forget to try to use **space** and **timing** in order to help you change the **focus** in this way.

Tension created by implication

What might a drama imply to an audience? That is, what will they see as being significant and meaningful about it?

The idea of some poor, half-starved man going to the gallows in front of a largely sympathetic crowd, for poaching a rabbit from a fat and bullying landowner to feed his family, is rather romanticised. It very rarely happened in real life. What *is* true, though, is that a great many people in the last century were extremely poor, many turned to crime and many were hanged. Public hanging was designed to remind such people of what would happen to them if they were caught. If a play suggested such hangings were unfair, what effect would it have

a on an audience of landowners?
b on an audience of poor people?

If a play suggested that the law was the same for everyone and therefore extremely fair, what effect would it have on the same audiences?

Dramatic style isn't just a question of what the audience expects. It also depends on what the audience is prepared to accept.

Reflection

10 Look back to Task 1, where you were asked to discuss recent news items. What implications do you think they have for various people? In small groups, choose one and try to develop a scene which shows what those implications are. Referring back to the section on *Evaluation* (p 31) in Project One will help you construct this scene.

11 Watch each other's scenes carefully and then discuss how you think different types of audiences might react. Would they, for example, think the scene was fair, sympathetic, offensive or what?

Melodrama

The most popular style of theatre in 1849 (the year in which 100,000 people were reported to have watched murderer John Gleeson hang) was **melodrama**. A close look at this particular style will help you see

a how the various ingredients of drama can be mixed into a particular style

b how a particular dramatic style reflects the audience at which it is aimed.

The term **melodrama** is simply a mixture of the two words *melody* and *drama*. Until 1843 there were only two theatres in London licensed to present 'dramas'. However, the regulations did not cover musical entertainments, so peppering 'dramas' with 'melodies' was a way around the law. In 1843 the Theatre Regulations Act made it possible for playwrights and acting companies to rely less on music. However, most writers and producers continued to use music for many years after, as they knew it could make the drama more emotive (appeal more to the emotions). Consider how much a good soundtrack can help the atmosphere of a horror or romantic film. Melodrama remained an immensely popular style of theatre right up to the end of the last century yet few melodramas are ever produced in the theatre now.

Typically, a melodrama would rely heavily on music, lighting, sound effects and stage trickery to produce a spectacle which would create strong emotions in the audience. The characters are often referred to as **stock characters**. That is, they are instantly recognisable character types like these:

The Hero
The Villain
The Heroine
The Comic Servant/Loveable Rogue
The Aged Parent

Melodrama plots are very predictable, for example:

The **Hero** is young and handsome and from a 'good family'. He is in love with the **Heroine** – a beautiful young girl whose family relies on his charity. The **Villain** accuses the **Hero** of some crime and through his treachery forces the **Hero** to flee. The **Villain** threatens the **Heroine** and her **Aged Parents** and will only be satisfied if the **Heroine** agrees to marry him. She resists as far as possible. Her only friend is a local **Loveable Rogue**. Just as the **Heroine** is about to give in to the **Villain**'s evil demands, the **Hero** reappears having cleared his name. The **Hero** fights the **Villain** and wins. The **Hero** declares his undying love for the **Heroine** and everyone lives happily ever after except for the **Villain** who is sent off to gaol.

1 In groups of five or six take on the roles listed above and improvise the story adding your own details wherever necessary. The improvisation should not take more than ten minutes. As you prepare it, try to
a make the characters instantly recognisable for what they are

b make the action as sensational as possible.

2 If you had the chance of providing your characters with costumes, what exactly would you give them?

3 Many writers of melodramas were paid as 'stock-writers', that is, they were paid a small weekly sum to produce material. Their method was often to fill up filing cabinets with snippets of dialogue gathered from court reports, newspaper stories, cheap novels and so on and rearrange these 'stock' lines into new plays adding suitable links wherever necessary. Look at the examples of typical 'stock' lines below.

On a large sheet of card, get everyone in the class to add a line which might appear in a melodrama. In groups of five or six rearrange *all* the lines written down into a melodrama adding your own wherever necessary. This exercise will obviously take time and thought. Don't hurry it. Remember to try to make the storyline simple, the characters instantly recognisable, the action sensational. Another key factor of melodramas was that **Heroes** won and **Villains** lost.

Prepare to meet your doom, Sir Jasper! You'll not escape this time!

Ungrateful wretch! Never darken my doorway again!

Alas! My heart is broken forever!

Ha Ha Ha! Now my beauty, you are mine, all mine!

Oh Lummy! I'm all in such a tiz, what with the young master coming home all of a sudden like!

STUDY EXTRACT ONE
Sweeney Todd or The string of pearls

Written by George Dibdin Pitt in the middle of the last century, *Sweeney Todd* illustrates very well the appeal of the melodrama to Victorian audiences and explains why so few are ever presented in modern theatres! The character of Sweeney Todd is quite well known and has been featured in numerous films and TV programmes in this century, perhaps because the idea of the story is so good.

Sweeney Todd

A common barber (Sweeney Todd) decides to get rich quick by slitting the throats of rich customers. The bodies are disposed of by an ingenious device which swivels the barber's chair around and drops the body into the cellar below. The corpses are then cut up and put into pies, sold by the lady next door!

So, if this is such a good story, why doesn't the original play get performed? Here is the first scene . . .

CHARACTERS
SWEENEY TODD The owner of a barber shop
TOBIAS His young assistant
MARK INGESTRIE A sea captain
JEAN PARMINE A jeweller

ACT 1, SCENE 1

Inside **SWEENEY TODD**'s *Shop. There is a barber's chair on a revolving trap door. When the trap door turns over a similar chair comes up on the other side.*

We first see **SWEENEY TODD** *dressing a wig, and* **TOBIAS RAGG** *attending him.*

SWEENEY You will remember now, Tobias Ragg, that you are my apprentice; that you have had of me board, lodging, and washing, save that you take your meals at home, that you don't sleep here, and that your mother gets up your linen. (*Fiercely*) Now, are you not a fortunate, happy dog?

TOBIAS (*Timidly*) Yes, sir.

SWEENEY You will acquire a first-rate profession, quite as good as the law, which your mother tells me that she would have put you to, only that a little weakness of the head-piece unqualified you. And now, Tobias, listen.

TOBIAS (*Trembling*) Yes, sir.

SWEENEY I'll cut your throat from ear to ear if you repeat one word of what passes in this shop, or are to make any supposition, or draw any conclusion from anything you may see or hear, or fancy you see or hear. Do you understand me?

TOBIAS I won't say anything, Mr Todd; if I do, may I be made into veal pies at Lovett's in Bell Yard.

SWEENEY (*Startled*) How dare you mention veal pies in my presence? Do you suspect?

TOBIAS Oh, sir; I don't suspect – indeed I don't! I meant no harm in making the remark.

SWEENEY (*Glares at* **TOBIAS**) Very good. I'm satisfied – quite satisfied; and, mark me, the shop, and the shop only, is your place.

TOBIAS Yes, sir.

Enter **MARK INGESTRIE**, *a sea-captain.*

MARK By the description, this should be the man I seek. He can doubtless give me some tidings of Johanna, and I can look forward to a happy meeting after an estrangement of many long and tedious years. Good morrow, friend; I have need of your craft. Let me get shaved at once, as I have to see a lady.

SWEENEY Happy to be of service to you, good gentleman. Will you be pleased to seat yourself? (*Brushes* **MARK**'s *hair*) You've been to sea, sir?

MARK Yes; and I have only now lately come up the river from an Indian voyage.

SWEENEY You carry some treasures, I presume?

MARK Among others, this small casket. (MARK *produces it*).

SWEENEY A piece of exquisite workmanship.

MARK It is not the box but its contents that must cause you wonder, for I must, in confidence, tell you it contains a string of veritable pearls of the value of twelve thousand pounds.

SWEENEY (*Chuckling aside, and whetting his razor on his hand*) I shall have to polish him off. Ha ha ha! heugh!

MARK What the devil noise was that?

SWEENEY It was only me. I laughed. By the way, Tobias, while I am operating upon this gentleman's chin, the figures at St Dunstan's are about to strike; the exhibition will excite your curiosity and allow me time to shave our customer without your interruption.

TOBIAS *exits.*

SWEENEY Now sir, we can proceed to business, if it so please you; it's well you came here, sir, for though I say it, there isn't a shaving shop in the City of London that ever thinks upon polishing off a customer as I do – fact – can assure you – ha, ha! heugh!

MARK Shiver the main-brace! I tell you what it is, Master Barber: if you come that laugh again, I will get up and go.

SWEENEY Very good, it won't occur again. (*He mixes lather*) If I am so bold, who are you? – where did you come from? – and wither are you going?

MARK You seem fond of asking questions, my friend; perhaps before I answer them, you will reply to one I'm about to put?

SWEENEY Oh, yes, of course; what is it?

MARK Do you know a Mr Oakley, who lives somewhere hereabouts? He is a spectacle maker.

SWEENEY Yes, to be sure I do – Jasper Oakley, in Fore Street. Bless me, where can my strop be? I had it this minute – I must have lain it down somewhere. What an odd thing I can't see it. Oh, I recollect – I took it into the parlour. Sit still, sir, I shan't be a minute; you can amuse yourself with the newspaper. I shall soon polish him off!

SWEENEY *gives him a newspaper and goes out. There is a roaring noise, and* MARK *and the chair sinks through stage. After a pause, the chair rises vacant, and* SWEENEY *enters. He examines the string of pearls which he holds in his hand.*

SWEENEY When a boy, the thirst of avarice was first awakened by the fair gift of a farthing; that farthing soon became a pound; the pound a hundred – so to a thousand, till I said to myself, I will possess a hundred thousand. This string of pearls will complete the sum. (*Starts*) Who's there?

SWEENEY *grabs* TOBIAS, *who has cautiously opened the door.*

Speak – and speak the truth, or your last hour has come! How long were you peeping through the door before you came in?

TOBIAS Please sir, I wasn't peeping at all.

SWEENEY Well, well, if you did peep, what then? It's no matter. I only wanted to know, that's all. It was quite a joke, wasn't it? Come now, there's no harm done, we'll be merry over it – very merry.

TOBIAS (*Puzzled*) Yes, very merry.

SWEENEY Who's that at the door?

TOBIAS It's only the black servant of the gentleman who came here to be shaved this morning.

SWEENEY Tell the fellow his master's not here; go – let him seek elsewhere, do you hear? (*Whets his razor on his hand*) I know I shall have to polish that boy off!

As SWEENEY *finishes* TOBIAS *finds the hat worn by* MARK. *He hides the hat and goes out.*

Enter JEAN PARMINE.

JEAN Good evening, neighbour; I would have you shave me.

SWEENEY Your servant, Mr Parmine – you deal in precious stones.

JEAN Yes, I do; but it's rather late for a bargain. Do you want to buy or sell?

SWEENEY To sell.

SWEENEY *gives a box to* JEAN.

JEAN (*Examining pearls*) Real, by heaven, all real.

SWEENEY I know they are real. Will you deal with me or not?

JEAN I'm not quite sure that they are real; let me look at them again? Oh, I see, counterfeit; but so well done that really for the curiosity of the thing I will give you £50.

SWEENEY £50? Who is joking now, I wonder? We cannot deal to-night.

JEAN Stay – I will give you a hundred.

SWEENEY Hark ye, friend, I know the value of pearls.

JEAN Well, since you know more than I gave you credit for I think I can find a customer who will pay £11,000 for them; if so, I have no objection to advance the sum of £8,000.

SWEENEY I am content – let me have the money early to-morrow.

JEAN Stop a bit; there are some rather important things to consider – you must know that a string of pearls is not to be bought like a few ounces of old silver, and the vendor must give satisfaction as to how he came by them.

SWEENEY (*Aside*) I am afraid I shall have to polish him off. (*Aloud*) In other words, you don't care how I possess the property, provided I sell it to you at a thief's price; but if, on the contrary, I want their real value, you mean to be particular.

JEAN I suspect you have no right to dispose of the pearls, and to satisfy myself I shall insist upon your accompanying me to a magistrate.

SWEENEY And what road shall you take?

JEAN The *right* path.

As JEAN *turns,* SWEENEY *jumps on him. They fight.* SWEENEY *forces* JEAN *into the chair.* SWEENEY *touches a spring, and the chair sinks with a crash.* SWEENEY *laughs and exclaims,* 'I've polished him off!' *as scene ends.*

Understanding the text

 1 Re-read the first piece of dialogue between Sweeney and Tobias and list what we find out about

- Sweeney
- Tobias
- the relationship between the two.

2 Who is Mark? Where has he come from and why has he arrived at Sweeney Todd's?

3 What 'sin' is the root cause of Sweeney's evil? What message might this be trying to give to the audience?

4 What 'moral' might lie behind the murder of Jean Parmine?

5 Just from reading this opening scene and matching it with what you have already learned about this style of play, write down a treatment of what you think will happen in the rest of it. Keep this work safe as you may wish to use it later.

Producing the scene

 6 In pairs, pick out those lines of Sweeney's which appear to be written for the audience's benefit, rather than directed towards another character in the scene. Help each other try out ways of delivering these lines in a way which will build the tension. Consider Sweeney's position on the stage (decide, in your pairs, where the audience will be), any actions or gestures he might make and his tone of voice.

7 There seem to be a great many lines which suggest that Sweeney is no ordinary barber well before he gets around to murdering anybody – which isn't long! (I particularly like the line 'How dare you mention veal pies in my presence?') In pairs, work through the first dialogue between Sweeney and Tobias in order to suggest to the audience that Sweeney is dangerously mad, yet trying to hide the fact from Tobias.

People often think that melodrama implies 'overacting'. Certainly, part of the style was to make big, obvious gestures and movements (part of the reason for this was a combination of poor lighting and acoustic in large theatres). Bear this in mind as you work on this scene.

8 Look at Sweeney's line

(*chuckling aside, and whetting his razor on his hand*) I shall have to polish him off. Ha ha ha! Heugh!

Organise a competition within your class to see who can deliver this line in the most 'appropriate' way given your knowledge of this style and how it is being used in this particular scene.

9 Draw a sketch or plan view of what a 'real' barber's shop might have looked like at the time.
What changes will you need to make to the set and the way things are positioned in order to allow an audience

- to see the whole room
- to see both Sweeney's face as he prepares the murders and his victims' faces as they sink through the floor?

10 Lighting in the theatre last century was quite poor by modern standards. How could you use make-up and costume in this scene to make it more obvious who the characters are and what they are like?

11 Theatres today use sophisticated lights to create atmosphere. Suggest places in this scene where different colours might be used. Refer back to the plan made in Task 9 and draw in where you would place the lights for best effect. (See the Special Assignment on p 109 for guidance.)

Reflection

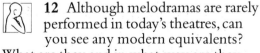 **12** Although melodramas are rarely performed in today's theatres, can you see any modern equivalents? What are they and in what way are they similar?

13 How do you think a modern audience would react to a production of this version of *Sweeney Todd*? What do you think would or would not appeal to them?

14 Discuss what you think plays like *Sweeney Todd* say about audiences in Victorian Britain.

 # Sensation and Escape

Why was melodrama so enormously popular as a dramatic style last century?

Look at the following statements about Victorian Britain and see if you can detect any possible links between them and the rise of melodrama.

- More working class people began to have some education.
- Stories spread more quickly owing to growth of newspapers and railways.
- Growing numbers of working people moved from the countryside into expanding towns and cities.
- Growing industrialisation meant more people worked together in factories. Factory work was tedious and depressing.
- There was a strong sense of right and wrong. Laws were harsh and religion was important.
- Improved communications meant that crimes and criminals could be reported throughout the land. Some achieved considerable fame.
- There was a demand for leisure.
- The number of theatres rose rapidly to meet this demand.

It may simply be that for many people life was so dull they needed to see something sensational to escape from the tedium of their real lives.

People were expected to live by harsh social and moral laws. Perhaps they also needed to see that there was good reason to stick to them – Heroes win, Villains lose.

Look back at the poster advertising the play called *Red Barn* (p 88). The play is often also called 'Maria Marten'. It is based on truth in so far as there really was a girl called Maria Marten who was murdered by her lover William Corder in a barn (which happened to be red). William and Maria had had a long and tempestuous affair. She was two years older than him and at the age of 24 she already had three children by different local men (one of whom was William Corder's brother) and was being sought by the police on an immorality charge. William fathered Maria's fourth child which died mysteriously after just two weeks and was secretly buried by William and Maria. Maria was known to have put pressure on William to marry her, but he wasn't so keen. He came from a fairly wealthy background and wanted to get away from the countryside to lead 'the high life' in London. She was a farm labourer's daughter and didn't easily fit into such plans.

The story of the murder quickly became popular, as church ministers used it to drive home their message that dreadful things would happen to 'young girls of loose morals' like Maria and 'seducers' like Corder. The story was picked up by showmen who at first used puppets to demonstrate the murder. However, audiences at the time preferred stories of Heroines and Villains which had a clear message, rather than dealing with the rather tacky morals and relationships of real life. Look at the short extract below from the play to see how the story was styled to fit the audience at the time.

CHARACTERS

WILLIAM CORDER A dastardly seducer

MARIA MARTEN An innocent country girl in love with William

INSIDE THE RED BARN

CORDER *discovered digging a grave. (Villain's music)*

CORDER All is complete, I await my victim. Will she come? Oh yes, a woman is fool enough to do anything for the man she loves. Hark, tis her footstep bounding across the fields! She comes, with hope in her heart, a song on her lips, little does she think that death is so near. *(He steps into a dark corner.)*

Enter **MARIA** *(The music turns soft and gentle.)*

MARIA William not here, where can he be, what ails me? A weight is at my heart as if it told some evil, and this old Barn – how like a vault it looks! Fear steals upon me, I tremble in every limb, I will return to my home at once.

CORDER *(advancing)* Stay, Maria!

MARIA I'm glad you are here, you don't know how frightened I've been.

CORDER Did any one see you cross the fields?

MARIA Not a soul, I remembered your instructions.

CORDER That's good. Now Maria, do you remember a few days ago threatening to betray me about the child to Constable Ayres? *(Tremolo fiddles)*

MARIA A girlish threat made in a heat of temper, because you refused to do justice to one you had wronged so greatly. Do not speak of that now, let us leave this place.

CORDER Not yet Maria, you don't think my life is to be held at the bidding of a silly girl. *No*, look what I have made here!

(He drags her to the grave. Slow music.)

MARIA A grave. Oh William, what do you mean?

CORDER To kill you, bury your body here. You are a clog upon my actions, a chain that keeps me from reaching ambitious height, you are to die.

MARIA *(kneels)* But not by your hand, the hand that I have clasped in love and confidence. Oh! think, William, how much I have sacrificed for you, think of our little child above, now in heaven, pleads for its mother's life. Oh spare, oh spare me!

CORDER 'Tis useless, my mind's resolved, you die tonight. *(Thunder and lightning)*

MARIA Wretch!
Since neither prayers nor tears will touch your stony heart,
Heaven will surely nerve my arm to battle for my life. *(She seizes* **CORDER***.)*

CORDER Foolish girl, desist!

MARIA Never with life!

They struggle, he shoots her, she falls in his arms.

MARIA (*soft music*)
William, I am dying, your cruel hand has stilled
The heart that beat in love alone for thee.
Think not to escape the hand of justice, for
When least expected it will mark you down,
At that moment think of Maria's wrongs.
Death claims me, and with my last breath I
die blessing and forgiving thee. (*Dies*)
CORDER Blessing and forgiveness! and for
me, her (*loud music*) murderer! What have I
done! Oh Maria, awake awake, do not look
so tenderly upon me, let indignation lighten
from your eyes and blast me!
Oh may this crime for ever stand accurst,
The last of murders, as it is the worst.

Understanding the text

1 What similarities can you see between the characterisation of Corder and that of Sweeney Todd? Look particularly at who his lines are directed at as well as what he says to his victim.

2 Pick out three lines which seem to suggest that Maria is a sweet and innocent girl.

3 What 'moral' would you say comes across as a result of Maria's last speech and Corder's reaction to it?

Producing the scene

4 What gestures could Corder make to suggest that he is an evil man? Similarly, how could Maria move and stand in order to suggest that she is innocence itself? In pairs, read through the scene again carefully and look for opportunities to make these 'overacted' gestures. Choose between 12 and 20 lines which you think offer such opportunities and rehearse them.

5 The stage directions indicate that some special effects could enhance the atmosphere of this scene. What sort of lighting and music would you use to do this? Either design a lighting plot, specifying colours and angles for this scene, or suggest some pieces of music which you think would be appropriate. You may wish to actually put these into action.

6 How could you heighten the tension in this scene by concentrating on the effects of time and space? At what moments, for example, would there be a lot of space between the characters/no space at all? How fast should different movements be made to create a feeling of suspense or a shock effect? Work in groups of three, electing one member as a director. Walk through the script concentrating on timing and use of space.

7 The Player in *Rosencrantz and Guildenstern Are Dead* claims that killing and dying are what his actors do best. In pairs, rehearse Maria's death making it as emotional as possible.

Reflection

8 To what extent do you think that audiences today still enjoy watching sensational stories in order to escape from 'real life'? Look back, for example, at the poster for *Les Maitresses de Dracula* (p 87). Is there a link? What are today's equivalents?

9 In addition to film, TV and the theatre, what examples of **sensationalism** and **escapism** in newspapers, books and magazines can you think of? Jot down as many as you can.

10 The real story of Maria Marten was, as you have seen, twisted considerably in order to suit the taste of the times. In small groups, find a newspaper headline which you think could be used as the basis for a sensational drama. Devise one scene as a 'taster'. The aim must be to produce some strong emotional response in the audience.

G The Natural and the Real

The style of writing, acting and presentation which we associate with melodramas began to be replaced towards the end of the last century with styles of drama that were altogether more subtle. Playwrights became increasingly disillusioned with the melodramatic style. The problem perhaps is that if a style relies on being sensational then each new work must be more sensational than the last (look back at your work in Study Unit B).

Looking back on the last century now, the excitement, fine sentiments and moral messages of the melodramas don't seem to match what we know about the way people lived. There was a good deal of hypocrisy in the way that some of the rich promoted a clean and moral life while behaving very differently themselves. The plays set moral targets which the poor couldn't afford to reach and some of the rich felt no need to.

The sensationalism of the melodrama may have offered audiences of the time an escape, but in many ways it exploited their real situation by hiding the truth of it. Look again, for example, at the way Maria Marten's story was used. The story isn't so much sensational, as simply unpleasant. Yet it asks no questions as to why the real characters behaved as they did, preferring to simply titillate the audience.

The way sex is treated in melodrama is important in our understanding of how the style reflects the Victorian society. As mentioned before, Victorian morals were very strict and so while cheerfully staging the most diabolical murders on stage, the role of sex in them had to be disguised in some way.

By the end of the century, attitudes began to change rapidly and many playwrights became more interested in showing what life was 'really like' on stage. They took away the sensationalism, the 'stock characters' and the simple moral solutions. Audiences began to be presented with more complex characters and situations which sometimes asked uncomfortable questions about the audience's own attitudes. This style of drama is sometimes called **naturalism** because it aims to represent the lives, concerns and behaviour of 'real' people. Of course, the fact that the drama still took place on a stage and the characters were played by actors still meant that the playmakers were controlling what an audience would see.

The Quare Fellow

The Quare Fellow is a play about a man who is soon to be hanged. It is set in the Irish prison where the hanging will take place, yet neither the audience nor the other prisoners get to see the condemned man. No one really knows him or what he has done, but the fact that he is going to be hanged dominates all the conversations in the prison in the days leading up to the execution. Dunlavin and Neighbour have been in the prison for a long time. Mickser is an Irish Republican and stirs up the warders. He is to be released on the day of the hanging.

Written by Brendan Behan and first produced in 1954, *The Quare Fellow* presents a stark and uncomfortable view of prison life. The photograph on the next page shows a scene from the original production. Notice how bleak it looks – a far call from the elaborate and tricksy sets of melodramas.

CHARACTERS	
WARDERS	I
	2
	CRIMMIN
	REGAN
	CHIEF
PRISONERS	MICKSER
	NEIGHBOUR
	DUNLAVIN
	ENGLISHMAN
	A B C D

Scene 2

The prison yard. It is morning.

WARDER 1 How's the time?

WARDER 2 Seven minutes.

WARDER 1 As soon as it goes five to eight they'll start. You'd think they were working with stop watches. I wish I was at home having my breakfast. How's the time?

WARDER 2 Just past six minutes.

MICKSER'S VOICE Bail o dhis orribh go leir a chairdre.

WARDER 1 I knew it. That's that bloody Mickser. I'll fix him this time.

MICKSER'S VOICE And we take you to the bottom of D. Wing.

WARDER 1 You bastard, I'll give you D. Wing.

MICKSER'S VOICE We're ready for the start, and in good time, and who do I see lined up for the off but the High Sheriff of this ancient city of ours, famous in song and story as the place where the pig ate the whitewash brushes and – (*The* **WARDERS** *remove their caps.*) We're off, in this order: the Governor, the Chief, two screws Regan and Crimmin, the Quare fellow between them, two more screws and three runners from across the Channel, getting well in front, now the Canon. He's making a big effort for the last two furlongs. He's got the white pudding bag on his head, just a short distance to go. He's in. (*A clock begins to chime the hour. Each quarter sounds louder.*) His feet to the chalk line. He'll be pinioned, his feet together. The bag will be pulled down over his face. The screws come off the trap and steady him. Himself goes to the lever and . . .

The hour strikes. The **WARDERS** *cross themselves and put on their caps. From the* **PRISONERS** *comes a ferocious howling.*

PRISONERS One off, one away, one off, one away.

WARDER 1 Shut up there.

WARDER 2 Shut up, shut up.

WARDER 1 I know your windows, I'll get you. Shut up.

The noise dies down and at last ceases altogether.

Now we'll go in and get that Mickser. (*Grimly.*) *I'll soften his cough. Come on . . .*

WARDER REGAN *comes out.*

WARDER REGAN Give us a hand with this fellow.

WARDER 1 We're going after that Mickser.

WARDER REGAN Never mind that now, give us a hand. He fainted when the trap was sprung.

WARDER 1 These young screws, not worth a light.

They carry **CRIMMIN** *across the yard.*

NEIGHBOUR'S VOICE Dunlavin, that's a Sunday bacon you owe me. Your man was topped, wasn't he?

PRISONER A.'S VOICE You won't be long after him.

DUNLAVIN'S VOICE Don't mind him, Neighbour.

NEIGHBOUR'S VOICE Don't you forget that bacon, Dunlavin.

Understanding the text

1 How would you describe the Warders' attitude in this scene towards

a the execution?

b Mickser?

2 What seems to be Dunlavin's and Neighbour's attitude towards the execution?

3 Look at Mickser's long speech. How is he describing the execution? Why do you think he is doing this? How would it make the Warders feel? How would it make an audience feel?

4 Why do the Prisoners shout 'One off, one away' at the moment of the execution?

Reflection and development

5 In what ways does the style of this scene appear to be more **naturalistic** than the extract from *Maria Marten*?

6 What emotional effect do you think this scene would have on a modern audience? Try to say why you think this.

7 What point do you think the scene makes about hanging? How does it do this?

8 Use what you now know about the play *The Quare Fellow* and the style it uses to develop another scene which could come from the same play. You may invent whatever characters you choose and set it wherever you wish. The important thing is that you try and make the scene seem 'natural' whilst putting over some message.

9 What differences would there be in the way a naturalistic scene like this is lit and the way a melodrama like *Sweeney Todd* should be lit? Would there be any differences in the sound effects and make-up used? Write up your ideas in your working notebook.

STUDY EXTRACT TWO
The Sally Ann Hallelujah Show

Melodrama sought above all else to entertain its audience by playing on their emotions. The plays concentrate on *what* is happening. Playwrights who wrote naturalistic dramas tried to present the audience with scenes which would reflect real life. They tend to concentrate more on *where* and *how* the story is happening as well as *who* it is happening to. As the twentieth century has gone on, many playwrights have begun to see that naturalism has its limitations. Like melodrama, it tends to present a story which can simply be watched and enjoyed by an audience without making them think about the implications of the story. Modern drama often uses a range of styles and techniques to make people think about *why* things happen, and what their implications might be.

The Sally Ann Hallelujah Show is a play that was originally written to be seen by teenagers in Nottingham. It tells the story of the growth of The Salvation Army and its founder William Booth (who came from Nottingham). In the play, writer Stephen Lowe blends the style of melodrama with other popular forms of entertainment at the time. From Music Hall he has adopted a 'Chairman' who introduces each part of the entertainment and talks freely to the audience. From pantomime he has adopted both typical storylines and characters, including the local Hero Robin Hood.

The play can be performed by as few as five people doubling up the parts and making the quick costume and character changes a part of the entertainment. The only required items of staging are

- four chairs
- a round table
- a coffin
- an easel with title cards
- a black and white reversible cloth
- a spittoon.

Some of the Salvation Army themselves developed Music Hall acts in order to try to get their message across.

Props may be mimed wherever possible and costumes can be suggested by different hats etc.

Of course, it is also possible to utilise many of the stage tricks and special effects discussed earlier and use the script as an exercise in capturing the style of Victorian theatre. Coincidentally, Stephen Lowe was born in the house next door to William Booth's.

The majority of people in Victorian Britain seemed to accept the way things were. After all, what else could they do about it apart from escaping through drink, entertainment or religion? Those in power certainly seemed to be in no great hurry to change things and often blamed the people for their own poverty and lack of morals. Some people, though, saw the injustice of the situation and fought for a change in attitudes towards the poor.

One such man was William Booth, the founder of The Salvation Army. The 'Sally Ann' was originally formed to combat the devastating effects of alcohol on the poor. Booth found out that many breweries and distillers 'pushed' alcohol in the same way as drug dealers today. Their victims were usually those who were most vulnerable: people who felt they had little to live for, the lonely, the hopeless, and often, children.

The campaign against such exploitation was a bitter and ongoing one but in 1885 Booth found another dark side of Victorian life to expose and fight – child prostitution.

CHARACTERS
CHAIRMAN A kind of Master of Ceremonies who stands to one side of the stage and uses a gavel to introduce each scene
BOOTH/ROBIN HOOD The hero
FLORENCE/MATA HARI The heroine
COUNT LEROI DRACULA The villain
OTHER MEN AND WOMEN OF THE SALVATION ARMY CHORUS

CHAIRMAN And now, friends in frailty, welcome to the very acme of our show as we transport you back into the days of yore, when Robin and his merry mirthful men disported in the woods and introduce a work that could most simply be described as a tragical-comical-historical-pastoral-melo-dramatical-pantomimical-horrifical little scene, entitled BABES IN THE WOOD.

A Caption Card reading BABES IN THE WOOD is placed on the easel.

FLORENCE In 1885, the Criminal Law Amendment Bill, which aimed to raise the age of consent for sexual intercourse from thirteen to sixteen, was thrown out of the House of Commons. In 1885 The Salvation Army went to war.

Caption: SCENE ONE. A WOODED GLADE

The next two scenes are mimed in pantomime/ melodrama fashion. The narrators encircle and enter into the action, sometimes pointing out a detail, sometimes speaking for the characters.

CHAIRMAN It is a fine and balmy day;
The vernal equinox blows clouds away.
It's fine and dry – an early but perfect harvest day.
And here we see a child at play,
Picking flowers fresh in May.

*A Little Girl – 'The **BABE**' dances, picks flowers.*

BOOTH May Day. Dawn. My daughter-in-law, Florence, found a distressed child on her doorstep. A young girl. Twelve. Thirteen. She told a strange tale.
CHAIRMAN But who have we here? Why, it's our Dame,
No doubt about to take the sun and walk.
She smiles so fondly at the maiden's game,
And then engages her in comic talk.

*The **DAME**, complete with comic props, bags full of sausages etc. 'talks' to the child.*

FLORENCE The girl was Annie Swan. One of a large family. It was a rare Sunday. A day on the Common. A treat. She half saw the old lady in conversation with her mother, caught a glimpse of something bright pass from hand to hand. Thought nothing of it. Why should she? She was a child on holiday.
CHAIRMAN The child was dancing wild.
Our Dame did make her laugh a lot.
The sun beat on the fair skinned child.
The old lady offered her a tot
Of something cool and mild.
FLORENCE A kind gesture.

*The **BABE** faints.*

A faint.
BOOTH The child faints.
FLORENCE Many a child faints in our cities.
BOOTH On a hot day. Through the heat.
FLORENCE With the hunger.

BOOTH With the sickness.

FLORENCE No-one stops to question.

BOOTH The kind old lady bears the child away.

The **DAME** *drags the* **BABE** *away.*

CHAIRMAN And now our scene doth swiftly fade
From gentle nature of that forest glade
To a dark and rat-infested cell,
Here rises from her sleep our tender maid
To find herself in dank and dismal Hell!

Caption: SCENE TWO. NOTTINGHAM CASTLE

The **BABE** *rises from the table where she has been placed under a black cloth. The* **DAME** *unwraps her dress and inverts it into a cloak. The following is full of melodramatic entreaties!*

FLORENCE She was trapped in the brothel of Madame Jeffares, a woman who catered for the best. The aristocrats. The artists.

CHAIRMAN The gaoler stood before her,
Which gave her a fearful shock.
But she was made of yeoman stock
And steeled herself for death rather than foul dishonour.

FLORENCE Jeffares was an inventive woman. Took some pride in the tools of her trade. Swinburne, the young poet, admired her handicraft of pain.

CHAIRMAN This evil sheriff
Threatened her with relish
Listing all the tortures
Of his own perfidious make –

They freeze in melodramatic positions.

FLORENCE Mrs Jeffares was in business. You couldn't afford too much waste. There was always someone who's taste would suit the merchandise, whether it be Monkton Milne, the MP, or Sir Richard Burton, the explorer. She allowed her girls no childish melodramatic choice between death and dishonour. She catered for the best, and the best liked virgins – willing or not.

BOOTH We checked this most fantastic of tales, and heard the same story from many girls. At first we doubted. The girls were often of an unsettled, imaginative, somewhat deranged frame of mind. We could not take their word for it.

CHAIRMAN Meanwhile in the forest something stirred –
It was a man in green, not an overlarge bird!
Let us go –
Deep into the Heart of England,
Into the Heart of Sherwood,
Into the Heart of an Olde Oak Tree. . .

Caption: SCENE THREE. THE ROYAL OAK

Everyone clambers onto the tables singing the 'Robin Hood' theme. Lots of good natured banter in the crush.

ROBIN I declare this council of war open. Agenda.

MAN 1 Male.

MAN 2 Female.

MEN Two genders!

ROBIN Very funny. Now, I'd like to pass a motion.

MAN 1 Clear the tree! Clear the tree!

ROBIN Very funny. I make the motion that this tree deplores the conduct of King John and his vassals in the castle, and strongly urges immediate action to put an end to it.

ALL Hear! Hear!

MAN 2 Let's ram his portcullis and storm up his battlements.

ROBIN No, Much the Miller's son. We are not yet sufficient in number for such a task. He is well served by surly thugs. We'll never beat him with the sword.

MAN 1 The pen is mightier than the sword.

ROBIN What does that mean, Friar Tuck.

MAN 1 It's a wise old saying, Robin.

ROBIN But what does it mean?

MAN 1 How would I know?

MAN 2 I know, Robin, I know.

ROBIN Speak forth, Alan a'Dale.

MAN 2 Well, it's like this. If we could find out more about his evil iniquities, we can write ballads about them and give out broadsheets, and let the people know, and then they'd all rally round us in support for our Holy war. It's only their ignorance that they can't see the real enemy that stops them from fighting.

ROBIN Well said, Alan a'Dale.

MAN 2 Thank you.

MAN 1 Creep!

GIRL 1 But how do we get this information? No-one can get into the castle except as a prisoner.

ROBIN We need somehow to plant a viper in his bosom. A spider in his nest. A spy in his midst.

GIRL 2 I'll go, Robin. Let me. I'll let myself be taken and smuggle out messages to you. Let me.

ROBIN Do you realise the dangers?

GIRL 2 I will use all my guile to preserve my innocence. But it is worth the risk, Robin, that others might be free.

ROBIN Well said, brave wench!

Much cheering, snippets of 'Robin Hood' theme etc as they fall off the table.

GIRL 1 We persuaded W.T. Stead, the editor of the influential *Pall Mall Gazette*, to publish the facts we uncovered. One of our officers, Jenny Turner, volunteered to enter a brothel, and smuggle out the true facts. The information she sent was even more horrific than we had ever dreamed.

Caption: SCENE FOUR. A CELL IN THE CASTLE

GIRL 2 *is writing a letter.*

GIRL 2 I have become the confidante of the madame here, and have, by my willingness and demeanour, persuaded her to save me for her own Master's pleasure, who is away at present. Meanwhile she has been talking openly to me of the White Slave Trade. Many thousands of girls, between 10 and 14, each year –

GIRL 1 (*reading*) are drugged and nailed down in coffins, with the barest minimum of ventilation holes, to escape detection. They are then despatched abroad to satisfy specific orders from Brussels to Bucharest. Some of the girls come to too early from their drugged sleep and die, screaming and clawing uselessly at the coffin lids.

GIRL 2 (*ties note to pigeon and tosses it out of the window where it is caught by Robin*) I do not know how long I can escape detection.

GIRL 1 We began publishing these stories in the Gazette, under the banner heading A MODERN BABYLON. Within hours a gang of thugs held the printers in siege, smashing every window and crying for the blood of Booth and Stead. On the streets the newsboys were attacked.

ROBIN Meanwhile back in the cell, Jenny had been discovered. In her sleep, her few possessions had been searched. She awoke to find the Master leaning over her.

The girl starts and backs away. The villain towers above her in a black cloak. She feels instinctively at her neck. Gasps.

VILLAIN Looking for something, little one? Could it be a crucifix to ward off evil spirits?

GIRL 1 She had kept hidden her Salvation Army medallion – it was this they had discovered.

VILLAIN Gone, my child. Gone. Buried fathoms deep in the primeval mud of my moat. Gone where no stray glint of sunlight may ever strike to ward away my evil intent. Now come, my child. Look into my eyes. You can not resist me. You are totally within my power. Come. Come. Come.

GIRL 1 At this moment, the girl's handsome fiancé, captain Frank Carpenter, was organising his men to besiege the tower.

ROBIN Once more unto the breach, dear friends –

VILLAIN Drat! A thousand drats! I have not time to slake my thirst. Well then, just a drop, my whitened sepulchre. (*He bears his fangs and bites the hypnotised virgin's neck. She faints away*) There, and now, into this coffin and then, by secret passages, to Transylvania. They do not catch old Dracula so easily. (*Hideous laughter*)

GIRL 1 The captain broke into the room and found his bride-to-be already drugged and in a coffin.

VILLAIN Gaze on her loveliness. You will not look on her face again, or any woman's!

ROBIN Free her, you devil-incarnate. There is no escape.

VILLAIN You think you have outdone me. But I have run from the sun before. Always the night comes and I am there, in the shadows, victorious. And now, my shining white knight, your light offends me. Your night has come.

He draws his sword.

VILLAIN You wear no sword?

ROBIN I need no sword of steel – (*produces pen*) – The Pen is Mightier Than The Sword!

VILLAIN You dare to come against Count Dracula with a pen? Prepare to die!

ROBIN (*leaping onto the table and freeing his bow*) But this is no ordinary pen, my friend. This pen is carved from the Heart of Royal Oak at midnight and has been consecrated by a friar. This is a pen that when strung to my bow will strike terror into your heart. A wooden stake for Vampires!

VILLAIN Ah! NO! NO!

ROBIN Repent, villain, of your deeds. Call on God for Grace.

VILLAIN Never! Never!

ROBIN Then die.

He looses the arrow. The **VILLAIN** *falls backwards with the arrow in his chest, staggers and disappears out of the window and Wheeeeee – SPLASH! into the moat!*

ROBIN An end to tyranny! (*releasing* **GIRL 2** *from coffin*). My love.

GIRL 2 My love.

General rejoicing, singing, **ROBIN** *carried around stage on shoulders.*

GIRL 1 In 1886, by dint of public demand, the Criminal Law Amendment Act was passed, raising the age of consent from thirteen to sixteen.

ALL Hallelujah!

Understanding the text

 1 What is there in the style of this extract that clearly indicates that the story is being 'performed' rather than happening in 'real life'? Find at least three things which show that this is not a **naturalistic** play.

2 What different settings are suggested in the stage directions? How do you suppose the author intends the audience to know where each scene is set?

3 What in particular do you think the writer has 'borrowed' from the style of melodrama?

4 What points do you think the scene is trying to make about

a life in Victorian England?
b William Booth?
c the actual style of 'melodrama'?

Producing the scene

 5 The stage directions suggest that several different sets could be used in this extract.

a What practical problems might this create for a small, travelling theatre company?
b How might this be overcome so that the audience get a 'sense' of the set without actually seeing it in detail?

6 In groups of four or five, devise a way of using timing and space to create tension in Scene 4. After you have walked through the scene and decided on these factors, consider how you could use melodramatic gestures to make the characters and the situation more obvious.

7 Design an appropriate costume for at least one of the following characters.
    The Dame   The Little Girl
    Robin Hood   Dracula

Reflection

 8 Not only has Stephen Lowe adopted the style of presentation used in pantomimes and melodramas in his play, he might also be said to have 'sensationalised' the facts in order to make a point. In truth very few girls were drawn into prostitution or shipped abroad in the way depicted here. Nevertheless, it did happen and the authorities were very slow to do anything about it even though they knew it happened. Do you think that playwrights are justified in using such unusual and possibly sensational examples in order to make their point?

9 In the play, the character of William Booth says:

'We live in melodramatic times. Too much is pushed into the dark and ignored.'

Are things still pushed into the dark and ignored? If you think they are, perhaps they could be exposed by using a melodramatic style of presentation.

Written tasks

 10 Rewrite the scene in which the girl, Annie Swan, is tricked by Madame Jeffares as a piece of naturalistic drama.

11 How would the Annie Swan story be reported at the time? Some newspapers, such as *The Pall Mall Gazette*, tried to make their readers aware of what was really going on. Others were not so keen on publishing what they might have seen as 'distasteful' stories. Write two contrasting articles based on The Salvation Army campaign against child prostitution which reflect these different attitudes.

12 Theatre programmes often include useful information on the style and historical background of the play they accompany. Design a programme for *The Sally Ann Hallelujah Show* and include information on the play's content, style and historical background.

SPECIAL ASSIGNMENT

Nineteenth-century theatre managers knew that in order to keep the audiences coming in they had to constantly offer something new. The problem was that once the audience had seen one good effect they expected something even more startling on their next visit. This had a damaging effect on the writers at the time who were called on to provide the theatres with an endless stream of new plays. The stories and characters became more tired and thin as more and more effort was put into inventing stunning tricks. There are examples of plays featuring horse races, exploding river boats and even steam trains racing towards some poor girl tied to the railway line!

In this Special Assignment you will consider how some of the inventions and tricks invented in Victorian times are still used today.

Set design

In Shakespeare's theatre the plays were performed on an open stage without scenery as we know it today. The Victorians, though, tried to create sets that looked like the real place. The plays were performed on a **proscenium arch** stage where the acting space was separated from the audience by a large archway which gave the effect of looking at a framed picture. You may well have a proscenium arch stage in your school hall.

The Victorians often used 'flats' to help create realistic sets. These were large wooden frames covered in canvas that could be painted to hide the wings of the stage from the audience and give more depth and detail to the set. These could be changed quite quickly by sliding them onto the stage in grooves or lowering them from the 'fly-tower' above the stage.

1 Using a cardboard box, make a simple model of a proscenium arch stage. Cut off the top so that you can get into the model from above, and cut a large square out of one side. Paint the inside of the box black.

2 Now look at the different scenes that would be needed to present the extract from *The Sally Ann Hallelujah Show*. Bearing in mind that if the play were to be performed in the Victorian style you would need very realistic sets, consider:

● What sort of backdrop would you need to hide the plain black wall at the back of the stage?
● What other furniture and scenery would you put on the stage for each scene?
● How could you use flats at the side of the stage to help create the different scenes?

a Sketch a design for at least one of the scenes in the extract from *The Sally Ann Hallelujah Show*.

b Make a 'plan view' of your design – that is, what it will look like from above. The symbols shown below are the ones commonly used by set designers to save them from having to make their drawings too elaborate. Make the backdrops and furniture for your model.

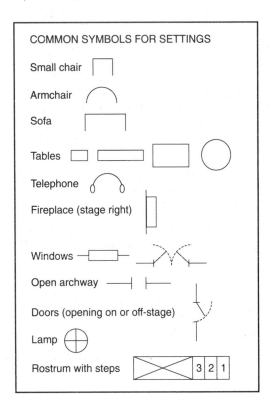

COMMON SYMBOLS FOR SETTINGS

Small chair
Armchair
Sofa
Tables
Telephone
Fireplace (stage right)
Windows
Open archway
Doors (opening on or off-stage)
Lamp
Rostrum with steps   3 2 1

3 Use your sketches and plans to make a model set for the show, and display it in your model box.

Composite sets

In recent years there has been a trend for theatre designers to build **composite sets**. This involves thinking of the key elements of all of the scenes in the plays and making just one set that can serve them all. Sometimes this involves working on a virtually bare stage and using just a few props and furnishings to create different scenes.

One production of *The Sally Ann Hallelujah Show* was performed in front of a backdrop which showed a Victorian street scene. A plain wooden table and two wooden chairs were used at various points for the Chairman to stand behind, to serve as the table in the castle, and to represent the cramped interior of the Royal Oak!

More complicated composite sets might involve

● using special flats called **book flats** which can open like a book so that they show one scene on the outside and a different one when they are opened
● using a line of triangular flats (**periaktoi**) which can be turned on spindles to show three different scenes
● using some structure which can be changed to represent different things (some of these work on the same kind of principle as a 'transformer' toy where bits can be pulled out and turned around to completely change the character)

• using a **revolve**, a part of the stage which can be turned around and even raised or lowered to show different settings.

Look at this picture from The Royal National Theatre's production of *The Shaughrean*. The play is a classic melodrama complete with scenes set in ruined castles and peasants' cottages.

4 Discuss what the advantages would be of having just one set rather than a number of different ones.

5 Design a composite set for *The Sally Ann Hallelujah Show* which it would be possible to use in the performance space in your school. You could make a model of the set to go into your model box or you might decide that the show could be played on an open stage (perhaps on the floor of the hall or on rostra blocks), in which case simply mounting it on a piece of board would be fine. If you choose an open stage, though, you will need to think about where the audience will be sitting.

Further reading

Create your Own Stage Sets Terry Thomas (A & C Black)
Stage Design and Properties Michael Holt (Phaidon)
Stage Design Kenneth Rowell (Studio Vista)

Lighting

At the beginning of the nineteenth century, lighting in theatres was achieved by using candles. The intensity of this light could be varied by placing the candle behind a glass lens but the number of effects possible was obviously limited and pretty dangerous! The introduction of gas lighting meant that more could be done with focusing and varying the lighting. Gas tends to give a rather yellow, hazy sort of light and the fumes thickened the atmosphere in the theatre. This might have been good in the spooky scenes but was probably rather stifling overall!

What the Victorian theatre managers discovered, though, were some principles of lighting that are still true today. Firstly, there are three reasons why lights should be used:

• to make sure that the actors and their expressions can be seen clearly
• to create different atmospheres
• to help the audience notice details about the set, costumes and props.

The lighting designer has three things to help achieve these aims:

• **Quantity of light:** How many lights should be on at any one time? This will obviously affect the total amount of light there is.
• **Colour of light:** Colour can be changed by putting filters in front of the lens. These are **gels**. Colours can be used in fairly obvious ways, for example blue to suggest night, green to suggest the depths of a forest. Some colours have special meanings: red can suggest blood, death and hell; white can suggest purity and heaven.
• **Distribution of light:** Where lights are positioned can have a big effect, as can the type (see the exercises below).

You can discover some useful things about lights just by using torches or, if you have the facility, a few different stage lights.

 6 Stand someone against a black wall or curtain and position a spotlight at their feet shining upwards. Look at their face and talk about the effect.

Compare this to what happens to their face if you shine the light down on them from above.

Get the character to change the angle of their face or put on different expressions.

Talk about the effects you are achieving.

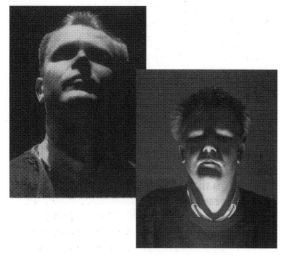

7 Dress some characters in different-coloured costumes. Try the same experiment again but this time with a number of different-coloured gels in front of the lights.

Pay particular attention to what happens when, for example, you put a red light onto a red costume.

Look at the chart at the bottom of the page which shows the main types of lights used in the theatre and describes what they do.

8 Create a simple still image in front of the black curtain. The scene should show three characters and should use a number of stage furnishings (table, chairs, ornaments etc).

Try lighting the scene with these different types of lights and on a grid like this make a note of their effect, but add as many different types, directions and angles as you have time for.

Type of light	Direction/angle	Effect
floodlight	head-on	
spotlight	front and above	
fresnel	behind	

Illusion

The Victorians were very keen on stage illusion. In addition to delighting in making characters appear or disappear through clever trap doors, they often used lighting to achieve the effect of people walking through

Name	Symbol	Description
Floodlight		Gives a wide wash of light to light the whole scene. Often used to light the backdrop or, when the right coloured gels are used, create a sinister atmosphere when used as floodlights at the front of the stage.
Profile spot		Gives a sharply defined circle of light the size of which can be changed but moving the bulb closer or further away from the lens. A shutter behind the lens can change the shape of the beam which is useful for suggesting, for example, light shining through an open doorway.
Fresnel spot		Gives a soft-edged beam of light like a car headlight. It can be focused in the same way as a profile but tends to look more natural.
FX lanterns		These are special projectors which can be used to give effects such as rain falling, clouds moving, fire flickering. One type is used specifically for creating lightning bolts.
Par can		Gives a strong but unfocused beam of light. Par cans are popular at concerts because of their intensity.

walls or appearing as ghosts. Sometimes this was indeed done with mirrors but another way was to use a special flat which was covered in thin gauze rather than thick canvas. The gauze could be painted and when lit from the front the audience would just see the painted scenery. However, when it was lit from behind the painted scene would effectively disappear. By placing a character behind the flat and lighting the figure it would seem as if they had magically appeared through the wall.

You can notice this same effect if you have net curtains on your windows. In daylight people in the street cannot see in, but once you put the room light on they can see through (remember this when you're getting changed!)

Lighting cues

Lighting today is electric and can be controlled very accurately through a dimmer board. Making sure that the right lights come on at the right time requires careful planning.

9 Read through the extract from *The Sally Ann Hallelujah Show* again and make notes on what sort of lighting effects you would use for the different scenes. Think about colours, angles and what sort of lights would give the right amount of light and the right sort of atmosphere.

You will also have to think about where on the stage the actors will be.

Plot your effects on a chart like this:

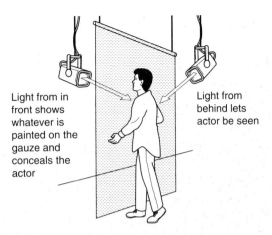

Light from in front shows whatever is painted on the gauze and conceals the actor

Light from behind lets actor be seen

10 Go back to the plan you made for the set of *The Sally Ann Hallelujah Show* and draw on it where you would need to place different lights in order to light the whole of this extract. Use the symbols shown above and give each light a number. These numbers can now be added to your cue sheet.

11 The next logical task would be to decide what channel on the dimmer board each light should be plugged into. Once this is done you would note that in the last column.

The lighting cue sheet you have produced here is a very basic one just to give you the idea of the process involved in designing and operating lights for a show. You will find much better examples of cue sheets and advice on designing and operating lights in the following books:

Lighting and Sound Neil Fraser (Phaidon)
The Stage Lighting Handbook Frances Reid (A & C Black)
Stages in Design Kenneth Kimber & David Wood (Hodder and Stoughton)

Cue no.	Cue	Effect	Light no.	Channel
1	Chairman speaks. Down stage right	Tight profile. White. Head-on/45°		
2	Florence on stage left	White fresnel on her and on card		
3	Chairman 'It is a fine & balmy day …'	Bring up general lighting centre stage		
4	Booth. Up stage centre	Add tight spot in blue		

Sound effects

The Victorians invented a number of quite ingenious machines and devices for creating sound effects. Electricity only came into use at the end of the last century. The wind-up phonograph – the forerunner of the gramophone – wasn't invented until 1877 and was of no use in the theatre because the sound couldn't be effectively amplified.

However, raging winds could be created by turning a large wheel made of wooden slats around in a drum of stretched canvas. Thunder was produced by shaking sheets of galvanised metal. In order to get a really good thunder effect one theatre manager had a wooden chute built behind the walls of the auditorium, going right from the roof of the theatre to the basement. He would have iron cannon balls rolled down the chute to give a truly quadraphonic surround sound. However, another manager pinched his idea before he patented it – hence the saying 'to steal someone's thunder'.

In melodramas an orchestra would also be available to provide appropriate music to the scenes. Because the plays were being produced so quickly there often wasn't enough time to write new music especially for the show, so the orchestra relied on using 'stock' pieces which fitted certain atmospheres. The same sort of music was used by pianists who played to silent films for the same reasons.

Today sound effects and background music can be taken straight from CDs. Modern amplifiers and graphic equalisers are used in the same way as lighting control boards to fade things in and out and control the volume and even the direction from which the sound appears to be coming.

12 No sound effects or pieces of music are mentioned in the extract of *The Sally Ann Hallelujah Show*. Go through the script and pick out:

a where special sound effects might help create atmosphere

b moments when some music in the background might be used.

A recording of *Music for Silent Movies* is available in the BBC sound collection and would be worth listening to for this task.

13 Design a sound cue sheet for this extract. Use the same format as you did for the lights stating clearly where the sound should come in, and what sort of sound it should be.

Further reading
Sound for the Theatre Graham Walne (A & C Black)
Lighting and Sound Neil Fraser (Phaidon)

Stage management

The role of the stage manager in a production is to make sure that everything happens when it is meant to happen. This means that he or she must have a copy of the script in which each sound effect and lighting effect is marked, as well as the positions the actors ought to be in at any given moment of the show. Called simply **the book**, the stage manager's script will also have a record of what props and furnishings are on stage at any one time, when they come on and when they go off, along with the names of which stage hands are responsible for them. In short, the book is the complete manual on how to run the show.

14 Working in groups, make a stage manager's book for the extract of *The Sally Ann Hallelujah Show*. You will need photocopies of the extract. Paste small sections of the extract onto the right-hand page of an exercise book. On the left-hand page make detailed notes on

a lighting cues and effects
b sound cues and effects
c props and furnishings needed.

15 Rehearse the extract and note down, in the book, more or less where each actor is standing at any given moment. This is best done by using a simple diagram like this:

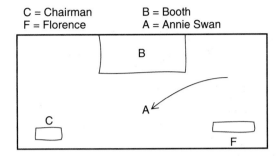

C = Chairman   B = Booth
F = Florence   A = Annie Swan

16 The real test of whether or not your book is accurate is to give it, along with your lighting and sound cue sheets, to another group. It will be their responsibility to operate the lights and sound and ensure that the stage looks right while your group performs the extract.

Reflection

17 Write an account of how you think lighting and sound can help bring a script like *The Sally Ann Hallelujah Show* alive on the stage.

18 Make notes on the practical difficulties you have encountered in this project and suggest ways that you might tackle these problems when you next have to produce a piece of theatre.

Further Reading

Plays

East Lynn by John Oxenford, in *The Golden Age of Melodrama* ed. Michael Kilgarrif (Wolfe)
Black Eyed Susan by D. W. Jerrold in *Nineteenth Century Plays* ed. George Rowell (OUP)
The Bells by Leopold Lewis
The Shaughraun by Dion Boucicault in *Selected Plays* ed. Peter Thomson (OUP)
These are all very typical Victorian melodramas. More are to be found in:
Victorian Melodramas ed. James Smith (Dent)
The Golden Age of Melodrama ed. Michael Kilgarrif (Wolfe)

Sweeney Todd by Chris Bond (Samuel French) is an excellent modern adaptation of the play
Jack Sheppard by Ken Campbell (Macmillan)   A play based on the true story of a young highwayman.
The Blood of Dracula by Chris Bond (Thomas Nelson) is a splendid spoof on the story of Dracula using a whole range of spectacular melodramatic stage tricks.

Poetry

'The Ballad of Charlotte Dymond' anon.
'Flannan Isle' by W. W. Gibson.

Fiction

The December Rose Leon Garfield (Puffin)
Smith Leon Garfield (Puffin)
Jack Diamond Leon Garfield (Puffin)
The Ruby in the Smoke Philip Pullman (Puffin)
Ask No Questions Ann Schlee (Macmillan)
A Chance Child Jill Paton Walsh (Puffin)
Oliver Twist Charles Dickens (Dent)

Non-fiction

Theatre in the Age of Irving by George Rowell (Basil Blackwell).   A readable and useful source book on the styles and techniques used last century.
The Illustrated Mayhew's London (Weidenfeld and Nicolson).   Henry Mayhew was one of the few journalists who reported on the conditions and lives of the poor in Victorian England. His reports are startlingly vivid and provide a wealth of material which could be explored through drama.
Victorian Melodrama by Robert Leach (Harrap).
The Fatal Shore by Robert Hughes.   This is a staggering account of how prisoners condemned to transportation were treated. The story of how they put on their own plays is told in Thomas Kenneally's book *The Playmaker*, and dramatised in *Our Country's Good* by Timberlake Werterbaker (Methuen).

The drama of images

The question of STYLE is explored further in this project and its relationship with FORM and CONTENT is made clearer.
The ideas of SIGN and SYMBOL are introduced by ANALYSING a number of VISUAL IMAGES.

The practical work will help you generate ideas for starting and deepening your own dramas.

 ## Every Picture Tells a Story

Chapter One introduced the idea of 'visual text' and suggested that pictures, or still images, could be 'deconstructed' in order to give us clues to
● what is happening in the image
● who it is happening to
● why it is happening.
(Look back to pp 5–6.)

Pictures can also be used to suggest things about characters and their relationships. (Look back to Chapter Two, pp 54–55.)

Making tableaux (still pictures in which you play the characters) can be used to mark key moments in personal or dramatic development. This Project looks at other ways of developing drama work from still images, in this case paintings.

The most obvious, and perhaps most useful, way of looking at a painting is simply to consider it as a whole and feel an atmosphere or an emotion in response to it. This might be the end of the matter as we conclude that we like it or don't like it, or the picture might make us want to express what we feel in a piece of our own work. Look at the three pictures of horses on the next page.

Their **form** is the same – they are all paintings.

Their **content** is similar – they are all horses.

Which one appeals to you most?

If you prefer one to another you are probably reacting to the picture's **style**.

To understand why we like or don't like the style of a painting, we can analyse it by concentrating on

- **form** eg the type, colour and quantity of paint used: the thickness and weave of the canvas, the sort of brush strokes used, the use of light and shade, the angle from which the scene/character is viewed and so on
- **content** eg what is actually shown in the painting, where it is set, what is in the background, what is being worn and so on.

What this sort of analysis doesn't explain is why the painters have chosen such different **styles**. To understand this we need to ask what the pictures seem to suggest to us.

1 On a blank piece of paper, copy out the three columns shown below and add as many ideas of your own about the feelings or thoughts that the pictures provoke in you.

Picture one	Picture two	Picture three
Pain	Fun	Speed
War	Childhood	Wealth
?	?	?

Your list shows what the paintings **symbolise** for you. By **symbol**, we mean something that has the power to suggest something else.

How exactly does a picture do that?

We can find out the answer by looking at the **signs** it is giving us. That is, the way it points out certain things (in exactly the same way as a roadsign tells us which way to go.)

2 On a second sheet of paper, fill in three new columns which note the different signs given by the pictures. For example, look at these descriptions of the three horses:

Picture one	Picture two	Picture three
wild	roly poly	sleek
screaming	nuzzling	upright
?	?	?

When we say that 'every picture tells a story' we should remember that the story is told by whoever is looking at it. How an audience interprets a picture depends upon how carefully they are looking at it.

- What knowledge do they have of its history?
- How much do they know about the techniques it uses?
- What mood are they in when they are looking at it?
- Do they like or dislike its content for some personal reason?
- Does it remind them of anything personal to them?

If you are prepared to let pictures remind you of other things and stir feeling within you then considering their **style** and **content** will give you some good starting points for drama. An awareness of how **signs** are read and can be used to **symbolise** other things will, as you will see in Chapter Four, increase the depth and interest of your drama work.

Study Examples

Pictured below are three contrasting paintings. The questions about each one do not require precise answers. They are for discussion and speculation and to give you a foothold from which to launch into your own work.

Waiting for the verdict

 1 Who is being tried? Why?

2 Look at the signs in the picture that seem to indicate relationships; for example, how close are they physically? What are they doing to each other? From this analysis suggest what the relationship is between the people in the picture. What do they think of each other? What do they think of the trial? What do they think the verdict will/should be?

3 What's going on in the background? What will happen next? What effect will the verdict have on these people's lives?

4 How would you describe the style of this picture? Does it seem to reflect 'real life' in a naturalistic way? Or does it seem heavily emotional in a melodramatic way?

Waiting for the verdict by Abraham Solomon (1857)

5 Imagine the artist is trying to make a social point through this picture. In other words, what might the picture symbolise?

6 What sort of feelings are being depicted here? Waiting, worry, regret . . .? What feelings does it evoke in us today?

Sympathy, boredom ('Oh no! Not another painting with a social message!') . . .?

7 The chart below shows how you can use one idea to spark off a number of others by considering similar situations. Try to add some of your own ideas to the lists suggested.

FOCUS ON SITUATION
Waiting

1 Waiting for a bus/train/'plane. It's an important appointment and you're already late.

2 Waiting for the results of a test. Exam? Driving? Blood? Pregnancy?

3 Waiting to be told what to do. New job? Army?

4 Waiting to see something happen. A secret meeting? A procession? The unveiling of a new invention?

FOCUS ON MOOD
Gloom

1 You've just lost all your money on a horse that was a 'dead cert'!

2 You have to leave someone you love.

3 You've just lost something precious.

4 You've had some terrible news.

FOCUS ON PLACE
A Courthouse

1 A place of judgement. Tutor's office? Exam room? Heaven's gate?

2 A place where truth is told. Friend's bedroom? Interrogation block?

3 A place of solemn ritual. Church? School assembly?

4 A place representing the society. A museum? A palace?

FOCUS ON CHARACTER
The man in the foreground

1 Someone who has reason to weep.

2 Someone who shares a trouble with their family.

3 Someone who must take the blame.

4 Someone who is inspected by others.

Ennui

 8 Look carefully for signs in the picture which suggest where these characters are and how long they have been there.

9 Where do you suppose the picture on the wall comes from? Who is if of?

10 What day of the week does this 'feel' like? What are they waiting for? Why aren't they talking?

11 What's their relationship to each other? To the artist? Do they know they're being painted? How do they feel about it?

12 What words might describe the atmosphere of this picture? Have you ever felt like this painting? When? Why?

13 What would you do if you found a picture like this in the attic or saw it on someone's wall?

14 What sound effects or music might fit this image?

Ennui by Walter Sickert (1914)

A bigger splash

 15 What signs suggest where and when this picture is set?

16 Who – or what – just landed in the pool? Where did they – or it – come from?

17 What sort of building is in the background? A house, a scenerey flat, a hotel? Where are its inhabitants (if it has any)?

18 Who put the chair on the pool side? What's happened to them?

19 What's beneath the surface of the pool? Will whatever went in come out again?

20 What's the weather like? Where is everybody?

21 What contrasts in sound and sight are implied here? How can we capture a contrast in drama in such a starling way?

A bigger splash by David Hockney (1963)

C Making Drama from Pictures

By considering the content and style of pictures, improvisations can be based around a number of themes. For example:

The characters in the picture – who are they, what are they doing, what's their relationship with each other, what might they be saying?

The setting – where is it, what is it like there, what else might happen there?

The artist – who is he, why is he painting this, what do others think of his work?

1 In pairs, look at the position of the characters in *Ennui*. Adopt the same positions. Consider what mood seems appropriate to that positioning. Whoever is playing 'the girl' counts to three, turns around and says . . .

2 In pairs or small groups, imagine you are on the other side of the room to the people shown in *Waiting for the verdict*. You know who they are and what they have done. Improvise your conversation as you sit watching them and listening to what they are saying. At some point in your improvisation, imagine that someone comes and gives them 'the verdict'. How does this affect your conversation?

3 In pairs, label yourselves **A** and **B**. **A** has spent several days of their summer holiday diving into this swimming pool for the artist – **B**. Improvise the scene in which **A** is invited to see the finished picture for the first time. She expects to see one of her beautiful dives but what **B** shows her is *A bigger splash*!

Look at the following approaches and use or adapt them for one of the three pictures.

● Imagine you are the models for the picture – why are you doing this job? What do you talk about as you pose?
● Imagine you are stuck in the painting.

When art lovers gaze at you they don't realise you are also looking at them!

● Imagine you, and characters in other paintings, have the ability to come alive and leave your paintings and talk to each other.

Responding to painting through your own feelings might lead you to:

● try to capture the atmosphere and feeling of the painting by blending simple movements and short lines together
● develop a series of tableaux which depict the emotions created in you by the work.
● devise a piece of movement or mime, perhaps involving a piece of music, which seems to you to match the picture.
● improvise a scene which illustrates a parallel situation or one that shares a 'brotherhood'.

You will find it helpful to refer back to Project Two – Structuring a presentation, if you want to develop this work further.

Further developments using pictures

4 As a whole group decide upon a theme or working title, for example:

> Us and them
> Alien
> Conflict
> Surprise!

a Gather as many photographs, prints, paintings etc which seem to relate to this theme in any way at all.
b Mount the images together into an exhibition, perhaps just on one wall, perhaps as a montage.
c Look at the whole collection and note
● similarities in technique/action/subject/ setting
● the total effect and atmosphere created
● your personal response to what you have created by assembling the exhibition.
d In pairs or small groups choose five or six of the images and weave a story around them to tie them together or find some other way of linking them through speech and movement.
e Imagine that this exhibition is all that remains of someone's life. Each image contains a special significance for that

person – in exactly the same way as a photograph album might. Investigate some of those moments of his/her life which led to them adding chosen images to this personal exhibition.

5 Make a collection within the group or, even better, throughout the school, of people's worst photographs: ones where people's heads are missing, something else has been superimposed, people are caught making stupid expressions etc. Use the resultant exhibition to generate small group improvisations which put some sort of story to the pictures. Possible titles might include

- OUR HOLIDAY
- THE CAMERA CLUB
- LIFE ON EARTH; AGENT KARG RETURNS TO ZARGON WITH EXTRAORDINARY EVIDENCE ABOUT THIS DISTANT PLANET

6 Experiment with ways of projecting pictures either as a backdrop to an improvisation or, unusually, onto an improvisation. Here are three methods which should be relatively easy to set up and could be experimented with.

Slide projection

Take a slide of your chosen picture then use a standard school projector to throw the image onto some sort of screen. Curtains and even black studio walls will give an image. If you can obtain a zoom lens so much the better as this will enable you to project a large image clearly (normally, the bigger the image the lower the quality).

A disadvantage of this method is that actors between the projector and the screen will pick up the image themselves and create a shadow behind them. However, this can be extremely effective.

Experiment making your own slides by placing clear acetate in slide mountings. Use felt or fibre-tip pens to create patterns or images (the ones used on OHPs are best for clear images though water-based pens can produce some weird effects).

Back projection

If you don't want projected images all over the actors, one answer might be to project onto a screen from behind. A normal school projector may be used but you will get the best image by using a wide-angle lens. The local teachers' centre or college should be able to help.

A special screen is needed but may be simply made by stretching thin cotton sheeting over a wooden frame. Man-made material tends to reflect the projected light and spoils the image. Screens like this can also be used for shadow plays.

Overhead projection

Some pictures can be copied straight onto acetate sheets for use on OHPs. The most successful are those which depend upon clear lines (you may know Edvard Munch's 'The Scream' or have seen old woodcuts etc). Alternatively, place an acetate sheet over your chosen picture and, using fibre-tip spirit pens, trace the lines or elements which most interest you.

Reflection

 7 What pictures do you have at home? What do you think their content and style would tell a stranger about you? Think about the signs that they give to their audience and what they may symbolise.

8 Think of a poster for a film or play that you have seen. To what extent is the content of the poster a true indication of what the film is about? How successful is the style of the poster in capturing the atmosphere and impact of the film?

9 Either design or describe a poster of your own for a play with which you are very familiar. Be aware when you are doing this of the signs you are using. Working on this task in pairs may be particularly interesting. Point out how your interpretation of the play's content and style is different from your partner's.

PROJECT SIX

Space, place and atmosphere

The ideas offered in this project relate as much to PERFORMANCE ART as they do to drama in its more traditional forms. The work draws attention to the SEMIOTICS of the performance space and the objects within it, leading to the possibility of creating SITE SPECIFIC work or more conventional forms of DEVISED THEATRE.

The Found Object

In 1917 the French artist Marcel Duchamp presented a new range of 'ready made' sculptures. One of them was called 'Fountain'. It was actually a plain porcelain urinal. Other objects on show were a shovel, a bicycle wheel and a bottle rack. Although these were everyday objects, placing them in an art gallery seemed to make people look at them in a new way. Of course, not everyone thinks this sort of thing is actually 'art'. When Carl Andre exhibited his sculpture, which consisted of nothing more than house bricks, at the Tate Gallery in London, somebody protested by throwing paint over it.

The point is that somehow whatever you put into a presentation space will acquire some sort of meaning. Experimenting with this idea can be very exciting in itself and can also generate ideas that can be developed into pieces of drama.

1 Look at this photograph. You can see that the items shown in it are fairly ordinary but what sort of meaning can you find in the way the picture has been composed?

2 Each member of your class should bring in one object that is personal to them. It may be a photograph, some sort of mascot or lucky charm or perhaps even something as simple as a hairbrush.

Work in groups of three. Place your three objects on a large sheet of plain white card. Move them around. Try to make different shapes out of them or see if one can rest up against another in some way. Try looking at the images from different angles. As you do this, talk about the different things the images remind you of.

Decide on one image you particularly like. You don't have to know why you like it – just so long as you like it! Give your work a title and write this on a separate piece of paper which should be placed next to your sculpture. Decide also how you want an audience to look at your sculpture.

3 Walk around the room and see what everyone else has done. Decide for yourself why they might have called their piece what they have.

Choose a piece, other than your own, that you find interesting (again, you may not know why). In this way you will form new groups. Imagine that you are either

a the artists who have created the piece or
b curators of the art gallery who know all about it.

Devise an 'explanation' of the sculpture. If you are the artists you might create a story or piece of performance that goes with the sculpture. If you are the curators you can invent a 'meaning' for the piece which it will be your job to give to visitors to the gallery.

4 Set up a definite performance area in your studio or classroom. Decide where an audience must sit to watch this space. Experiment with what happens when you place certain objects in this space, for example a chair, or a hat stand, or a telephone.

Discuss what different meanings these objects seem to have. For example, if you just placed a telephone on the floor someone might say that it conjures up an image of an empty house where all the furniture has been taken away. A chair lying on its side would seem to suggest something very different to a chair standing in its normal way.

Having tried just one object at a time, try putting two or three in the space together. Again, discuss what sort of stories seem to be hinted at by the very way they are positioned.

5 If you have the facility to use stage lights, see what happens when you light the objects from different angles or with different colours. You can sometimes find the most extraordinary things happen when you do this. A candlestick standing on an old table with a wooden chair next to it can seem perfectly innocent under fluorescent lights, but lit from the side by a dim spotlight it can take on quite a sinister aspect.

A science of signs

What you have been doing here is playing about with **semiotics**. This is the term used for what can be described as 'the science of signs'. Everything we see, hear or touch carries some sort of meaning for us. Most of the time we take this for granted as the meanings do not seem particularly interesting. A red traffic light means we have to stop – nothing very interesting about that. Somebody wearing a pair of jeans is probably working in a place where it's OK to wear jeans, or they are relaxing – nothing very interesting about that. On the other hand, somebody turning up at the Queen's garden party in jeans will probably be thought to be making some kind of anti-establishment statement. A red light suddenly shining on the face of a character in a play will not mean 'stop' but may suggest all sorts of things about the character.

An important word here is **context**. When you experience something 'out of context' you tend to notice it and ask questions about it. So if you went to see a Shakespeare play and the only thing on the stage was a mop and bucket, you would have to decide whether it had some special meaning relating to the play or whether a stage hand had just forgotten to take it off! Another important word is **convention**, meaning what is expected and is 'accepted' as the usual thing. You will not, I hope, be having too much trouble reading this because you understand the conventions of the English language. If I suddenly diceded to strart spolling fings as I flelt like rarder than in the wee you are youst to – you might start having more trouble. If I went further and told you that @@@!^^^ ★★&)—>< : @@!§, you'd have no idea at all what I was saying.

Breaking conventions deliberately can be fun and can give an audience a new way of looking at things. If you break too many at once, though, the result will just be confusion and you'll end up communicating nothing at all. It is crucial that you bear this in mind when you are making and performing drama. You need to ask yourself what an audience will make of the signs you are giving them – _you_ might have decided what using a particular light or sound means, but will they?

Environments

We are used to seeing drama being performed on a conventional stage. Most of the plays shown in theatres are quite conventional in the way they tell a story, explore the lives of characters, raise questions about certain issues, and so on. In most cases, the set for the play is designed and created after the play has been written. But not always!

'Forkbeard Fantasy' is one theatre company that sometimes starts the other way round. Their play _Work Ethic_ is based in a loading bay of a factory. Pretty much the whole set was made from cardboard boxes and the play was all about boxes being shifted from one place to another. In this way it seemed to be making a comment on the more absurd aspects of international commerce. Below is a picture of the set drawn by a member of the company.

Work Ethic was born after Forkbeard Fantasy decided it would be interesting to see what came out of collecting hundreds of cardboard boxes together and spending the afternoon playing with them. For a different show they did the same with piles and piles of old books (perhaps you are beginning to realise what kind of people these are!).

1 Without causing any damage, change the environment of your studio or classroom by repositioning the furniture. Can you make the chairs look like a forest or a lunar landscape? How about trying to use piles of books (or whatever) to create a miniature city?

From this starting point you may find that characters and situations spring to mind. For example, two hungry giants might be carefully stepping through the miniature city in search of something or someone to eat. An exploration party from the Starship Enterprise might have beamed down onto the surface of a new planet which appears to be made entirely of – well, plastic chairs!

Be open to suggestions. Try out anything and everything.

C Defining the Performance

When you go to the theatre the performance is usually already well defined. It's likely to be on a stage that is raised above floor level, and the audience's seats will be arranged so that they are facing it. In Ancient Greece, the performance space was round and the audience sat in a tiered **amphitheatre** which made a semi-circle around the stage. Some theatre today is performed with the audience sitting or standing in a circle (**theatre in the round**). But how could you set up a performance space in a place where people were not expecting to see a performance?

1 Work in small groups. Your first task is to find a way of defining a performance space by using objects. For this, it would be enormously helpful to have a good collection of things like ropes, brooms, poles, sheets, warning tape, pipes, tubes, maybe even books and boxes – pretty much anything really.

Your group should pick a selection of objects and see how these might be placed on the floor in a way that would make it clear to an unsuspecting audience that something unusual is about to happen in this space.

Try to create some sort of ritual to go with the placing of the objects. This might involve moving in a special way or making some kind of sound. The audience of a play in Ancient Greece would know when a performance was about to start because a chorus would stand around the edge of the stage gently tamping poles on the ground. Bit by bit the audience would fall silent and begin to focus on the rhythmical beating sound and the silent figures. In Japanese Noh theatre the audience see the musical instruments which are to be used being brought onto the stage in a careful and ceremonious way. Try to give your setting of the space some kind of magical quality.

2 Through setting up your performance space in this ritualistic way you may be reminded of some particular place. The next job is to find a way of suggesting this place by using one or two pieces of white card. Imagine, for example, folding the card into a paper jet and having one performer bringing it onto the stage, flying it around once then 'landing' it. This action could be followed by someone making a 'bing-bong' noise followed by a muffled announcement. Suddenly, the audience know that they are watching an airport.

You might use your card to make a castle, a house, a cross. One group recently managed to make a little guillotine which worked!

Having decided what place you want to suggest and made the card into a suitable **signifier** – something that will give the audience a clear sign – you will need to find an interesting and dramatic way of bringing the object into the performance space.

3 How can you now introduce yourselves as performers? Sometimes actors introduce themselves directly to the audience before adopting their character:

> 'Hello. My name is Kevin and in this play I play the part of the King.'
> (*He takes up a stately position at the back of the stage.*)

(Look at the extract from *Drink the Mercury* on p 176 for another example of this.)

In the circus, of course, all the performers parade around the ring before the show proper begins. You need to think of something that will fit with both the ritual you devised for setting the performance space and the way you have defined the place.

Once you have made it clear that you are the performers and not people who have just accidentally walked onto the stage, you will need to signal clearly that you have become certain characters. This means that you need to decide what sort of characters it would be interesting to find in the place you have suggested. Experiment with establishing the characters, for example by adopting a certain pose, or by saying something that only that type of character would say, or by changing the way you move.

So now you have the opening of a piece of theatre. You have set a performance space, suggested a place for the action and introduced some characters. One way of moving forward would be to put the question:

> *If this is how the play opens, how does it end?*

Having designed a suitable ending you could try to structure the middle section. Alternatively you could just use this exercise to make the way you start your next piece of performance work more interesting.

Reflection

What has been suggested here is a very open-ended way of working. Its success relies on you being very open-minded, willing to experiment, and prepared to accept that sometimes ideas just will not seem to gel. On the other hand, simply playing around in this way can be a great deal of fun and can feed into your future work – *but only if you reflect on it!*

 4 Write notes on what you found exciting, frustrating or confusing about working in this way. If you managed to come up with something that you personally found pleasing or fascinating, try to identify how it happened.

5 Think of a piece of drama that you have previously been involved in. Have you discovered anything in this workshop that would have made that piece of drama more interesting for an audience? Talk or write about how you could use your new ideas if you were to perform that drama again.

Four

Drama in movement and sound

Drama's roots lie deep in human history and are linked closely with
MYTHS and RITUALS.
This chapter looks at these links and further explores the use of
SYMBOLS in drama.
The activities concentrate on RHYTHM, MOVEMENT and MASKS.
The underlying theme of the work is concerned with the destructive
side of human nature.

Most theatre in the Western world has tended to place a greater importance on what is said in words than on what is captured by movement and sound. This certainly isn't true of theatre in other parts of the world where movement and sound are seen as holding tremendous meaning. Recently many writers, actors and directors here have begun to feel that theatre which relies heavily on words is limited. They have begun to use movement and sound to communicate ideas which can't be expressed so well in words.

This chapter will show you how you can use your body more effectively to communicate ideas and feelings. Some activities look closely at the sort of gestures and movements we use every day to communicate meaning. Some of these are so much a part of our nature that we often don't realise that we are using them. Other activities may seem closely linked with mime and dance though none demand the highly specialised skills often associated with those art forms.

 # Expressing Yourself

Have you ever noticed how people rock themselves for comfort when they are tired or distressed?

Rocking seems to be a movement that stays with us from the cradle to the grave. It is a common image both of new life (think of a mother rocking her baby) and old age (think of someone in a rocking chair).

In between these extremes we can see children playing on swings or rocking horses and enjoying the motion, or people squatting and rocking with their heads in their hands after some tragedy.

Psychologists have suggested that this urge to rock is linked with the first rhythm we ever feel in life as embryos in the womb where the mother's heartbeat provides a gentle rhythm. Rocking is comforting and

This theatre company, called The Right Size, *has chosen to use some of the movement techniques which have been known to circus clowns for many years*

enjoyable because it reminds us of this safety and warmth.

Rocking is just one of the ways in which humans express themselves quite naturally through the way they move. Some sounds also commonly express inner feelings about certain situations. Consider, for example, how people sometimes moan in grief, sigh through frustration or make a 'Mmmmmmmmm' in appreciation.

1 In pairs, discuss other movements or sounds which you think have a clear meaning. Improvise a scene in which all the communication is done in this fashion. For example, two drivers who have just bumped their cars and are surveying the damage might

sigh	shake their heads
tut tut	look to the sky
draw in breath heavily	put their hands to their head...

Try not to use gestures such as pointing or sticking two fingers up. Similarly, try not to replace words with sounds.

2 As a whole class, add to this list of emotions, moods or feelings on a large piece of card or blackboard.

love   sadness
boredom   frustration
          hysteria
   pain   greed
      confusion
fear   disgust
   anger   horror

3 Get into pairs, **A** and **B**. **A** selects one word from the list and poses as if they are a statue carved to illustrate that particular feeling. **B** must guess what feeling the statue is showing and then takes a turn. Keep this going for a maximum of five minutes.

4 Change partners. In this exercise **A** selects any one word from the list and uses appropriate movements and sound to suggest that they are feeling that particular emotion. It may help to think of being in a particular situation, for example sitting at a desk sighing heavily and wringing your hands as if you are trying to write something but are frustrated by not knowing what to write. Again, **B** considers the list and guesses which one **A** is depicting. Swap over and keep going for five minutes.

Signatures

There are a number of things which distinguish one person from another. Fingerprints are one example, signatures another. Even though people may share a name, the way they write that name says something about them. The exercises that follow use this idea and illustrate how something as simple as your own name can become the foundation of a performance.

5 Stand in a space on your own and write your first name in the air with your fingertip. Keep this going again and again developing a rhythmical movement. Make the movement larger by using firstly your whole forearm and then your arm – imagine that you are using an aerosol can to spray your name on a wall. Make the movement bigger still, using your whole body to paint your name on a wall. The bottom of each letter will be on the floor, the top at the very end of your reach.

6 Find a way of making your body into the shape of each letter of your name.

7 Write your name on the floor capturing, in your movement, something of the nature of each letter. An 'S', for example, might suggest a sliding, smooth movement whereas an 'E' might be stiffer and more regimented.

8 Experiment with ways of saying each letter which also seem appropriate to their shape and sound. An 'S' could hissssssed. An 'E' as in SUSIE could be elongated to become 'Eeeeeeeeeee'.

9 Finally, combine the last four exercises to produce a performance of your own name – a personal signature in sound and movement.

Playing music as a background to this activity will make the whole thing feel somehow less unnatural and more like a theatrical experience.

10 Working in pairs or small groups, choose two of the emotions from your list which you think either contrast with each other (Love/Hate) or complement each other (Sadness/Pity). Find a way of using the words themselves as the foundation for a sequence of movements and sounds which will capture the meanings and feelings of those words.

Reflection

11 Watch each other's work and comment on how successfully the sounds and movements captured the emotions. How much agreement is there in the class on this? Do some sounds and movements seem to have a 'universal' meaning – that is, are they interpreted in exactly the same way by everyone?

12 Look back to the section on Evaluation in Project One (p 31). How possible is it to separate **form** and **content** when watching work like this? What might this suggest about the nature of the movements and sounds?

 # Rhythm and Ritual

Rhythms

Although some rhythms, like rocking, are a natural response to some situations, in others they are used deliberately – compare someone rocking themselves in despair to a child on a rocking horse. In drama, rhythms can be used deliberately to create and communicate meanings or feeling.

The following games will help you see how rhythms can be used to create tension.

> **1 ZING ZING ZING** Divide into groups of six or seven and number yourselves as you stand in a small circle. In this game, as in the last, the aim is to keep a rhythm going whilst at the same time trying to catch other people out. It works like a dialogue spoken to a simple bouncy rhythm. Number 1 starts the game by saying:
>
> No **1** Zing Zing Zing and a One Two Three
> Number 6 (or any other)
> No **6** (*replies*) Who me?
> No **1** Yes you.
> No **6** Not me!
> No **1** Then who?
> No **6** Number 4 (*or any other number*)
> No **4** Who me?
> No **6** Yes you.
> etc etc
>
> The conversation keeps going like this until someone falters or gets it wrong in which case Number 1 starts the whole thing over again. The whole group can help keep the rhythm going by clapping their hands, clicking their fingers or tapping their feet. You may know another version of this game which is sometimes called 'Who stole the cookie from the cookie jar?'

2 CLAPTRAP Sit in a circle and number everyone in sequence. The game requires everyone to set up a rhythm which will keep going all the time. The rhythm consists of
a patting your thighs with the flats of your hands
b clapping both hands together
c clicking the fingers on your left hand
d clicking the fingers on your right hand.

Start the sequence and speak the following as you do the actions until you get used to it:

> pat, clap, left click, right click
> pat, clap, left click, right click

etc.

To actually play the game everybody keeps this rhythm going but the player who is Number One says their number as they click their left finger and someone else's number as they click their right. For example on the left click Number One says 'one', and on the right click they add 'six'.

Number Six will then say their number on the left click and someone else's on the right click, 'six, nine'. And so on. So, with everyone keeping the pat, clap, left, right rhythm going the whole time the sequence should look like this:

> pat, clap, left (1), right (6)
> pat, clap, left (6), right (9)
> pat, clap, left (9), right (3)
> pat, clap, left (3), right (14) etc

Keep the rhythm slow at first but speed up as you get better at the game. The ultimate aim is to produce a smooth rhythm in which no one is 'caught out' forgetting what number they are or muddling the sequence.

3 ZOOF, HO, ZAP! Play this game in a circle as a whole group. Imagine that there is a ball of energy which is so full of power that you can't bear to keep hold of it for more than a split second. As a result the imaginary ball is passed clockwise around the circle using an action as if you were passing a rugby ball and shouting ZOOF! For practice, send the ball around a few times trying to get the rhythm smooth.

The game takes on a competitive element because players can bounce the ball back to the person who is passing to them by spreading out their arms as if to make a wall and saying HO! The ball would then have to be ZOOFED around anti-clockwise until someone said HO! to change its direction again. A third option is to take up a James Bond stance and 'fire' the ball across the circle to someone else shouting ZAP!

The aim, as before, is to keep a steady rhythm going while still trying to trick people who aren't awake.

Of course these games are just a bit of fun to get you used to creating and mastering simple rhythms. There are rhythms to many aspects of our real lives, though. Often we are largely unaware of them, even though they govern much of what we do. Consider, for example, the constant rhythms of
- your heartbeat
- your breathing

or those rhythms which govern
- your eating
- your sleeping.

In the world around us we are affected by the rhythms of
- day and night
- the seasons
- the tides.

Rituals

A great many of these 'natural rhythms' lie behind rituals or ceremonies which have been created by people to celebrate or mark important moments in some natural rhythmical cycle. You may tend to think of rituals concerning aboriginal rain or hunting dances or being somehow linked to 'primitive' man. This would be taking a very narrow view of both rituals and the people who perform them. Rituals and ceremonies which mark special occasions can be found in all cultures. Sometimes, people have almost forgotten what the ritual was for in the first place. In Britain, for example, many villages mark the coming of spring by dancing around a Maypole or performing special folk or Morris dances. The origins of these rituals lie in fertility rites. In some parts of India, a girl's first menstruation is cause for great celebration. Every July in the Spanish town of Pamplona the young men show their courage by allowing young bulls to chase them down the street. In the Catholic communion, churchgoers are invited to eat the body of Christ and drink his blood in the form of a wafer and some wine. The deepest roots of drama lie in the 'performances' of these rituals. Like other drama performances, rituals are a way of capturing and expressing in a controlled way an idea about what is important in the real world.

Look at the list of natural rhythms at the bottom of the last page. Do any of these lie behind any rituals or ceremonies with which you are familiar? For example, Christmas as a Christian Holy Day marks the birth of Christ and is thus an important point in the calendar of Christians. It also approximately marks mid-winter in the seasonal cycle and has been celebrated for this reason since before Christ's birth. The fact that the year has turned seems a good reason to dip into the winter stores and have a slap-up meal (you might like to discuss why eating such a lot at this time also made good practical sense in days gone by).

4 In small groups, choose a special occasion and note down its particular features, that is, things which happen on that occasion which don't tend to happen elsewhere. Choosing Christmas dinner as your special occasion might give you a list like this.

- Carving the turkey.
- Pulling crackers.
- Wearing stupid hats.
- Lighting the pudding.
- Taking a little sherry.

Such a list would represent the 'essence' or special flavour of the occasion – its **signature** perhaps.

Put a mimed action to each line you have chosen. Decide carefully on how to position the group in order to reflect something about Christmas. Develop the lines and actions into a sequence which can be repeated again and again. This type of sequence is sometimes called an **Essence machine**.

5 Without changing the lines or the actions too much, how could you develop this sequence to show another element of the occasion? On the Christmas dinner example, you might have

- the person carving the turkey making more and more of a mess of it

- the person lighting the pudding becoming more and more frustrated because it won't light

- the person sipping sherry more and more. . .

well, you've got the idea!

Take your time to develop this idea into a performance. As you work, what is said should become less and less important but the movements and sounds people make to express their feelings should become more important.

6 Look at this sequence of movements and sounds.

- A group of school children stand shoulder to shoulder in line chattering.
- Someone gently thumps a stick onto the floor three times.
- A hush falls magically over the group.
- The line becomes straighter and each child stands smartly upright facing blankly forwards.
- An adult, majestically caped, sweeps down the aisle.
- With the merest nod, the pupils sit.
- One pupil shuffles noisily into her chair. The adult coughs and looks at her. Complete silence.

School assemblies may not be quite like that in your school but this example shows how they can be extremely 'ritualistic'. The movements and noises are very significant – everyone seems to know what they mean and what to do in response to them.

Using this or an example of your own choice, work as a whole group and enact a ritual/ceremony with which you are all familiar. Emphasise each key action to show its importance and meaning in the situation.

Music

Not only are **rituals** often performed in response to some natural **rhythm**, many actually involve using rhythms deliberately produced by humans. This is perhaps most obviously true when we think of the role music plays. What music, for example, do you associate with weddings or funerals?

7 What sort of music is used to accompany the ceremonies or rituals of cultures other than white British culture? If possible, listen to some examples and try to find out how they fit into the ceremony.

It's difficult to talk about the use of music as a resource for drama in a book, but something you could do is think about any pieces of music which seem to imply, through their rhythm, some kind of ritual or ceremony. For some examples, listen to any of the following:

The film soundtracks of

> *The Mission* by Ennio Morricone
> *The Killing Fields* by Mike Oldfield
> *Cry Freedom* by George Fenton
> *Koyaanisqatsi* by Philip Glass

Music accompanying the BBC series *Flight of the Condor*

Adagio for strings by Albinoni (arranged by Giazotto)

Mahler's *First symphony* (there is an amusing section where the children's song *'Frère Jacques'* is rearranged as a funeral march)

The Rite of Spring by Stravinsky
Prospero's Books, The Piano and *The Draftsman's Contract,* all by Michael Nyman

Born – Never Asked by Laurie Anderson
Outback by Outback

8 In small groups, choose a piece of music which you think is suggestive of some kind of ritual. Devise a sequence of movements and sound which reflects the mood and purpose of the occasion. This work may have links with both dance and mime but isn't exactly either.

9 Working as a whole group, listen to a selected piece of music once through. Without commenting on it, choose for yourself a starting position and spontaneously improvise fitting appropriate movements when the music is played through again.

Discuss what the music suggested to you and what your response was after working through just once. Is there any way you could draw your different ideas together? If there are others in the class who seem to have had approximately the same idea, team up. Play the music through again and try to work together complementing each other's movements.

Reflection

 10 What other 'rituals' do you have in your life? Are there any particular to your family, for example something you do together every day or week? How have these rituals been developed and what purpose do you think they serve?

11 Some rituals are so much a part of our lives and seem so ordinary that it is difficult to actually see them as rituals at all. Imagine that you are an alien visiting Earth for the first time. Either write, tape or make an oral report on these situations which you take to be rituals:

- A teenage disco
- A coastal resort on Bank Holiday
- The M25 at rush hour.

Describe what actually happens in them and try to assess the purpose of the ritual.

STUDY EXTRACT ONE
Zigger Zagger

Written especially for the National Youth Theatre in 1967 by Peter Terson, *Zigger Zagger* made a huge impact through both its content and form.

The play tells the story of a teenage boy called Harry who has a passionate love of the local football team. He is drawn into a core of supporters led by a character called Zigger Zagger. Their love, it seems, isn't so much for the actual game of football as for the 'kick' they get out of its rituals: the singing and taunting, the clapping and stamping, the cheering and jeering.

When it was first produced, the insight it gave into the obsessional behaviour of young football fans was stunningly new. In performance, a cast of almost ninety was used to create a vibrant and sometimes threatening image on the stage. The play gives an opportunity to use **rhythmic** and **ritualised** sounds and movements in a modern and familiar context.

In this scene, Harry has become carried away by the crowd feeling and thrown a bottle at a policeman. He is led away to a room under the stands. As Harry and the policeman talk, the sounds of the crowd can still be heard in the background.

CHARACTERS
HARRY A teenage football supporter who likes to think of himself as 'one of the boys'
POLICEMAN Experienced in working at football matches and particularly familiar with dealing with boys like Harry

Scene Nine

Under the stand.
[HARRY *and* FIRST POLICEMAN.]
POLICEMAN: You sit there.
HARRY: Torture chamber this is, then?
POLICEMAN: Yeah.
HARRY: I'll miss the match here.
POLICEMAN: So will I.
HARRY: We under the stands, are we?
POLICEMAN: Yeah, hear that murmur? That's the simultaneous breathing of fifty thousand idiots.
HARRY: Suppose I'm done now, am I? Shopped?
POLICEMAN: Yeah. You've had it now. That was a near shot.
HARRY: I suppose, you fellers, when somebody throws a bottle at you, you lean on them hard?
POLICEMAN: Yeah. The copper's press. They're over the other side now. He's dribbling down the wing. It's a corner.
HARRY: After the match, I'll be taken away in a black maria, eh?
POLICEMAN: Oh, yeah. Armed escort. That was a lovely corner, it's a scramble, but no, it's over the bar. Listen for the goal kick. Must have been a nice one.
HARRY: I'll get the third degree, will I, when it's all over? The dripping tap and all that?
POLICEMAN: Yeah. You'll get all that. We're on the attack, yes, they're going upfield. That was a bad decision.
HARRY: You'll beat me up and knock me around, won't you? You fellers don't like it when one of you gets the knock.
POLICEMAN: We don't like that.

HARRY: You better not show any marks.
POLICEMAN: You what?
HARRY: When you beat me up. Marks. Or the magistrate will see them.
POLICEMAN: We have special methods, see. We'll beat you about the legs with foam rubber truncheons. Oooh, that was a save.
HARRY: Do they hurt?
POLICEMAN: What?
HARRY: Foam rubber truncheons.
POLICEMAN: Oh yeah, they're specially made for the job in Hong Kong. They're stiffened with bamboo.
HARRY: How many of you will there be?
POLICEMAN: Now, here they go. They're on the right wing, listen to the stand above us, he's getting there, near the penalty box, he's going to shoot. No. He can't. He's manoeuvring for position now, he can't find a way through, he slips it back to his winger again, he lobs a high one over and it's a shot, it's a shot, it's a goal! We've done it.
HARRY: How many of you will there be?
POLICEMAN: Many what?
HARRY: At the beating up?
POLICEMAN: Oh, half a dozen of us biggest fellers. They usually put the police boxing team on that job.
HARRY: Will there be handcuffs?
POLICEMAN: Yeah. Big ones for you. Special hard case.
HARRY: And an appearance.
POLICEMAN: Appearance?
HARRY: Before the magistrates.
POLICEMAN: Oh, yeah. There'll be all that.
HARRY: I wish I'd never done it.
POLICEMAN: You what?
HARRY: I wish I'd never done it. I'll be banned.
POLICEMAN: Yeah, you'll be banned all right.
HARRY: Banned for life from the City End.
POLICEMAN: Yeah.
HARRY: I'll be an outcast.
POLICEMAN: Yeah. Are you crying?
HARRY: No. I just got wet eyes. They water easily in the wind.
POLICEMAN: H'm.

Understanding the text

1 Pick out three lines which suggest that the policeman is actually more interested in following the game than talking to Harry.

2 Do you think the policeman is being serious in everything he says to Harry or just 'winding him up'? Choose three examples to illustrate your answer.

3 The policeman makes a number of comments about what is happening in the match. How can he possibly know?

4 What sort of character is Harry? Has he been in trouble before? Pick out three of his lines and explain why you think they say a lot about him.

Producing the scene

5 This play requires a large cast to act as a crowd of supporters. Getting them on and off stage would present a big problem. One solution would be to leave them on stage the whole time. However, if you did this, how would you stage this scene which happens under the terraces? Design a set for *Zigger Zagger* which would allow a number of different scenes to take place whilst keeping the crowd on stage.

6 Look carefully at the policeman's lines in which he seems to be commentating on the match. What particular sounds could the crowd make in the background which suggest certain things happening? For example, the line 'Oooh, that was a save' could come immediately after hearing the crowd gasp then clap in appreciation. Make a note of all the places where such a sound could be used. Simply listening to the crowd sounds on a televised football match will give you some ideas about how each one might differ.

7 Working as a whole class, try to produce the crowd sounds which would be in the background between the lines 'Yeah, hear that murmur?' and 'Oooh, that was a save'.

Two people should read out the parts of Harry and the policeman. Remember that the crowd sound must come before the policeman says his line. Remember also that the sound of the crowd must appear to come from some distance.

8 Rehearse the section between lines 7 and 35 again. This time try to add some movement in the crowd which, like the sound, suggests

a that the crowd operates as one body
b that they are in the background of the Harry/policeman scene and therefore somehow distant.

Further development

9 In small groups, devise a sequence of movements and sounds which suggest threat. The piece should not actually show violence, but capture the idea that violence is just below the surface and will happen at any moment. (You may have seen the film musical *West Side Story* in which an impending gang fight is suggested by the actors slowly walking towards each other clicking their fingers rhythmically.)

10 Invent, either in groups or as a whole class, a ritual which involves the group working together in rhythmical movement and sound. Decide

- what the aim of the ritual is
- what the mood of the ritual is
- where the tension in the ritual is (if any)
- who, or what, is the focus of the ritual.

11 In small groups, choose another place which could be easily identified by the type of sounds generated there, such as:

A busy office   A fairground
          A sailing ship in stormy seas
A haunted house   A lonely hill farm

Give your idea to another group who must then rehearse some appropriate sounds to create a 'sound signature' for the place.

Watch the work and reflect on how the presentations have managed to capture the atmosphere of the places given.

D Symbols and Myths

Symbols

The work so far in this chapter has shown how sound and movement can be used to represent particular places, or reflect certain moods and emotions. How can sound and movement be used to express **ideas**? Ideas don't have any solid, instantly recognisable form.

The following exercises look at symbols – that is, images which seem to stand for something else. (Look back to Project Five if you are unclear what is meant by the term 'symbol').

 1 As a whole class, stand in a circle. One volunteer enters the circle and takes up some sort of pose. They should not plan it or even have any idea themselves of what it might be. The rest of the class look at the image and suggest a title for this 'statue'. A second person enters and joins the first somehow. They must be physically connected as if carved from the same lump of stone. A new title is found and a third person enters, and so on.

When everyone has joined the statue and a final appropriate title has been found, discuss what it was about various images that suggested the changing titles.

2 Look at the words below. In pairs or small groups try to make a simple drawing or diagram which captures the idea of each word. (You may have played a game called 'Pictionary' which gives useful practice in thinking in pictures rather than words).

CREATION	CONFLICT	SPACE
WINTER	PEACE	DEATH
TIME	NIGHT	VIOLENCE
KNOWLEDGE	EVIL	LOVE

Using one of your 'pictographs' as a guide, try to create a tableau with your own bodies which will capture the idea of the word. Add just one sound to the tableau which you think will help create an appropriate atmosphere for the image. Share your work with the rest of the group and discuss how the most successful pieces worked.

3 Working on your own, divide a piece of paper into two columns. Copy out the list in Task 2 into the first column. In the second column suggest an object which could be used to represent or **symbolise** that idea. For example:

Idea	Object or symbol
Winter	A snowflake
Violence	A gun

Symbols are ways of reminding an audience of other things. They can only do this if the audience shares some knowledge or attitude about the thing being **symbolised**. Using a snowflake to symbolise winter may not make much sense to an Australian Aborigine. Similarly, some people might see a gun as symbolising peace whereas others see it as a symbol of violence or oppression – it depends on the situation and the experience of the person seeing it.

Symbols are a language. Like written and spoken languages, they have to be decoded in order to be understood. But unlike a language of words which can only be written or spoken, symbols can be communicated in other ways, through movement, sounds, shapes, colours and objects. The ideas can be made solid.

A way of finding an appropriate symbol for an idea is to consider the different qualities we give to actual solid objects.

Ask yourselves the following questions about winter.

- Is it sharp or soft?
- Is it tight or loose?

- What colour is it?
- Does it move slowly, quickly or both?
- Is it large or small?
- Is it heavy or light?
- Is it pleasing or ugly?
- Is it comforting or frightening?

There are no 'right' answers to the above. Your experience of winter is probably different from everyone else's – it will remind you of different things. Nevertheless, there may be certain things about your vision of winter which could remind people with similar general experiences of winter too. It's the process of recognising, capturing and expressing these slight differences which makes drama so interesting – the fact that we don't see the same things in exactly the same way but can understand how others see them.

One group of four working on the title 'winter' came up with the following simple yet powerful image.

Two of the group stood behind two others who were crouched. The standing pair set up a gentle swaying rhythm with their bodies and continually fluttered their fingers to capture the idea of falling snow. Below, the two crouched figures very slowly began to spread and grow both across the floor and up from it. Their rhythm was less predictable and one was given the impression that the gently falling snow was in fact feeding some kind of unstoppable monster.

The image seemed to capture both the charm and softness of snow as well as its potential power and danger.

Reflection

4 In what ways does this symbolisation of winter rely on the audience sharing some knowledge with the actors?

5 Look back at the ideas in Task 2 again. In small groups, choose a different one, or add one of your own, and ask a series of questions about it to try to make it 'solid'. Use your answers to develop a short sequence of movements and sounds which will symbolise the idea you have selected.

Myths

People are inquisitive. They like to find out why things happen. Some of our experiences though are very hard to understand.

Events such as winter seem clear in one sense: we feel the cold, the trees are bare, snow falls and so on. In another sense, they tickle our curiosity; why does this happen every year? Different cultures through history have found their own way of answering such a question. Compared with our understanding which is based on scientific evidence, some of the explanations used by other cultures seem to us to be no more than quaint stories. They are often referred to as myths. It is quite easy to imagine a tribe of Amazonian Indians finding our equations about the origins of the universe pretty nonsensical. Perhaps to them, our equations are a hard way of looking at an easily accepted fact of life.

The myth below is an Ancient Greek one.

Demeter was Goddess of the Earth. With her daughter, the beautiful Persephone, she kept the world green and fruitful. People and beasts smiled and played in the sunshine.

But Hades, the God of the Underworld, fell in love with Persephone. As all things that grew on earth started their life in his domain, why shouldn't the beautiful Persephone be his wife and bring joy to his dark world?

One day, while Persephone was picking flowers in a meadow, Hades came and took her.

When Demeter found her gone she wept and forbade the trees and plants to grow and bear fruit until Persephone was found.

In time, Zeus – the God of all the Gods who lived high on Mount Olympus – commanded his brother Hades to restore Persephone to the dying Earth. Hades agreed but on the condition that the girl had tasted no food during her stay.

Persephone was overjoyed to hear that she was

to be released, forgetting that she had been tricked into eating seven seeds of a pomegranate – the food of the dead. Persephone must stay in the Underworld!

Zeus persuaded the jubilant Hades to accept a compromise. For half of the year Persephone would live on Earth. All life there would flourish in that time. For the second half of the year, Persephone must go to the Underworld. On Earth, all would wither and die.

6 What does this myth seek to explain? List the different characters who appear in the story. What does each one appear to symbolise?

7 Working in groups of four, discuss how you could present each character to make it clear what they symbolise. Design a costume for each one and suggest how they might be made up. Give each character an object which seems to match their 'personality'.

8 How might each character stand and move in a way that reflects their 'personality'?

9 Pick out the different places referred to in the story and note down some ideas on what each one might look like. Experiment with ways of showing these places by using movement and sound. How could you contrast Earth with Persephone there, to Earth when she is in the Underworld?

10 Try to combine all your ideas from Tasks 6–9 to find a way of presenting the Persephone myth through movement and sound. You may, if you wish, add either dialogue or narration but try to keep this to a minimum. The Special Assignment on p 146 describes how this work could be developed further by using masks.

11 Do you know any other myths? As a whole group note down all the myths which come to mind and discuss what they are trying to explain. How much do we still use the symbols attached to these myths? For example, Eros is a character from Greek mythology who fired arrows into people's hearts to make them fall in love (you may know him as Cupid).

Discuss how the characters of myths are represented. In Norse mythology, for example, Thor is the God of thunder. Look at the picture of him below.

In what way is Thor an appropriate representation of thunder? Why do you suppose he is always seen with a hammer – what is it about thunder that it might represent?

Masks and Movement

A way of representing ideas as ancient as myths themselves is to use masks. Like certain pieces of costume or objects they have the power to instantly signify that the person wearing or holding it has become something or someone else.

• A man wearing a crown becomes a king.
• A man holding a bow and arrow is a hunter.
• A man wearing the mask of a horse is a horse.

The picture below comes from a modern play called *Equus* by Peter Shaffer.

1 In what way is this 'horse' different from the sort of horse you might see in a pantomime? Do you think it is more effective in capturing the essence of a horse? Try to explain your answer.

2 What sort of movement and sound could the actor wearing this mask use to further *suggest* a horse while not actually trying to convince the audience that he is one?

The work which follows shows how masks can be used to suggest characters and ideas and help an audience see things in a new way.

A word of warning is needed here. Wearing masks is unfamiliar – it's not something we do every day, after all! Because using masks is a new experience it will make you feel differently. As you work through this unit try to make notes on how you are feeling so that you can compare your experience with those of others in the class.

3 Perhaps the simplest introduction of all to masks is by using a LARGE plain paper bag (the stiffer oblong grocery bags are ideal). DO NOT use plastic bags or ones that are at all tight – suffocated students are bad for business! Each member of the class should have a bag – if they are all exactly the same to start with then so much the better.

Cut two small eye holes in the bag and, wearing this simplest of masks, move around the room not talking to anyone or touching them. Just get the feeling that the mask is a barrier between you and everything outside of you.

Keep this going in silence for several minutes. Build on the sense that you are a stranger in a strange land.

Put on one of the pieces of music selected earlier which suggested a ritual. Allow yourself to develop a movement which seems to combine the feelings induced by the music and by the mask.

4 Without discussing this session, find a space in the room on your own and lay out your mask in front of you. How can you make the mask reflect what you felt during this ritual? Cut out the eyes, mouth and nose and devise a pattern over the mask. Use different colours, patterns and shapes to try to represent how you felt.

5 Having spent some time making your mask more personal to you, consider what sort of movements it seems to suggest. Put it on again and once more start to move around the room in this way. Don't say anything but each time you come close to another mask stop, look at it and make a movement in reaction to it. Some other masks will make you feel more powerful, some less. Some may make you feel sympathy, others disdain. Keep this going for at least five minutes. A number of mirrors placed around the room can produce interesting reactions through the masks.

6 Get into groups of three or four. Place your masks in a line in front of you and discuss what the relationship between them might be. Do these masks like each other? How do they react to each other? After discussing this briefly adopt one of the masks other than your own and using movement only improvise a very brief scene in which the masks are brought together, react to each other and part.

Making and using masks

You may already know several ways to make masks. A common one is to gradually build up layers of papier-maché onto an inflated balloon. Each thin layer must be left to dry properly before the next is added. When you think the coating is thick enough to serve as the base for a mask, simply burst the balloon. Other features can then be added by using more papier-maché or other objects which can be attached and moulded on. A more sophisticated, yet quite easy way of making masks, is to acquire the head of a tailor's/dressmaker's dummy. A material called 'Mod-Rock' can be bought quite cheaply from art shops. This is a length of thin crêpe bandage impregnated with plaster. Simply dip the bandage into a bowl of water and mould it onto the dummy's face. Dry the bandage with a hairdryer for speed. Once it is dry peel it off the face and use it as the basis for adding other features.

The picture below shows a number of simple masks which could be made in this way.

Masks for myths

7 In small groups, remind yourself of the Persephone myth on page 142 and each pick one of the characters to work on. (You may, if you prefer, choose a character from any other myth you know.)

On your own, take a sheet of A4 paper and draw a simple face shape on it. Now draw a number of simple human features on the face which you think are appropriate for the mythical character you have chosen. Label this side FACE.

Turn the paper over and draw another face shape (you should be able to trace through from the first side). Inside this face, draw a series of lines and shapes in different colours. These should show the inner character of what you have chosen, not the outward appearance. Should Hades, for example, be shown in bright or dull colours, straight or curled lines, small or bold shapes? Label this side CHARACTER.

8 Make a simple mask in one of the ways described above and give it the features you designed for the FACE.

9 Look again at the design you made for CHARACTER. Use the shapes and patterns to give you an idea of how you might express this character in movement. Remember, once you put a mask on, your own face can no longer be used to express feelings and thoughts – only your body can show this. Spend some time on your own developing movements which fit the mask. Working in front of a mirror is enormously helpful for this.

10 Use these masks to help re-enact the myth you have chosen.

SPECIAL ASSIGNMENT

The task in this Special Assignment is to find a way of using movement and sound (and perhaps masks) to explore an issue and express what you feel about it in a way which will make an audience think about it from a new angle.

By way of an introduction to this task, look at the picture above.

In what ways is the horse in this picture different to those in other paintings you have seen of horses? (Look back to p 117 in Project Five.) Is it in any way similar to the horse mask shown on p 144?

What does the style of the painting suggest about this particular horse?

What effect does it have on you?

The picture is a large painting by Picasso called *Guernica*.

Guernica is a town in Spain. In 1937 during the Spanish Civil War, the Fascists launched an unexpected air attack on the town. It was the first time such a large-scale bombing raid had taken place on a civilian target. The incident was seen as outrageous. The famous artist Picasso wanted to show the world the horror of the incident, so he painted *Guernica*.

Look again at the picture. To what extent do you think it (especially the horse) captures Picasso's feelings about the incident?

Tasks

1 Work as a whole group using movement and sound to try to capture the incident at Guernica. The following sequence of events might be a useful guide.

> *Morning in Guernica. A quite ordinary day.*
> *The market place slowly comes alive.*
> *An unusual noise is heard in the distance.*
> *It gets closer and closer*
> *becomes deafening*
> *bombs start to fall*
> *chaos*
> *fear*
> *pain . . .*

Add other words to this list which could suggest movement and sound. Develop your ideas into a sequence of images. Rather than simply miming the incident, try to show the feelings the incident produced. This may mean using sounds and movements which are not **naturalistic** but grotesque and strange (like Picasso's horse, for example).

2 In some ways Picasso's painting *Guernica* has become a symbol. The one incident, as shown in the painting, seems to sum up, or symbolise, all the horrors and atrocities of oppression and war.

Working in small groups, consider any other incidents which seem to you to somehow symbolise some aspect of human life. There may be a current news item which does this or you may be able to think of some minor incident in your own life which seems typical of some bigger issue.

How can you show what this incident was and, more importantly, what it seems to mean, by using movement and sound?

STUDY EXTRACT TWO
Savages

An issue that keeps cropping up in the news headlines is the destruction of the world's forests. Every month an area the size of Wales is being stripped of its trees. Even though scientists around the globe have warned that such destruction could bring about catastrophic changes in the climate, the forest clearance goes on.

Of course, it is not only the trees themselves that are being destroyed but also the lives of the people and creatures who have lived there for thousands of years. The destruction of the forests is perhaps symbolic of the way in which 'civilisation' ignores history and nature, living only for today without regard for what may happen tomorrow.

This particular issue certainly isn't a new one. A newspaper article 30 years ago inspired Christopher Hampton to write the play *Savages*. This is how he introduces the published version:

> On 23rd February 1969, the *Sunday Times* Colour Magazine published an article by Norman Lewis called 'Genocide', which dealt with the destruction of the Brazilian Indians. Among the many appalling examples of systematic extermination discussed by Mr. Lewis and ranging from the sixteenth century to the present day was one which involved the slaughter of large numbers of the Cintas Largas tribe. 'It was seen as essential,' Mr Lewis writes, 'to produce the maximum number of casualties in one single devastating attack, at a time when as many Indians as possible would be present in the village, and an expert was found to advise that this could best be done at the annual feast of the "Quarup". This great ceremony lasts for a day and a night, and under one name or another it is conducted by almost all the Indian tribes whose culture has not been destroyed. The "Quarup" is a theatrical representation of the legends of creation interwoven with those of the tribe itself, both a mystery play and a family reunion attended not only by the living but also by the ancestral spirits. These appear as dancers in masquerade, to be consulted on immediate problems, to comfort the mourners, to testify that not even death can disrupt the unity of the tribe.
>
> A Cessna light 'plane used for ordinary commercial services was hired for the attack, and its normal pilot replaced by an adventurer. It was loaded with sticks of dynamite – "bananas" they are called in Brazil – and took off from a jungle airstrip near Aripuana. The Cessna arrived over the village at about midday. The Indians had been preparing themselves all night by prayer and singing, and now they were all gathered in the open space in the village's centre. On the first run packets of sugar were dropped to calm the fears of those who had scattered and run for shelter at the sight of the 'plane. They had opened the packets and were tasting the sugar ten minutes later when it returned to carry out the attack. No-one has ever been able to find out how many Indians were killed, because the bodies were buried in the bank of the river and the village deserted.'
>
> It is this incident which forms, and which I knew as I read the article would form, the climax of this play.

The play that arose out of this harrowing article tells the story of a British diplomat called West. Posted in Brazil, West has an interest in the myths and legends of the Amazonian Indians. A number of these are retold throughout the play, which also documents what is happening to such tribes as Western civilisation forces itself into the heart of the forest.

In the play, West is kidnapped by a revolutionary movement which is trying to draw the world's attention to the terrible poverty suffered by most Brazilians. The spokesman for the kidnappers is an educated Brazilian called Carlos. As the play develops the two men build a respect and perhaps even some liking for each other.

However, by the end of the play it becomes increasingly obvious that the demands set by the kidnappers are not going to be met. Neither West nor his captors have been able to use their logic or their language to change anything. Their politics and ideas are no more able to understand or change the world than the Indians' myths. West and Carlos are, in a way, stuck inside masks. Whereas, according to the legend, the Indians use real masks to protect themselves, West and Carlos wear invisible masks, made out of their culture and politics. Unable to remove them they destroy themselves.

Like *Zigger Zagger* (Study Extract One), *Savages* requires a number of different scenes to be played on the same set. The stage directions at the start of the play describe how three posts are placed towards the back of the stage. They are used to represent various Indian symbols throughout the play.

CHARACTERS

WEST An English diplomat. He remains calm, confident and even quite good-humoured despite being kept hostage.

CARLOS A key member of an organisation trying to draw attention to the plight of the Brazilians. Well-educated, intelligent and sensitive but not as confident in his manner as West.

TWO MEN White mercenaries.

INDIANS

NINETEEN

The guerrilla hideout. **WEST**, *handcuffed, looks furious.* **CARLOS** *paces uneasily up and down.*

CARLOS: Well, look, I'm very sorry, that's all I can say.

WEST: It's not enough, I want to know why.

CARLOS: I told you, there's been a hitch. A minor hitch, which means we have to delay everything for twenty-four hours.

WEST: Listen, I've been very patient cooped up here all these weeks listening to your dreary propaganda, but there's just so much I can take.

CARLOS: I'm very sorry, it was my fault, I should never have said anything to you about it yesterday. I thought you'd be pleased to know.

WEST: I was, of course I was, I thought it was true.

CARLOS: It's only another twenty-four hours. I promise you you'll be out tomorrow.

WEST: You'd better give me that in writing.

CARLOS: We all have to suffer for the cause, comrade.

WEST: I don't see why I should suffer for your wretched cause.

CARLOS: Because it's essential.

WEST: That's a matter of opinion.

CARLOS: It's a matter of fact.

WEST: Look, as far as I'm concerned, there are causes in Brazil which are far more essential. Like, for instance the extermination of the people who used to own this country. That seems to me far more important than replacing one authoritarian government with another.

CARLOS: Is that what you think we're trying to do?

WEST: Well, I hardly imagined you had parliamentary democracy in mind.

CARLOS: Whatever makes you think democracy would be any use to us? Mm? Democracy is a luxury for countries rich enough so it doesn't matter who they elect. You don't think we're risking our lives so we can put in some bumbling idiot who'll waste all his energy trying not to upset anyone? We're fighting this war on behalf of the people. What could be more democratic than that?

WEST: Letting the people choose.

CARLOS: Don't be absurd. How do you expect people to choose when all they're worried about is where the next crust of bread is coming from? There are children of eight on the streets of Rio offering themselves to anyone in a suit, you think they're going to turn into good Democrats? You make me laugh. All this crap about the Indians, it's just romantic bourgeois sentimentality. Listen, there are ninety million people in this country, and there aren't enough Indians left to fill up Maracana football stadium. So you say, look after the

Indians, after all, poor things, it used to be their country, didn't it, and they'll never cause much trouble, because there are hardly any of them left, and they're not interested anyway. Look after the Indians, you say, but for Christ's sake don't look after the ninety million, or you never know what they might start wanting. All your liberal hearts bleed at the thought of those poor naked savages fading away, but it never begins to dribble across your apology for a mind that half a million children under five starved to death in Brazil last year.

WEST: That is a complete perversion of my point of view.

(**CARLOS** *responds with sounds mimicking* **WEST**'s *pomposity*.)

(*Indignant.*) You people are all the same.

CARLOS (*enraged*): So are you people.

(*He storms out.* **WEST** *sits, frowning, staring blankly into space. A moment later,* **CARLOS** *returns with the chess-board.*)

Better we don't have any more discussion, don't you think? Better we just play chess. (*Pause. He begins setting up the board.*) You might even win this time.

WEST: I don't really feel like it just now.

(**CARLOS** *goes on calmly distributing the pieces.*)

CARLOS: I don't have anything particular against you. It's just I can't help trying.

WEST: What do you mean?

CARLOS: Che said, if a man is honest, you can make a revolutionary out of him. You seem honest enough.

(*He selects two pawns and holds his closed fists out towards* **WEST**. *Long pause. Finally* **WEST** *indicates one, and* **CARLOS** *opens his fist to show the white pawn.* **WEST** *takes it from him.*)

Off you go.

(**WEST** *makes an opening move.*)

WEST: I've a feeling I am going to win.

BLACKOUT

TWENTY

The **CHIEF** *and his* **WIFE** *sit, waiting.* **WEST** *appears.*

WEST: Origin of the masks.
In the middle of the night
After a bad day's hunting and hungry to bed
A man heard something moving around near his hut
And running out found a giant paca which he killed.

There was enough meat for everyone in the village
But two did not join in the feast
A woman who that night was giving birth
And her husband.

The next day when the men had set off hunting
A devil wearing a bark mask appeared in the woman's hut
He told her that the villagers had killed and eaten his son
And that he must be revenged.

She and her husband and child he said would be spared
And told her to gather the bark from a certain tree
That night the devils came and killed every villager
But the three who hid their faces behind the bark.

Now it is known that the wearing of the bark masks
Is certain protection against the devils.
For who seeing his own image, his own skin,
Could destroy his own kind?

(**WEST** *exits.*)
(*Music. Two* **INDIANS** *appear, playing ten-foot flutes and dancing. Behind them, with their right hands on the* **MEN**'s *shoulders, two* **GIRLS** *dance in time. They circle and weave around the posts and across the stage. The* **CHIEF** *rises and moves behind the posts. As he does so, the other* **INDIANS** *rise and join the dance. The* **CHIEF** *emerges from behind the posts wearing a mask, dancing his own dance. The ceremony is reaching*

a climax of excitement and exhilaration.)
(Cutting through this the sound of a light aircraft. The INDIANS falter, continue, falter again, and, as the sound of the aeroplane increases in intensity, gradually stop. The 'plane is now overhead.)
(It drops bombs.)
(Explosions, panic, chaos. The sound of the 'plane diminishes, then increases again as it turns and flies back over the village even lower.)
(More bombs.)
(Screams of pain and fear.)

BLACKOUT

TWENTY ONE

The guerrilla hideout. WEST, handcuffed, contemplating the chess-board. CARLOS watching him. A knock at the door. CARLOS gets up and leaves the room. Long pause, during which WEST gives out a little grunt of pleasure and makes a move. Then the door bursts open and CARLOS re-enters, white and tense. In his hand, though at first concealed from WEST, the pistol with silencer. WEST looks up, triumphant, indicates the chess-board.

WEST: Pick the bones out of that.
CARLOS: I. . .
WEST: I think I've. . . *(He sees the gun and breaks off suddenly.)* What's erm. . .?
CARLOS: I. . . *(He levels the pistol at WEST.)*
WEST: *(feebly)* Don't.
CARLOS: Sorry.

(He shoots WEST three times. WEST slumps grotesquely to the floor, still dangling from his handcuff. CARLOS looks at him for a second, desolate. Then, from outside, the wail of a police siren. CARLOS starts, then rushes out. A hail of machine-gun fire in the BLACKOUT.)
(Fanfares, reminiscent of the opening of a TV news bulletin. A white frontcloth drops in. On it are projected, one by one, overlapping, innumerable photographs of WEST, black and white, colour, family snaps, headlines in several languages, until the whole cloth is covered with images of WEST.)

TWENTY TWO

The frontcloth rises to reveal a bloody heap of Indian bodies. Silence. Then a groan of pain. Two MEN enter with sub-machine guns, one, as is clear from his goggles and flying-jacket, the pilot of the 'plane, the other his co-pilot. One of the INDIANS in the pile of bodies onstage groans, and begins painfully to rise to his feet. It is the CHIEF, still wearing his mask. One of the men shoots down the CHIEF and fires a burst into the heap of bodies, then they pass across the stage and off. A cry followed by another burst of machine-gun fire offstage. Silence. The MEN return, looking well pleased. The PILOT pauses, tucks the gun under his arm, produces a packet of cigarettes, offers one to his companion, takes one himself and lights them. Pause. Then he throws the box of matches to his companion who nods and leaves the stage. A moment later, he returns without his gun, but with two torches headed with rags soaked in kerosene. He lights one and hands it to the PILOT, then lights the other. They leave the stage in the direction of the village. Silence. An animal cry, another soft groan, the light drone of flies. The crackle of flames. Effect of flames as the LIGHTS DIM to BLACKOUT.

Note: 'Che' referred to at the end of Scene Nineteen is Che Guevara, a revolutionary leader who, with Fidel Castro, overthrew a corrupt and oppressive regime in Cuba in 1958. He went on to inspire popular revolutions in other South American countries before being murdered in 1968. He has become a popular symbol of revolution.

Understanding the text

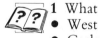

1 What impression do you get of
● West
● Carlos
● their relationship
from Scene Nineteen? In what ways are their characters similar?

2 Explain in your own words why Carlos doesn't think that 'democracy' is capable of providing a solution to the people's problems.

3 Look at the stage direction in which Carlos selects two pawns for the chess game. In what way does this action symbolise the situation West and Carlos are in?

4 The impact of these last few scenes depends a great deal on the way images are contrasted. Read through the scenes again, noting where the contrasts seem to be.

5 Why do you think this play was called *Savages?* Who do you think the title refers to?

6 In what ways could the characters of West, Carlos and the Indians be said to be symbolic?

Producing the scenes

7 Make two lists showing
a the feeling and atmosphere of the guerrilla hideout
b the feeling and atmosphere of the forest clearing before the attack.
Given that there is a need to move quite quickly from one to the other, suggest how this contrast could be achieved through stage setting and lighting.

8 How would you move from Scene Nineteen to Scene Twenty in a way that wouldn't confuse the audience? (West is, after all, still a captive of the guerrillas, yet he suddenly appears among the Indians.)

9 Go through the whole of the extract and note where sound effects will be needed. If you have the facility, make up a soundtrack.

10 As a whole group, work on ways of presenting the attack. Guard against being comically melodramatic as people pretend to die in a noisy writhing agony. Consider what the 'essence' of the attack is. You could then concentrate on the essence and perhaps find a particular stylised and uncomical way of showing this.

11 There seems to be an interesting and pointed contrast between the way in which the murder of one man – West – is broadcast across the world, yet the slaughter of the Indians happens 'behind' the screen and seems to have been ignored. It is marked only by the 'light drone of flies'. What do these contrasting effects seem to say about the attitude of the Western press? How else could you contrast the impact of West's death with the impact of the slaughter of the Indians? Work in groups of six to suggest a variety of solutions blending sound, movement and still image.

Reflection

12 Dramas based on documentary material can be very powerful and actually help change situations. TV writer Jimmy McGovern made such a film about the Hillsborough disaster which effectively re-opened the case made by families of the victims for compensation. Some people think that this kind of drama can be dangerous because audiences take as truth what may be in part fiction. The film *In the Name of the Father*, which was about men arrested for an IRA bombing, was controversial for this reason. Do you think playwrights and film makers have the right to add their own interpretation to the facts in order to make a good drama?

13 The audience of *Savages* are faced with lots of different images at the end of the play. A lot of different sound effects are used, as well as projected pictures and headlines and a powerful tableau. What might be the advantages of using these images rather than just telling the story in dialogue?

STUDY EXTRACT THREE
The Last Tree

Since Christopher Hampton wrote *Savages* in response to that *Sunday Times* article, a new dimension to the issue of deforestation has arisen and given a new phrase to our language – 'acid rain'.

Acid rain is caused by chemicals such as sulphur dioxide being pumped into the atmosphere. The chemicals dissolve into the water vapour in the atmosphere which then falls back to earth with increasingly devastating effects.

- In Pitlochry, Scotland, in 1974 rain fell which was more acidic than vinegar.

- The average raindrop in Europe is now up to twice as acidic as it was 30 years ago.

- In 1982, 7.7% of West Germany's forests showed signs of damage caused by acid rain. By 1984 almost 50% were showing signs of damage.

- In the early 1980s damaged trees were taking two or three years to die. By 1985 it was seen that trees were dying in as little as five weeks.

- 18,000 of Sweden's lakes have been affected. Many can no longer support fish.

- Wood damaged by acid rain is of little use. In West Germany, in 1984, it was estimated that the cost of such damage was DM 7–10 billion (£2–3 billion).

This new factor caught the attention of playwright Angie Farrow. She was already concerned about the deliberate destruction of the world's forests. This seemingly accidental destruction led her to speculate how long it would be before all the forests were totally destroyed, which would force us to change every aspect of our lives.

After researching both the causes and effects of acid rain, Angie tried to identify what caused her to react so sharply to her findings. The result was a play for children called *Green Deserts* in which the audience are given a stark picture of a future world where people have been forced to live inside huge domes to shield themselves from the poisonous atmosphere outside – an atmosphere poisoned by their own greed and short-sightedness.

Printed here is an adaptation of a section of the play in which one of the inhabitants of this frightening underworld escapes and sees, for the first time, what's left outside.

What is printed here is no more than a part of the image. The rest is dependent on how the performers add rhythmical sounds and movements to capture the nightmarish journey and the ultimate dicovery.

The Last Tree

by Angie Farrow
A piece for movement, voice and percussion

Three decades ago the Ministry of Health declared that it would be an offence henceforth for mortals to venture into the outside.

It's Tuesday – one of those days when you wake up and it's like you're in someone else's skin. I'm hardly listening to the tee 2 screen . . . to the roboid from communications who says, 'Rise and shine it's Tuesday!'. I can't even hear the shmaltzy music which pours through the speaker like sweet semolina. It's like I'm cut off. I keep thinking, 'I'll open the door, I'll open the door, I'll open the door and I'll just walk out.'

And then I do.

Picture a yellow corridor which never ends
Flanked with shiney doors
Each one conceals a neighbour I've never met.

11136   11137   11138

Picture a man in a skin suit
Stalking on unsteady legs,
His face a mask of intent.
That's me!
On and on he treads, each step, a lurch of guilt.

11260   11261   11262

Picture an endless row of tee 2 screens
Chorusing this fleeting form.

11490 11492 11493

Picture him now as he halts
Picture a heart which leaps in its own stillness
Picture an eye which skids to rest to
Picture a square pocket in the yellow wall.

11600

The panel is about half a metre square. I press the four support buttons which hold it firm and carefully remove it from the wall. And there, through the darkness I make out the frame of the lift schaft. Sachel told me, 'Just keep going upwards. Keep. Keep. Keep going upwards. Keep going. Keep going. Keep going upwards. Upwards. Keep. Keep. Keep going upwards.'

Imagine a smell that's warm
And a darkness that's thick like blood
And leads ever upwards.
Feel if you can the rusty crossbars of an ancient shaft
And a clutching animal figure in fitful climb.
That's me!

I'm thinking, 'Rise and shine it's Tuesday! Rise and shine it's Tuesday!' to kind of remind myself that it's all real. The rust is eating my hands and my body's feeling like it's someone else's. But I keep going. Keep. Keep. Keep going. I keep going.

Three decades ago. Three decades ago and one year precisely the Ministry of Health declared that it would be an offence hence an offence hence an offence hence an offence henceforth for mortals to venture into the outside. I wipe the sweat from my face. The rust tastes of flesh-wounds.

Outside air is bad for you
Outside air is bad
Outside air is
Outside air
Outside.

See if you can a needle of light
Which pricks the blackness
A heaving body which searches its source.
Listen as the lead bolt gives way
And releases the trap door.

Outside
Outside
Outside.

A kind of creamy light pours in. It could be water except you can breathe it. It could be wetness except it isn't. And I'm thinking, 'What if it kills me!'

You'll see now a huge, flat plane
A vastness that reduces you to a speck of dust.
You'll feel a wind that gushes and stings your cheek
And a sky too big for you to take.

And then a tiny figure will emerge
From a hole in the ground
That's me!
And you'll see how he squints
And how he staggers and stutters
Towards a shape in the distance
The only
The only
The only shape
The only shape
The only shape in the distance.

And when I get there it's like I knew it all along. This breathing thing stuck and sucking to the ground. It's stuck, but it's free as well, like a bird. I know it. I know the rustle it makes when the wind blows and the green curly hands that tremble on these massive arms.

And as I stand
As I stand
As I stand transfixed
It breathes to me its name
Tree
Tree
Tree
Tree
Tree
Tree
Tree
Tree
Tree
Tree

Understanding the text

1 Go through the text picking out all the places where rhyme and repetition are used. What sort of atmosphere do they seem to suggest? What movements would seem appropriate here?

2 Are there any other clues in the text about movement and facial expression? One

example is the line
  'Stalking on unsteady legs
  His face a mask of intent.'
Note down any others even if they aren't as obvious as this one.

3 Try to explain in your own words how the tree can possibly be
  'stuck . . . but free as well, like a bird'.
Think again of how a group of actors might represent this.

4 The line
  'It breathes to me its name'
again suggests that the tree has a kind of human quality. Can you suggest a movement and a sound which could be attached to this line?
The movement and sound need to make the tree seem partly human, but they should still be clearly reminiscent of a tree.

5 What might the tree symbolise? In other words, what meaning can we attach to the idea

a that it is the last tree
b that it is 'stuck to the ground yet free'
c that it breathes its name
d that it has 'green curly hands that tremble'?

Producing the scene

6 Although the text is written as one continuous piece, the action takes place in a number of different places. Working in groups or on your own, pick out those different places and briefly describe or sketch each one. The sound and movement you select later will need to reflect these images.

7 Although only one character seems to be speaking this whole speech, one way of enlivening a performance would be to use a number of different voices.

a Go through the text and pick out any lines that you think could use a special type of voice.

b Look out for any places where people could be saying some lines as a background noise to the main speech.

c Are there any lines which could be repeated as an echo by actors other than the main speaker?

d Are there any lines which the whole group could come together and say?

Working in small groups, go through the text allocating lines to either individuals, pairs, smaller groups or the whole group. Then practise reading the lines so that we get a 'collage' of voices building the various atmospheres.

8 Devise a rhythm for the numbers of the passing rooms. Experiment with ways of keeping this going: clapping, finger clicking, foot tapping, perhaps using a tambor or some other percussion instrument.

As you prepare the rhythm try to make it reflect the idea of stalking down a corridor which never ends.

Finally, try to put the rhythm with a walking action, either with all of you walking and making the rhythm or some walking while others keep the rhythm going in the background.

9 How, through movement and physical stance, can you capture the contrast between the cramped, dark vertical of the shaft and the endless empty horizontal plain outside?

10 What other background noises are suggested? Feel free to invent your own possibilities here. Experiment with using human voices to make the noises, rather than pre-recorded material. What, for example, does the 'schmaltzy music' sound like? What half-heard domestic sounds might be faintly escaping from the rows of shiny doors which conceal the neighbours? What echoes will drift up or down the shaft?

11 Consider the space you have available carefully. If you were to move this text to a performance, where would you want the audience in relation to the actors? No actual set or props are mentioned so you really do only have the space and yourselves to create the images.

Further development

12 Working in small groups, improvise or write a piece of text which shows another element of life in the futureworld of *The Last Tree*. As in the extract above, try to find ways of using rhythmic sounds and movements in addition to the spoken word in order to communicate the atmosphere of that world.

13 Find a poem or story which you think would lend itself to being dramatised in this very 'physical' way. Try to bring the piece to life by breaking it down and using different voices for different lines or by adding background rhythms or sounds and carefully selected stances and movements.

14 Look at the opening page of The Book of Genesis in the Bible in which the Creation of the world over seven days is described. How could you use movement and sound images to depict that? In small groups, use any of the techniques you have discovered in this chapter to try to present just one small part of the Christian Creation myth.

Written tasks

15 Look back to the painting on p 146. Note down all the words that come into your mind in response to that image. Make a large drawing of the horse's head and arrange your words inside it so that the words themselves seem to form the visual image.

You may have worked on 'Shape Poems' like this before. Consider how you could combine words and shape to capture an image from either *Savages* or *The Last Tree*.

16 There are some words which try to capture various sounds, for example:

BANG   CRASH   SPLASH
CRUNCH

This device is called **onomatopoeia**.

Imagine you are trying to write a new dictionary of such words. Invent both the words and the meanings. For example, what word would adequately describe the sound of a bowlful of custard hitting the floor?

17 Write a short scene for a radio play in which all the audience will hear is a sequence of sounds with only the occasional line of speech to indicate who is in the scene and what is happening. Suitable scenes might include 'THE NIGHT AT CASTLE DRACULA', 'ESCAPE FROM COLDITZ', 'REVENGE OF THE BBC SOUND EFFECTS WOMAN'. The dictionary devised in Task 16 will be useful in your writing of the stage directions.

18 Devise and write a myth which offers an explanation of some natural event. There must be a number of characters in the myth who, like Thor or Persephone, symbolise certain ideas. Give them appropriate names and say something about their characters.

19 Develop the story from Task 18 into an outline for a play which will use movement and sound in preference to speech (though you may use some speech). Write part of the story, with precise stage directions, so that a team of actors would understand exactly how you wished them to move and what noises you wished them to make.

Reflection

20 Do you know of any plays which rely heavily on movement and sound? Try to describe how the play used these techniques and assess how effective they were. You may know of some dances which successfully tell a story or capture a certain atmosphere. A good example is the Northern Ballet's production called *A Simple Man* which brings to life the paintings of L S Lowry.

21 What advantages and disadvantages do you think dramas that use the kind of techniques discussed in this chapter have over dramas which depend mostly on the spoken word?

Further Reading

Plays

Not surprisingly, texts which aim directly at using sounds and movements are rarely published; all you can print really are the words and, as you have seen, these are just a small part of the whole. However, the following texts offer some interesting opportunities:

Act Without Words and
Act Without Words 2 by Samuel Beckett (Faber).
Power in 'Power Plays' ed. David Self (Hutchinson). Tells the story of American anti-nuclear campaigner Karen Silkwood through a sequence of visual images.
Rainbow's Ending by Noel Greig (Cambridge University Press). An example of 'story theatre' which enables the performers to adopt a range of characters and encourages the invention of visual images in much the same way as *The Last Tree*. The story is a fable which reflects the state of the modern world. 812.34/cop
Indians by Arthur Kopit (Methuen). This moving play tells the story of 'the Wild West' through a powerful mixture of circus and documentary. It emphasises the Indians' point of view and uses many striking visual images. 822.914/sha
Equus by Peter Shaffer (Andre Deutsch). The story of a teenage boy who blinded a number of horses with a hoof pick. The horses themselves must be played by actors, giving an interesting opportunity for using carefully researched movement.
Rare Earth by Belgrade TIE Company (Methuen). This TIE programme is, in fact, two plays which focus on the issues of conservation and pollution. The first play tells the story of the white man's invasion of the American plains and the second (called *Drink the Mercury*) is about the devastating pollution of Minamata Bay in Japan. Both plays make extensive use of movement and theatre forms from the cultures they depict.

Fiction

The following novels may be of interest in that they all address political issues such as pollution, animal rights, nuclear war, homelessness.

Goggleyes Ann Fines (Hamish Hamilton)
Z for Zacharia Robert O'Brian (Victor Gollancz)
Brother in the Land Robert Swindell (Puffin)
Future Track 5 Robert Westall (Puffin)
Talking in Whispers James Watson (Victor Gollancz)
A Serpent's Tooth Robert Swindell (Hamish Hamilton)
The Wave Morton Rhue (Puffin)
Who has Poisoned the Sea? Audrey Coppard (Heinemann)
Nancebuke John Branfield (Victor Gollancz)
The Guilty Party Joan Lingard (Hamish Hamilton)
Stone Cold Robert Swindells (Hamish Hamilton)

Poetry

Whale Nation Heathcote Williams (Jonathan Cape)
Elephant World Heathcote Williams (Jonathan Cape)

Non-fiction

Impro by Keith Johnstone (Methuen). This has a very useful and interesting chapter on the use of masks.
The Actor and His Body by Litz Pisk (Harrap). Full of movement exercises and ideas for their development.
Voice and the Actor by Cecily Berry (Harrap). A comprehensive and imaginative range of exercises for developing the voice as a tool in drama.
Worlds of English and Drama by Bird and Norris (Oxford University Press). This is an interesting collection of stories from around the world with ideas for creative work based on them.

Words in rhythm

> This project develops the work on RHYTHM and looks at its effect when used with words.
>
> The activities help develop a sense of FOCUS and involve COMPOSING 'songs' to serve different functions in plays.

A Musical Play or Play With Music?

In the last 20 years musical plays – often just called 'musicals' – have enjoyed an enormous revival of interest. This may largely be due to the astonishing success of Andrew Lloyd Webber and his former partner Tim Rice. In the early 1970s this partnership shot to success with a then controversial piece of theatre called *Jesus Christ Superstar*. The show was described as a 'rock opera' and was soon followed by *Evita, Cats, Starlight Express, Chess, The Phantom of the Opera* and *Aspects of Love*. Numerous other new musicals have appeared along with revivals of older shows such as *42nd Street, Guys and Dolls* and *Me and my Girl* to name but a few.

'Musicals' such as these have their origins in the 'operettas' of the last century (you may have heard of Gilbert and Sullivan who became particularly well-known as writers of operetta). They are characterised by the use of song and dance as a central focus of the piece and are often remembered for their best-known songs (often referred to as 'show stoppers') rather than for the stories they tell and the themes they deal with.

Tasks

1 Find the Entertainments Guide in any national daily newspaper and count the number of shows in the West End of London which you know to be, or think might be, 'musicals'. What proportion of all the shows advertised do musicals account for?

2 Discuss with your group any other plays or films you may have seen where music was used in the background to effectively create an atmosphere.

3 Discuss what you think the differences are between plays (or films) that have music in them, and 'musicals'.

4 Do you know of any plays which contain songs but can't really be described as 'musicals'? If you know any, try to say why they are not 'musicals'.

B Chorus

In everyday language, people tend to think of the chorus as the part of the song in which everyone joins in. In 'musicals' there are usually a number of actors and singers who are only there to join in the chorus – they too are called 'The Chorus'.

The origin of the word goes back to the beginnings of organised theatre in Ancient Greece. The organisation and presentation of the plays was quite ritualised. The Chorus was actually a character in the plays who talked directly to the audience, telling them what they were about to see or pointing out the significance of what they had just seen. The lines were written in verse and their presentation could be likened to a chant.

In time, the lines came to be spoken by a group of actors who used varying tones of voice to make the meaning of the lines clearer and more interesting to listen to.

The following short extract is spoken by the Chorus at the end of the play *Oedipus Rex*. It shows very clearly what the purpose of the Chorus was. Even without knowing the story of *Oedipus Rex* it is possible to get a fairly clear idea of the main theme of the play just from these last few lines. Read it through carefully then answer the questions.

> Sons and daughters of Thebes, behold; this was Oedipus,
> Greatest of men; he held the key to the deepest mysteries;
> Was envied by all his fellow-men for his great prosperity;
> Behold, what a full tide of misfortune swept over his head.
> Then learn that mortal man must always look to his ending.
> And none can be called happy until that day when he carries
> His happiness down to the grave in peace.
>
> (from *The Theban Plays* by Sophocles, translated by E F Watling, Penguin)

Understanding the text

1 Where is the play set?

2 What sort of man do you suppose Oedipus was?

3 What seems to have happened to him?

4 What is the moral of the story?

5 Would you say this play was a comedy or a tragedy?

6 In groups of six, experiment with ways of presenting this Chorus. Remember, the aim is to get across that Oedipus's story is a warning to us all. To achieve this, try changing the tone and pace of your voices.

- Should they be deep and slow?
- Light and fast?
- Should the tone and pace change for different parts?

A chorus of Trojan Women from the Royal Shakespeare Company's The Greeks *(1980)*

This type of work is sometimes called **choral speech** – not simply because a group of people are speaking it together, but because, like the original Chorus, they are using the rhythm of the lines to make the meaning clearer.

Reflection

 7 Do you know of any other plays that use a Chorus? Look at, for example, *Henry the Fifth* by Shakespeare and *Murder in the Cathedral* by T. S. Eliot.

The role of the Chorus is not dissimilar to the Narrator figure found in some plays (the typical children's Nativity play, for example). Another recent variation is the Chairman or Master of Ceremonies. Look back to the extract from *The Sally Ann Hallelujah Show* on p 105 and compare the lines of the Chairman there with the ones from *Oedipus Rex* above.

8 The naturally musical quality of a group of voices working together has been exploited not only in the theatre, but by a number of poets. Poems which provide particularly interesting opportunities for **choral speech** include:

Night Mail	W. H. Auden
Limbo	Edward Braithwaite
The Highwayman	Alfred Noyes
Tarantella	Hilaire Belloc
Hornpipes	Edith Sitwell

Poems by Benjamin Zephaniah

(The collection of pieces by Edith Sitwell, set to music by William Walton and known as *Façade*, is an unusual and entertaining experiment in the use of voice.)

The work of modern Afro-Caribbean poets such as Lynton Kwesi-Johnson is certainly worth experimenting with in this way.

Find and experiment with some of these pieces and discuss the differences between reading them privately and reading them aloud.

 ## Songs to Focus Attention

Bertolt Brecht was a German writer and director who has had an enormous influence on modern theatre. Working in Germany in the 1920s and 30s he was bitterly opposed to Hitler and the Nazis and eventually had to escape from them. Brecht saw the theatre as a means of expressing ideas about current issues (which made him an enemy of the Nazis). He realised that audiences often took the stories told in the theatre at face value and missed the point they were really trying to make. The trouble was partly due to the way in which Western audiences had come to expect plays to be **naturalistic**. In such plays the characters tend to talk to one another as if they are living through a piece of real life and the audience isn't actually there at all.

To overcome this, he used in his plays a number of techniques which would *remind* the audience that they were watching a play rather than some snippet of real life. Projecting slides, using the minimum of scenery and harsh lighting, not hiding or disguising technical equipment, were just some ways of doing this. Another way was to have the actors talking directly to the audience or even speaking aloud stage directions. This technique is often referred to as the 'Verfremdungseffekt' or 'Alienation Effect' as it was intended to stop the audience feeling so closely involved with the fiction that they missed what the play might mean for them in their own lives.

A key device in Brecht's work was song. You would only rarely tap your feet to his songs, or jive in the aisles with them. In fact, they may not even have to be sung. They can be presented in a way similar to the Chorus of Greek plays. The aim is always to focus the audience's attention on a particular incident or theme. The presentation must challenge the audience rather than excite or lull them.

Read the example below from the short play *The Exception and the Rule*.

> We are about to tell you
> The story of a journey. An exploiter
> And two of the exploited are the travellers.
> Examine carefully the behaviour of these people:
> Find it surprising though not unusual
> Inexplicable though normal
> Incomprehensible though it is the rule.
> Consider even the most insignificant, seemingly simple
> Action with distrust. Ask yourselves whether it is necessary
> Especially if it is usual.
> We ask you expressly to discover
> That what happens all the time is not natural.
> For to say that something is natural
> In such times of bloody confusion
> Of ordained disorder, of systematic arbitrariness
> Of inhuman humanity is to
> Regard it as unchangeable
>
> (from *The Exception and the Rule*, by Bertolt Brecht, translated by John Willett, Methuen)

Understanding the text

1 This is how the play opens.
a Who is the song addressed to?
b What is it telling them to do?

2 Discuss what the following lines mean.
a Inexplicable though normal
b Incomprehensible though it is the rule.

3 The last five lines seem particularly difficult. In simpler terms I think that what it is saying is that if we accept chaos, violence and unfairness as 'normal human behaviour' or even law, then we are assuming that we can't change it. Why do you think Brecht is saying this at the very start of this play?

Producing the scene

4 In groups of at least four, experiment with the following ways of reading the lines out in order to help them make most sense.

- Each actor says one line in turn.
- Each actor speaks one sentence in turn.
- Divide the lines into units of meaning, for example:

  'An exploiter / And two of the exploited / are the travellers'.

- Divide the lines in order to add emphasis to some words over others, for example:

  'Find it surprising though / not unusual / Inexplicable / though normal'

You may decide to speak some of the lines together, as a Chorus.

5 Having decided which way of speaking seems most effective, experiment with ways of adding shape and movement to the piece. Compare
- standing in a straight line
- having some standing, some sitting, some kneeling
- facing different directions as if talking to different groups of people
- moving on your line then freezing.

6 Finally, try to add a rhythm to the way you present the lines. It may not be a constant, repetitious beat, but it should aim to make the audience listen, and to help them understand what it means.

Ballads

The extract from *The Exception and the Rule* told the audience what ideas to watch out for in the play to come. Brecht often broke up his plays with sections like this in order to comment on the story that was being told or to challenge the audience to think more carefully about something that had just happened. Sometimes, he used songs to actually tell parts of the story. Like his use of Chorus-type songs, this was not an original idea but simply a re-introduction of the 'ballad' into the theatre. 'Ballads' are simply songs that tell a story. Their rhythms are very easy and repetitive. Originally they were sung by minstrels who could probably read neither music nor words. The simple rhythms were easy to learn and remember. Examples of ballads can be found in Shakespeare's plays where they are used to focus the audience's attention on certain themes or emotions occurring in the story or to provide a break from the main action. Ballads are certainly still popular today.

 1 Think about your own favourite pop songs and note down any that you would consider to be a ballad – that is, it tells a story and uses a simple repeated pattern.

2 Working in small groups, choose one ballad with which you are all familiar and write down the words (you may already have a copy of them, of course). If you were making a new pop video to accompany this ballad, how would you show the story it tells? Work through the lyrics of the ballad and break it into 'scenes'. Who would be in each one? What would they be doing? Each visual image must be very tight – that is, it must be immediately apparent what is going on in order to keep up with the song.

Either write a **treatment** for such a video or develop a sequence of **tableaux** to tell the story. Find ways of moving swiftly and smoothly from one tableau to the next.

The simplicity of ballad rhythms makes it possible to rewrite the words in order to suit a particular dramatic purpose better. The play *Oh Dear What Can the Matter Be?* in Chapter One used this very technique at the end by changing the well-known song *Da Do Ron Ron* into a lively plea for girls to stick up for their rights called *The Pressure's On*. Here is an extract (if you know the tune you will see that the words fit fairly well).

> The minute I was born they dressed me all in pink
> The pressure's on yeah the pressure's on.
> And when I asked them why they told me not to think
> The pressure's on yeah the pressure's on.
>
> Yeah, I learned to cook and sew
> Yeah, I learned to tie my bow
> And when I said it wasn't fair
> They made me dress in lacy underwear.
>
> When I reached my teens I had to get a lad
> The pressure's on yeah the pressure's on
> And when I didn't get one I felt so bad
> The pressure's on yeah the pressure's on.
>
> Yeah, I had to change my hair
> Yeah, they told me what to wear
> I had to get slim and use the beauty creams
> So men could think I was the woman of their dreams.

You probably know other songs which have undergone a change in order to suit a new situation, for example, those used by football crowds or in TV adverts.

 3 What movements could be used in the song above to make the meaning of each line clearer? Work in groups of four on any two of the verses, developing a particular movement for each line.

4 Staying in the same groups, use the rhythm of a well-known popular song and devise two more verses which reflect an aspect of your own lives. Look at the way certain lines rhyme in the extract and note how many beats each lines has.

When you have written your own verses, add appropriate movements.

Rapping

A recent trend in pop music which is now proving to be an extremely useful tool in the theatre is 'rapping' or singing 'a cappella' (without accompaniment). By using simple rhythms and rhyme schemes rapping can allow actors to tell stories or make points in a lively way without demanding musical backing. The form seems to be able to combine traditional ballad forms with the kind of commentary Brecht needed. It allows the actor/singers to break up the lines and perform them through use of Chorus and movement.

The following example comes from a recent play called *It's a Girl!* which tells the story of a woman called Linda who finds herself fighting for two basic rights. Her first fight is against her husband who wants her to have their baby in hospital. Linda wants to have it at home. Linda leaves him and moves in with a friend in a village called Bradstow only to discover that the NIREX company are planning to dump nuclear waste there. Linda becomes drawn into a second fight. . .

I've had enough

Tell you a little story
About a woman who travelled down South
Quiet little lady
Didn't like to open her mouth
Well one fine day
She got tough
She said Man
I've had enough.

Chorus
I've had enough
Lord, oh Lord
I've had enough
Well this woman gets going
When the going gets tough
I've had enough.

She came to stay with Evie
She kipped down on her floor
That man don't change his mind

He'll never see me no more
I can mend a fuse
Fix a shelf
Have that baby
By myself.

(*Chorus*)

She went to a meeting
With the NIREX company
Listen to the man
Spout a load of old baloney
You want the truth
Right in your lap
What you say
Is really total crap.

(*Chorus*)

The meeting erupted
The Bradstow cats went wild
Who's that crazy woman
Got the boss man really riled.
Hell she's angry
Hell she's mad
Goes by the name
Of Linda Bragg.

(*Chorus*)

Listen all you people
From the North down to the South
Don't take it lying down
Stand up and open your mouth.

Today's the day
We get tough
Listen man
We've had enough.

(*Chorus*)

---

 1 Summarise in your own words what incident is described in the rap.

2 What could be the advantages of telling the audience about this incident in a rap rather than showing them in a conventional scene?

3 In small groups, try to devise a rhythm which would fit at least two verses of this rap. Develop this into a performance which would make an audience concentrate on the words and what they mean. Use movement and positioning as well as tone, pace and volume of voice to help make the story and attitudes clear.

4 Experiment with ways of keeping the rhythm going by using your own bodies as instruments. Clapping hands, clicking fingers and stamping feet are obvious ways, but can you make other sounds, with your mouth, for example, that would add a sense of rhythm?

Further development

5 Look back to the extract in Chapter Four entitled *The Last Tree*. Either using the words as they are printed, or simply as a basis, experiment with 'rapping'. Add other rhythmic sounds to build an atmosphere.

6 Choose any improvisation you have done recently and, in the groups in which you worked then, try to reproduce it in the form of a 'rap'.

7 Recall any piece of live theatre you have seen recently. Write down briefly
- the story it told
- the theme it was tackling
- what you thought of it.

Rather than presenting such a review as an essay, write or record it as either a rap or a ballad.

8 Brainstorm a list of products which are advertised on TV.

CARS   PERFUME   WASHING POWDER   BEER

and so on.

Choose one and rewrite the words of a well-known song (just one short verse would be enough) to accompany an advert for that product. Improvise the whole advert, choosing carefully where the song should fit in for best effect.

9 An alternative to Task 8 would be to look through a local newspaper and pick out one of the adverts placed by a local trader. Imagine that trader has approached the local radio station and asked them to produce a 'jingle' to advertise the trader's shop/business on the air. Use rapping or invent your own tune as the basis for the advertising jingle.

Reflection

 10 What is your opinion of the use of songs in plays? Do you prefer a play to have a musical element or not? In what ways do songs or the use of some kind of Chorus add to the play?

11 Consider the way songs and jingles are used in advertising. Why do you think so many advertisements use this device? Which ones stick in your mind the most? Do you think this is because of
- the tune?
- the visual images that go with the tune?
- the actual product being advertised?

Discussing your thoughts on this may help you see how you can successfully adapt the same devices for your own drama work.

Performing poems

> Poems work by using words very economically. Playing with the actual SOUNDS of words and their RHYTHMS can help bring out a sense of MOOD, CHARACTER and TENSION – elements that are needed in all improvisation and script work.

The poet Michael Rosen has said that 'A poem is an idea'. Samuel Taylor Coleridge wrote that a poem is 'the best words in the best order', and Suzanne Langer, a philosopher in the arts, describes drama as 'an enacted poem'.

A good play, like a poem, needs to be tight. It should use words and images economically so that the audience doesn't become distracted by things that are not important to what the play is trying to say. In this sense, looking at poems can point out some useful things about what works in drama.

Few Words, Big Ideas

Haiku poetry originates in Japan. The idea is to capture an image by using a very strict constraint. The poems are written in three lines and have a total of seventeen syllables – five in the first line, seven in the second and five in the third. Not all of the examples below stick rigidly to this rule but you will see, I hope, that in just a very few words they do conjure up some powerful images.

 1 Read these example of haiku through silently for yourself a few times, then experiment with how you might use different tones of voice and pauses when reading them aloud.

Coffee
in a paper cup —
a long way from home
        Gary Hotham

Home early —
your empty coat hanger
in the closet

        Gary Hotham

Crying
she moves deeper
into the mirror
        Scott Montgomery

Library closing —
the sleeping wino wakes up
holding a shut book

        Sydell Rosenberg

In the laundermat
she peers into the machine
as the sun goes down
        Sydell Rosenberg

Behind sunglasses
I doze and wake . . .
the friendly man talks on
        Anita Virgil

2 Work in small groups. First of all, find a way of acting out what is going on in the poem. For example, it could just involve a girl sitting on a chair gently sobbing as she look into a mirror then leaning further forward to look more closely.

Simply doing this may not be a particularly good way of capturing very much about the poem. Why is the girl crying? What does it mean 'she moves deeper into the mirror'? You need to talk about how these poems make you feel and what they remind you of. The next stage is to try to find a movement or mime sequence that captures your personal responses. Don't worry too much about telling a clear story to the audience; focus more on how to convey the atmosphere and emotions the poem you have chosen have conjured up for you.

3 Experiment with ways of adding the words of the poem to your movement sequence. Should the poem come first? After? During? Will you have one person speaking it or all of you? Try repeating it or having some words/line echoed. Try using it as a round so that as one speaker finishes the first line, a second one starts, and so on.

4 Choose one type and colour of light that will suit your performance. Can you think of/find a piece of music that would act as a suitable background to the performance?

B Trust the Sounds

1 In groups, read this poem aloud by taking a line each. You will think it's nonsense but never mind – just try to speak the words aloud according to how they are spelt.

KARAWANE

jolifanto bambla ô falli bambla
grossiga m'pfa habla horem
égiga goramen
higo bloiko russula huju
hollaka hollala
anlogo bung
blago bung
blago bung
bosso fataka
ü üü ü
schampa wulla wussa ólobo
hej tatta gôrem
eschige zunbada
wulubu ssubudu uluw ssubudu
tumba ba- umf
kusagauma
ba - umf

Hugo Ball, 1917

2 Read it through again and this time pay attention to the typeface that has been used for each line. What clues does the way it is printed give about how it might be spoken? For example, you might decide that *anlogo bung* suggests that the speaker is making the words sound longer, perhaps to stress the importance of whatever *anlogo bung* is! The boldness of the next line – *blago bung* – looks more blunt. Maybe the speaker is being

dismissive. The next *blago bung* doesn't look so confident – perhaps it is spoken by somebody who is just weakly agreeing. Keep on trying this through until you get a clear idea of how the lines should sound.

3 The poem is called 'Karawane' – that's 'caravan' in English. As well as being something you get stuck behind on Cornish roads in the summer, a caravan is a trail of camels used to transport people and goods across the desert. With that in mind, imagine this conversation is taking place between the Arabs in the caravan:

> as they trudge across the sand in the heat of the sun
> as they sit around a camp fire at night
> as they are loading up their camels for the journey
> as they are buying/selling their goods in a desert village

Although we have no real idea of what on earth these words actually mean, try using them as a script for one of the scenes suggested above. The actions and gestures you use might make it clear what some words mean but, more importantly, the way you say the words will give a sense of character and what their attitude is to the situation they are in.

4 Write and perform a short script of your own using a made-up language. To do this you may choose to pick a situation first, for example:

> cavemen picking over the last scraps of an animal they've killed
> aliens exploring the weird and wonderful world of your drama room

Stick to no more than 20 lines and write out the words so that they look like you want them to sound.

5 Now look at this speech from Shakespeare's *Macbeth*. Again, don't worry about what the lines mean for the time being, just think about the sounds they make.

She should have died hereafter.
There would have been a time for such a
word –
Tomorrow, and tomorrow, and tomorrow,
Creeps in this petty pace from day to day
To the last syllable of recorded time;
And all our yesterdays have lighted fools
The way to dusty death. Out, out, brief
candle!
Life's but a walking shadow, a poor player
That struts and frets his hour upon the stage
And then is heard no more. It is a tale
Told by an idiot, full of sound and fury,
Signifying nothing.

- Try speaking lines 2, 3 and 4 quickly. How easy is it without becoming tongue-tied or gabbling?
- What movement is suggested by line 4?
- What sort of atmosphere does the line 'Tomorrow, and tomorrow, and tomorrow' have? What effect does the repetition of this word have?
- Compare the sound of this line to 'Out, out, brief candle!' Talk about how the sound of the two lines suggests a mood for the speaker.

The very last word – *nothing* – sounds somehow very final. The hard 'g' is almost like a full stop in itself. Compare it with the *ba-umf* at the end of 'Karawane'.

6 Although this speech was written to be performed just by the actor playing Macbeth, work in a group to see if you can find some images or a movement sequence that would fit it in the way you did with the haiku. Try splitting up the lines and giving them different characters in the way you did with 'Karawane'. Perhaps echoing certain words or lines would help you emphasise the mood you feel the piece has.

C Finding the Rhythm

Some words seem to demand to be spoken in a certain way. Compare the way your mouth works and what happens to your face when you say 'huge' and 'tiny', or how the sounds of the words 'grip' and 'slide' seem to capture what they mean. Good writers are well aware of the sounds words make, though this is often more apparent in poems than in plays.

1 Read these two verses from a poem through to yourself and then, in groups, try to perform them as if

they were a radio jingle
they were the verses in a cheap birthday card
they were a children's skipping rhyme
they were a piece of really juicy gossip.

Miller's End
When we moved to Miller's End
Every afternoon at four
A thin shadow of a shade
Quavered through the garden-door.

Dressed in black from top to toe
And a veil about her head
To us all it seemed as though
She came walking from the dead.

Talk about how these different rhythms affect the poem. Do they suit the words that are actually being spoken?

Now read the rest of the poem.

With a basket on her arm
Through the hedge-gap she would pass
Never a mark that we could spy
On the flagstone or the grass.

When we told the garden-boy
How we saw the phantom glide,
With a grin his face was bright
As the pool he stood beside.

'That's no ghost-walk,' Billy said,
'Nor a ghost you fear to stop –
Only old Miss Wickerby
On a short cut to the shop.'

So next day we lay in wait,
Passed a civil time of day,
Said how pleased we were she came
Daily down our garden-way.

Suddenly her cheek it paled,
Turned, as quick, from ice to flame.
'Tell me,' said Miss Wickerby,
'Who spoke of me, and my name?'

'Bill the garden-boy.'
She sighed,
Said, 'Of course, you could not know
How he drowned – that very pool –
A frozen winter – long ago.'

Charles Causley

Now you know the whole poem, go back to
the first two verses and find a way of reading
them aloud which you think is more
suitable.

2 Pick out all of the words in the poem that
suggest different types of movement. Talk
about what they seem to have in common,
and experiment with ways of saying these
aloud so that the sound matches the
movement.

3 Talk about how the tension in the poem
works. Does it build up steadily or does the
poem work through some kind of shock
tactic? Rehearse a reading of the poem again,
using movement and space along with the
words, but this time be very aware of where
an audience would be sitting. Think about
ways of using your voices, positioning, and
where you are looking, in order to draw the
audience into the tale and send a shiver down
their spines at the end.

Idea to Story

In the haiku used at the start of this project,
you were given very few words but the
images were so strong that you were
probably able to feel some sort of emotion in
response to them. 'Karawane' focused your
attention on the sounds of the words, and
'Miller's End' made you think about
capturing the appropriate rhythm. The poem
below raises different questions in that it tells
a story but the story doesn't seem complete.

Magic Box
There at the bar sat the magic man
Who, not very long ago,
had bowed with his most impressive grace
At the end of his little show.
His beautiful moustache had lost its curl
And drooped into his beer.
His eyes that in the footlights glowed
Were bleary and unclear.
And I had a drink with the wonderful magic man.

'That really was a remarkable trick,
Please tell me how it's done.'
He didn't seem to hear at first
He downed his beer and another one.
Then, in a voice that still retained
the glamour of his show,
He said to me with half a smile,
'It's not a trick, you know.'

'Those volunteers from the audience
You'll never see them again.
There's no trap door or phony floor
From beginning to the end.
No trickery at all,' he said,
'I wouldn't have you on.
They step inside that magic box
And, damn it, they're gone.'

Well, we sat and drank a little while,
I thought about the show
And all I'd heard and then I said,
'Well, just where do they go?'
Then he said, 'I just don't know
But they're glad enough to go.
I've travelled far and near
And everywhere
They beg me to make them disappear.'

Pete McCabe

1 Work in pairs. In your own way, improvise the scene between the magic man and the person from the audience.

2 Now use all the words of the poem. Find a way for the person who is telling the story to cut between telling his audience the tale and cutting back to the conversation with the magic man. How can you change your voice and position to show when you are in the scene at the bar and when you are talking about what happened in the bar?

3 Work in groups of four. As two of you perform the poem, the other two should act out, in silence, the scene from the magic show in which an audience member is made to disappear. Where would you place these two actors to show that this scene has happened in the past? If you have the opportunity to use lighting, experiment with ways of dividing the stage up by using coloured or different types of lights.

4 This poem lends itself to other improvisations, for example:

● Imagine the narrator is telling this story to her friends. What reaction would she get? How could she try to convince them she was telling the truth?
● Where do the audience members go? Imagine that when they arrive on the other side of the magic box, they meet up. Where are they? What would they say to each other?
● Imagine someone goes to the police with their story about how their friend or partner has disappeared in this way. What would the scene in the police station be like?

Reflection and development

5 Write out your own thoughts on how working with these poems may help you in your work on

● improvisation
● dealing with play scripts.

6 Find three poems that would lend themselves to performance. One of them should give you the chance to play with the sounds of the words, one should have a strong rhythm, and one should be a narrative poem – that is, it tells a story that could be acted out.

Five

Means to an end

Tackling issues through drama

STUDY UNITS

This chapter looks at what AUDIENCES expect a play to be, and what they expect to get from it. The aim is to show you how you can meet those expectations without changing what you want to say as playmakers.

The chapter explores the processes behind PRODUCING and PRESENTING a play.

The tasks involve considering how THEMES and ISSUES can be communicated to a chosen audience.

Central to all the work in this chapter is an exploration of the type of drama known as THEATRE IN EDUCATION (TIE).

You will find it useful to record your thoughts and ideas in Units A and B and keep them safe. These can then be used to inform and guide your work in the later units.

Targeting an Audience

Here are two phrases which are often used to describe plays and films.

'A SHOW FOR ALL THE FAMILY!'

'UNSUITABLE FOR CHILDREN!'

These are obvious examples of an audience being **targeted**. Whoever is presenting the drama has already decided who it is most suitable for and is either trying to attract them or, alternatively, to stop certain people from seeing it.

Sometimes, of course, the reasons for not allowing certain things to be shown to audiences are not up to the playmakers at all – a point that is investigated later.

Use the following questions to try to clear up your own ideas on the different expectations audiences have.

1 What do audiences expect to get from watching a play? Working in small groups, write the following onto a slip of paper:

When we go to see a play we expect to. . .

Cut some paper or card into strips and copy out the following then arrange them in order of importance under your title slip. (You may wish to add some more possibilities.)

| RECEIVE USEFUL INFORMATION |
| GET AN INSIGHT INTO INTERESTING CHARACTERS |
| BE EXCITED | EXPERIENCE TENSION |
| FEEL EMOTIONAL | HAVE A LAUGH |
| SEE A GOOD STORY |
| EXPERIENCE SOMETHING NEW |
| LEARN SOMETHING ABOUT OURSELVES |
| BE ASKED QUESTIONS |
| BE GIVEN ANSWERS |

2 As a whole group, discuss how your lists differ. Is it possible to agree on one thing that plays should offer an audience above all else? Which statement would all of you be prepared to accept as being the most important?

3 In small groups, look at the television guide on next page.

Which programmes, would you say, are directed towards a particular sort of audience?

Complete the following grid.

A Audience	B Programme
Children not yet at school	Playdays
?	Sesame Street
Housewives	Daytime Live
Teenagers 14–16	?
Whole family	?
?	CinemAttractions

Use recent television guides to make your own target audience grid for one day.

4 Choose any two of the types of audience that you have identified other than yourselves, for example, pre-school children and housewives.

Rearrange the list from Task 1 in a way which you think would show what those two types of audience expect from television.

How are they different from your list and from each other? How would you explain these differences?

5 Sometimes there is a difference between what audiences say they *want* and what other people say they *need* or can have. Divide the class into two groups. Group One should imagine that they work for a television company which is intending to make a new drama series for young school children. Group Two are people who, for various

BBC1

6.0 Business Breakfast *48183* **7.0** Breakfast News **(T)** *362519* **9.0** Breakfast News Extra **(T)** *3133676* **9.20** Style Challenge (S) *6677893* **9.45** Kilroy (S) *7922541* **10.30** Can't Cook, Won't Cook (S) *88541* **11.0** News; **(T)** Weather *7773386* **11.05** The Great Escape *7130386* **11.35** Change That (S) *6341760* **12.0** News; **(T)** Weather *8300657* **12.05** Call My Bluff (S) *8048763* **12.35** Going For A Song (S) *9489763* **1.0** News; **(T)** Weather *46638* **1.30** Regional News *86723676* **1.40** The Weather Show (S) *99992763* **1.45** Neighbours **(T)** *40812305*

2.10 **Quincy Walk** Softly Through The Night (S) **(R)** First in a two-part episode in which the forensic pathologist (Jack Klugman) investigates campus drug-dealing. *6651367*

2.55 Through The Keyhole (S) *6310560*
3.20 Skipper On Style (S) *6454831*
3.30 Children's BBC: Playdays *8273831* **3.50** Monster Café **(R)** *6794725* **4.05** The New Yogi Bear Show *5633473* **4.10** Casper (S) *4157015* **4.35** 50/50 **(T)** (S) *9526980* **5.05** Newsround **(T)** *5964657* **5.10** Blue Peter **(T)** (S) *6329589*

5.35 Neighbours **(T)** (R) *203855*
6.0 News; **(T)** Weather *265*
6.30 Regional News Magazine *367*
7.0 **Auntie's TV Favourites** **(T)** (S) Steve Wright with more snippets and trivia concerning programmes past and present.

7.30 **Here And Now** **(T)** (S) Including a report on the growing level of violence faced by NHS staff in hospital accident and emergency departments, and a visit to Fair Isle, where a four-generation family tradition will end when Angus Hutchison ceases to be Scotland's last lighthouse keeper. *251*

8.0 **EastEnders** **(T)** (S) *2980*
8.30 **Only Fools And Horses** The Second Time Around **(T)** (S) **(R)** *1015*
9.0 News; **(T)** *2657*
9.30 **Panorama** Water Torture **(T)** With all the signs pointing to another summer of water shortages, Michael Robinson reports on the crisis in the pipeline, asking water industry chiefs to defend their record. *424594*

10.10 **One Of Her Own** (Armand Mastroianni, 1994 TVM) Rookie policewoman, raped by a colleague, insists on making a case of the incident, thereby ruining her life and career. Lori Loughlin plays the young officer in a telemovie that is based on fact but treated without subtlety. *1052183*

11.40 **Absent Without Leave** (John Lang, 1992) (S) Another Real People drama, this time from New Zealand and reasonably well done, with Craig McLachlan as WW2 conscript who deserts to be with his pregnant young wife. *329831*

1.15 Weather *4646110* **1.20** Close

BBC2

6.0 Open University: Images Of Education *8492831* **6.25** Rich Mathematical Activities *8488638* **6.50** Play And The Social World *8962251* **7.15** See Hear Breakfast News **(T)** *3854541* **7.30** Teenage Mutant Hero Turtles *8076893* **7.55** Blue Peter **(T)** (S) **(R)** *1166251* **8.20** Bump *3175522* **8.25** Open A Door **(R)** *6389102* **8.35** Raccoons *3267725* **9.0** TV6 *97299* **9.30** Ici Paris (S) *7516928* **9.45** Watch Out (S) *7504183* **10.0** Teletubbies *21831* **10.30** Go For It! *4768347* **10.50** Look And Read Special (S) *4771831* **11.10** Zig Zag (S) *6636725* **11.30** Ghostwriter (S) *2102* **12.0** Teaching Today (S) *54873* **12.30** Working Lunch *37305* **1.0** History File *22371638* **1.25** Landmarks (S) *70520251* **1.45** Storytime (S) *86700725* **2.0** Bump *30095928* **2.05** Open A Door **(R)** *30094299*

2.10 **Alias Smith And Jones** **(R)** *7340580*
3.0 News; **(T)** Weather *6458657*
3.05 **The Phil Silvers Show** Dinner At Sowicis **(R)** *7165909*
3.30 Blockbusters (S) *2488893*
3.55 News; **(T)** Weather *5537831*
4.0 Blockbusters (S) *5514980*
4.25 Ready, Steady, Cook (S) *5524367*
4.55 Esther Meeting The Queen Mother (S) *1412893*

5.30 **Today's The Day** (S) *744*
6.0 **The Simpsons** Dancin' Homer **(T)** (S) *476134*
6.25 **Space Precinct** The Fire Within **(T)** **(R)** *684657*
7.10 **The Ren And Stimpy Show** Galoot Wranglers/Ren Needs Help **(T)** (S) *404386*

7.30 **Computers Don't Bite: The Beginner's Guide** **(T)** (S) See Watching Brief. *893*
8.0 **Top Gear Motorsport** **(T)** (S) Tiff Needell with the motor-racing magazine. *9562*

8.30 **The Antiques Show** **(T)** (S) Joining a weekend package trip to the Paris antique markets, and meeting some very young collectors. *9657*

9.0 **Till Death Us Do Part** **(T)** **(R)** *8909*
9.30 **Tales From The Riverbank** If You Want To Be Happy, Learn To Fish (S) Actor and accomplished fly-fisherman Geoffrey Palmer presents this new series on the natural history of angling. *17541*

10.0 **Game On** (S) **(R)** *78164*
10.30 **Newsnight** **(T)** *365657*
11.15 **Ruby** (S) Chat with Wax and guests — including Marianne Faithfull and Eddie Izzard — in the first edition of the pushy one's new talk show. *690015*

11.55 **The Phil Silvers Show** Army Memoirs **(R)** *153164*
12.25 **Weather** *9610955*
12.30 **Learning Zone:** Open University: Outsiders In — Muslims In Europe *42508* **1.30** Picasso's Collages *96357* **2.0** Nightschool TV: Cats' Eyes *65431* **4.0** BBC Focus: Italia 2000 *21416* **4.30** Royal Institution Discourse *23665* **5.30** RCN Nursing Update *16394*

Carlton

6.0 GMTV *4786034* **9.25** Supermarket Sweep **(T)** (S) *6685812* **9.55** Regional News **(T)** *3010947* **10.0** The Time, The Place (S) *25657* **10.30** This Morning (S) *62939218* **12.20** Your Shout *8315589* **12.25** Regional News **(T)** *8307560* **12.30** News; **(T)** Weather *9475560* **12.55** London Today **(T)** *9450251* **1.25** Home And Away **(T)** (S) *70548657*

1.50 **Capital Woman** (S) *40895638*
2.20 **Blue Heelers** (S) *7324522*
3.15 **Breakaways** **(R)** *6469034*
3.20 **News Headlines** **(T)** *6465947*
3.25 **Regional News** **(T)** *6464218*
3.30 **Children's ITV:** Tots TV *6718305* **3.40** Caribou Kitchen (S) *7339812* **3.50** Cartoon Time *7335096* **4.0** Scooby Doo *5541034* **4.25** The Famous Five (S) *4147638* **4.50** The Big Bang **(T)** (S) *1804522*

5.10 **Home And Away** (S) **(R)** *7038473*
5.40 **News;** **(T)** Weather *260183*
6.0 **London Tonight** *183*
6.30 **London Bridge** (S) *763*
7.0 **Wish You Were Here..?** **(T)** (S) Including a visit to Kenya which takes in a safari, snorkelling and a balloon ride, and a bargain mini-cruise from Harwich to Hamburg with a look at Lubeck. *8928*

7.30 **Coronation Street** **(T)** *947*
8.0 **World In Action** **(T)** (S) First in the new series reports on the growing tendency for communities to take vigilante action against paedophiles in their midst, through campaigns to identify known sex offenders. The police and probation service, it claims, are increasingly concerned that this only serves to drive dangerous men underground. *7676*

8.30 **The Freddie Starr Show** **(T)** (S) **(R)** Re-run revelry with trusting snake Freda. *6183*

9.0 **Bramwell** **(T)** (S) More costume doctoring, with poor neglected Mrs Marsham's condition causing her husband belated concern, and the Bramwells having to operate. With Jemma Redgrave, David Calder. *5305*

10.0 **News;** **(T)** Weather *11198*
10.30 **Regional News** **(T)** *763305*
10.40 **The Island** (Michael Ritchie, 1980) Calculated to make Jaws seem plausible, this movie version of another Peter Benchley oeuvre is as daft as they come. Michael Caine plays the journo whose investigation into Caribbean disappearances leads him to a lost tribe of pirates in need of a new leader. *31070831*

12.45 **War Of The Worlds** The Resurrection, Part 1 **(R)** *433619*
1.45 **Stand And Deliver** *422503*
2.45 **Real Stories Of The Highway Patrol** *8901874*
3.10 **The Lost Hours** (David MacDonald, 1952) British b-and-w crime drama with imported lead Mark Stevens. *6816771*
4.30 **Curtis Calls** (S) *64693042*
4.35 **World In Action** **(T)** (S) *72926665*
5.0 **The Time, The Place** (S) **(R)** *43023*
5.30 **News** *16348*

Channel 4

6.0 Sesame Street **(R)** *31893* **7.0** The Big Breakfast *69589* **9.0** Bewitched **(T)** **(R)** *82367* **9.30** Schools: Geography Junction *7501096* **9.45** Book Box *7599251* **10.0** Stage Two Science *2829893* **10.15** Schools At Work *2783454* **10.20** Off the Walls *2830909* **10.40** The English Programme *23288947* **11.05** Encyclopedia Galactica *7789947* **11.15** The Mix *5326831* **11.30** Rat-A-Tat-Tat *4321831* **11.45** Living and Growing *4326386* **12.0** Right To Reply **(T)** (S) *95831* **12.30** Light Lunch (S) *25299*

1.30 **Man On A Tightrope** (Elia Kazan, 1953) **(T)** Cold War propaganda drama in which the proprietor of a rundown Czech circus hopes to escape from behind the Iron Curtain. With Fredric March, Gloria Grahame, Adolphe Menjou. *35872*

3.30 Collector's Lot **(T)** (S) *541*
4.0 Fifteen-To-One **(T)** (S) *676*
4.30 Countdown **(T)** (S) *560*
5.0 Montel Williams Mixed Race Teens Torn Between Two Worlds **(T)** (S) *9034*
5.30 Pet Rescue **(T)** (S) *812*
6.0 Hangin' With Mr Cooper Will She Or Won't She? (S) *725*
6.30 Hollyoaks (S) *305*
7.0 News; **(T)** Weather *626928*
7.50 Rhyme And Reason **(T)** *824386*
8.0 **Mrs Cohen's Money** Savings **(T)** (S) "Think about the future with the same sense of urgency as you think about the present," urges Bernice C, complaining that as a nation we haven't got the hang of saving. In this penultimate programme of the personal finance series she explains things like PEPs and TESSAs and explores the pitfalls of ready-packaged pension plans. *5218*

8.30 **The Entertainers** **(T)** (S) The women performers of the north-eastern artistes' agency are in the spotlight tonight, with young Tara facing her first pro show, and Lynn and Penny bowing out as a duo. *4725*

9.0 **Melissa** **(T)** (S) See Watching Brief. *7457270*
10.25 **Dark Skies** Both Sides Now **(T)** (S) *931454*
11.25 **Cheers** Those Lips, Those Ice **(T)** (S) *100812*
11.55 **NBA Raw** (S) Basketball action. *793676*
12.55 **NYPD Blue** Bombs Away **(T)** (S) **(R)** *7021955*
1.45 **10-7 For Life** (S) **(R)** Following a Toronto policewoman as she prepares to pack it in after 15 years in the force. *5240077*

2.50 **My Learned Friend** (Basil Dearden, Will Hay, 1943) Hay stars as a lawyer/murder target in this black farce. *5391394*
4.10 **Watching The Detectives** **(T)** (S) *5519597*
5.10 **There Lived A Man Called Kozyavin** Animation attacking bureaucracy. *8031313*
5.20 **Backdate** **(T)** (S) **(R)** *9900348*

reasons, are concerned with looking after young school children (teachers, parents and so on).

Each group should rearrange the list from Task 1 to fit their priorities. Group One should base their arrangement on what they think young children *want* in the hope that this will boost the popularity of their programme.

Group Two should arrange their list according to what they think young children *need*.

Try to develop a specific role in the discussion. This will allow you to argue from a position which isn't necessarily your own and contribute information which may be fictitious yet interesting.

6 Having made a list, each group should consider and note down any subjects which they think would be unsuitable for an audience of young school children.

Stay in role during this discussion. What evidence/arguments would the character you have adopted give to support their views?

7 Organise a meeting between Groups One and Two. Discuss, first of all, those areas that you think would be unsuitable for young children. To what extent do you agree about this? Go on to compare what you think the main aim of the new drama series should be and possibly what it should be about. Do you agree about this?

Up until 1968 all plays and films had to be given the approval of the Lord Chancellor. If he considered that the piece would cause offence or would not be in the public's interest, he could censor or ban it. The Lord Chancellor no longer has this power but some things are still not shown by law or by common consent (that is, people just seem to agree that some things should not be shown openly).

Reflection

8 The picture below shows a scene from a play by Edward Bond called *Saved*. The play was originally banned because of this scene in which a group of youths mindlessly stone a baby to death. The play is now regarded as something of a modern classic.

Some people thought the scene was simply too repulsive and offensive to show in public. Others argued that by showing how low humans can sink, it jolted the consciousness of audiences who would rather pretend such things didn't happen.

Do you think there is ever a good reason to show such horrid things on stage?

9 Can you think of any subjects which are not available for everyone to see because of

a common consent?
b law?

Do you agree that there should be such restrictions, or can you think of any examples when audiences are not allowed to see something which you *think* they should see if they wished?

The balance between giving an audience what it wants and providing something it needs is a delicate one. It might be true to say that in both cases the decision isn't really up to the audience at all. It is up to whoever is making the drama and what they think the audience wants or needs to see.

 ## Challenging the Audience

Challenging the imagination

Chapter Three showed how drama and real life are fundamentally different. Drama involves pretending. Even if the subject of the drama may be documented fact, the presentation of the fact in a play requires careful selection of what the audience will see and how they will see it.

What the audience see in a play is fictitious – it's not really happening.

Through drama the impossible can happen before an audience's very eyes, they can hear what people are thinking, see what people are dreaming and witness the same event from different points of view.
Audiences are often happy to 'believe' that what they are watching is really happening. They are said to 'suspend their disbelief'. For an audience to 'believe' in this way, the playmakers need to prepare them for the imaginary world to which they are being taken. Sometimes this is achieved in a very direct way. Look at this extract from Shakespeare's *Henry the Fifth* in which the Chorus tells the audience that they are going to be taken to France and back!

> The King is set from London, and the scene
> Is now transported, gentles, to Southampton;
> There is the play-house now, there must you sit,
> And thence to France shall we convey you safe
> And bring you back, charming the narrow seas
> To give you gentle pass; for, if we may,
> We'll not offend one stomach with our play.

 1 What reasons might Shakespeare have had not to actually show the King on the journey to France?

2 Who is the Chorus referring to when he uses the word 'we'?

3 Compare this short extract with the examples of choral speech in Project Seven.

This century, the 'impossibility' of drama has been frequently used to fire an audience's imagination in the most spectacular ways. Film makers have transported audiences much further than Southampton and on to whole new universes. Sometimes, the film/play makers fail to make an audience 'suspend their disbelief' by rushing them into the fictitious world without preparing them carefully enough. The result is often that the drama appears ridiculous. You may wish to discuss any films or plays you have seen where you feel this has happened and try to pinpoint what stopped you 'suspending your disbelief'.

Challenging the conscience

Many playwrights have tried to use the 'impossibility' of drama to challenge the audience in a different way. Their aim has been to make audiences consciously think about certain issues. Although the drama happens in a fictitious world, the issues it explores can be relevant to the real one.

Look at the following introduction from a play called *Drink the Mercury*.

> We are here today to tell you the story of what happened very recently in a small fishing village in Japan called Minamata. You'll see in a short while why the people of that village want all the world to know what has happened to them. We are not from Japan. But we want to try to tell this story in a Japanese way. It is the story of a girl called Ioka, a girl of about your age, who lived in the village of Minamata. Ioka is dead now. She died when she was nine years old. When she died, she was looking forward to going to school. She never went to school and you'll soon see why.
>
> (from *Drink the Mercury*, the Belgrade TIE, Amber Lane Press)

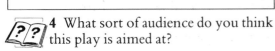 **4** What sort of audience do you think this play is aimed at?

5 What is going to be unusual about the way this play is performed?

Why do you think the audience are being told this?

6 This introduction seems to tell the audience exactly what the play is going to be about. What would be the point of them watching it?

Whatever else they expect from drama, most audiences expect to be entertained in some way. Your discussions in Unit A of this chapter probably revealed that different people regard different things as being entertaining.

Some dramas present a kaleidoscope of different techniques and features simply to entertain the audience. Entertainment is the end result.

In other dramas entertainment is used as a way of exposing the audience to issues that the playmakers themselves think are important – it is a means to another end. (By 'issues' I mean questions that feel important and need to be answered.) The different elements of drama are used as a kind of microscope through which an issue can be inspected. *Drink the Mercury* tells the story of Ioka. Its aim isn't to keep the audience wondering whether or not she is going to die, but to explore the reasons why she died. The purpose of the play is really to make the audience consciously aware of the deadly effects of pollution.

7 Working in small groups, divide a sheet of paper into two columns. In the first column note down any plays or films which you think are principally designed to entertain the audience. In the second column note down any films or plays which deliberately drew your attention towards some issue.

Reflection

 8 Do you think a drama that deals with issues such as pollution can be entertaining? Think about what sort of things could still hold an audience's attention even though they have been told what happens in the end. Have you, for example, ever seen a film or play more than once yet still enjoyed watching it a second or even a third time? What made you watch it again?

Theatre through the kaleidoscope

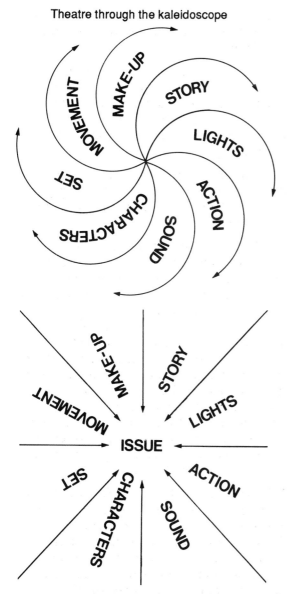

Theatre through the microscope

The Tasks in Units A and B have tried to make you start thinking about what the *purpose* of plays might be, for both the audience and the playmakers. The units which follow look more closely at how an audience's attention can be drawn to issues that the playmakers think are important. Your notes from the Tasks in Units A and B should help you to *say what you want to say* in ways that will entertain the audience and keep their attention.

 # Raising Issues

Below is a treatment of a story which raises a number of issues. There are only three characters in the story:

- a teenage girl
- her father
- her stepmother.

In groups of three, improvise each scene in sequence. Try to develop a sense of the characters in order to see why they might be doing the things they do. Each scene should only last three minutes or so. Go straight on to answer the questions which follow.

SCENE ONE
A room in a large house. A teenage girl is teasing her stepmother by unfairly comparing her with her real mother. The girl is extremely attractive and it is obvious that she knows it. The stepmother knows that all the local boys fancy her but know her to be a notorious tease. The stepmother threatens to tell the girl's rich and powerful father about her cruel teasing but the girl laughs and suggests that her father dotes on her too much to believe the tale.

SCENE TWO
At the breakfast table. The poor woman has become increasingly distressed by the unkindness of her stepdaughter and has decided to talk about it to her husband. However, just as the girl predicted, he can see no wrong in his daughter and feels that the stepmother is being oversensitive. He suggests that the pressures of coming into a new family are great and that she is not as young as she used to be and therefore is simply feeling the strain. The scene ends with the appearance of the daughter who, realising the nature of the conversation, uses it to cruelly tease the woman further.

SCENE THREE
A bedroom. The mother is making herself up in the dressing table mirror. Bit by bit she looks at herself more carefully and

notices the bags under her eyes, the dullness of her eyes and the worry lines creeping over her forehead. The closer she looks the worse it seems to be. In a sinister way, the image in the mirror begins to change from being her sad and tired face to being that of her stepdaughter laughing and mocking her.

SCENE FOUR

A forest. The girl is out walking when she notices that a handsome young man is following her. Taking him for yet another admirer she deliberately lures him into an encounter. It becomes apparent that the man intends to murder her. By playing the innocent, defenceless little girl she manages not only to escape his intention but also to get him to admit that he has been hired by her stepmother to do the job. The girl decides not to go home.

SCENE FIVE

The breakfast table. The stepmother has a new air of relaxation about her and when her husband asks where his daughter is she is able to lie convincingly. However, the morning mail arrives and with it comes a letter from his daughter accusing the stepmother of attempted murder. She adds that she will not return home while the stepmother is in the house.

SCENE SIX

A city street. The stepmother, now in very ordinary clothing and looking terribly haggard after being thrown out by her husband, is looking for the girl. It is obvious that she has suffered terribly and is no longer in complete control of her senses.
After asking a number of local people she discovers that the girl is living in a commune with seven miners. She decides to go and seek her revenge. . .

Understanding the text

1 Remind yourself of the original story of *Snow White and the Seven Dwarves*. In what way are the events of this story similar?

2 Compare the way the characters were presented in this story with the way they appear in the original tale of *Snow White*. In what ways are they similar/different?

3 Who do the audience tend to sympathise with in the original story? Who are they encouraged to sympathise with here? What is there about the way the stories are told that encourages the audience to side with one particular character?

4 What would you say was the 'moral' of the original story of Snow White? Is the moral of this story different?

5 Given that in fairy tales people generally get their just deserts in the end, write or improvise an appropriate ending for this treatment.

6 What questions do you think this story raises about

a what an audience expects of a fairy story?
b the way certain types of character are shown in fairy stories?
c the typical 'moral' of a fairy story?

The aim of this new version is to try to retell the traditional *Snow White* story from a new **perspective**. That is, it tries to tell the story by focusing on the same events but in a new way. The new perspective might make the audience consider the events in a new light and make new judgements about them. It becomes the stepmother's story instead of Snow White's.

Changing the focus of a story can raise a number of issues for an audience if they are used to hearing just one version.

Reflection

7 Think of another well-known fairy story. Decide what you think the moral of that story is and who the story is focused upon. Now write or improvise a new version which focuses on a different character. In what way does the moral change in your version? Fairy stories are generally thought to be aimed at very

young audiences. Is your version still suitable for young children or has the new focus changed the target audience?

Another war story?

Chapter Two investigated the way the Second World War has been portrayed in films and plays. Rather than focusing on the men who fought the war and the action they saw, it looked at the women and life on the 'Home Front'. This in itself raised a number of questions like these.

• Why were women expected to work the same as men to help the war effort yet were paid much less?
• Why were women who had proved their ability to do certain jobs during the war removed from them once the war was over?

• Why is it that few war films recognise that there were so many deserters, or that crime actually increased during the war?
• Why is it that people often talk fondly of the wartime spirit and describe how everyone pulled together, yet there were a great many strikes over pay and conditions?

At the time of the Second World War, the British ruled over the whole of India (this included Pakistan and Bangladesh at the time). As citizens of the British Empire, India's men were allowed to join the British Army. Many volunteered and fought the Japanese in South East Asia. Some even paid for their own fares to Britain in order to train for specialist services like the RAF. . .

A squad of Sikh volunteers in the British Army during the Second World War

This snippet of information also raises a number of questions.

- Why would Indian men volunteer to fight in the British Army?
- What did the men expect to get in return for their volunteering?
- What sacrifices did they and their families make to pay for the passage to Britain?
- To what extent were they accepted into the services?
- Were they actively encouraged to volunteer?
- What promises might have been made to them?

Below and on the right are a number of possible scenes inspired by this information. They are not in any particular sequence.

THE SCENES

A British officer has been sent to India to recruit keen young men for training as RAF mechanics. He has never been to India before and has high hopes of finding plenty of volunteers. On arrival in India he is met by an older officer who has spent many years in the country and does not share his enthusiasm and high hopes.

A bundle of leaflets arrive in a small Indian town. They explain that the British King needs men to volunteer for special training in order to fight the war against Germany. Since the leaflets are printed in English, the people in the village are uncertain of exactly what they mean. What action do they take?

A British recruiting officer explains to an Indian man why he should volunteer for the special training. What doubts does the Indian have. How does the officer reassure him?

A number of British servicemen at a training base in Britain have been told to prepare for the arrival of the first group of Indian volunteers. Some of the servicemen have been to India. What is their attitude? What action do they take?

An Indian man considers with his family whether or not to volunteer. What arguments for and against do different members of the family give?

A group of Indian men arrive at the docks in Bombay ready to volunteer. They are interviewed by British officers who have been told to make sure that no shirkers or troublemakers are accepted. How do they 'screen' the volunteers?

An Indian man wants to volunteer. He explains his reasons to the committee in his village in the hope that they will raise the money for his passage. What sacrifices will they have to make in order to help him? Do they think it's a good idea?

A group of British instructors are talking about their new Indian charges. What attitudes do they have towards their progress?

An Indian volunteer from a wealthy and powerful family is billeted in a poor English rural community. No one in the village has ever met an Indian before. What incidents occur and what attitudes develop as a result of this meeting?

An Indian serviceman is taken prisoner of war and questioned by a German officer as to why he volunteered.

A group of Indian women whose husbands have volunteered, are told they must leave their homes. The Japanese are advancing rapidly towards the area. A troop of British soldiers will shortly be arriving to take up positions in and around the town. How co-operative are the women? What is the attitude of the Army towards them?

A highly skilled Indian volunteer tries to get a job in England after the war. What happens?

APPROACHES

8 Working in small groups, improvise just one of the scenes. Discuss the content of your improvisation and develop a second scene of your own which might follow on from it.

9 Select and improvise two scenes which you think, when shown together, may raise some interesting issues because of the different perspectives they seem to show.

10 Arrange a number of the scenes into a sequence which will tell the story of just one character of your own choice.

11 Decide as a whole class a particular issue which you would like to explore through the frame of this story. Choose one of the scenes as a starting point and develop a drama which will offer a new perspective on some aspect of the Second World War.

Reflection

12 If you worked on the scenes above in small groups, share your work and discuss the issues which seemed most interesting to you. Look back to the section on Evaluation in Project One.

Evaluate each other's work in terms of how successfully it made the audience consider a new aspect of the Second World War.

STUDY EXTRACT ONE
RAJ

Raj was devised and written by Leeds Playhouse Theatre in Education Company.

Theatre in Education (or TIE) is a special form of theatre which aims to raise particular issues with specially targeted audiences. Rather than being called a play, TIE companies usually refer to their work as 'a programme'. This is because it often actively involves the audience in some discussion or decision-making process in order to help them pick out and understand the issues being raised. These issues are usually social, historical or political ones which the TIE company consider have a relevance for their audience (which usually consists of young people).

Sometimes the problems raised by the programme can't actually be solved. However, simply making an audience consciously aware of them might help change or develop attitudes in such a way that the same problems can be avoided in the future (the same argument was used in defence of the play *Saved* mentioned on p 174). This is largely true of the play *Raj*.

Set in India at the end of the Second World War, *Raj* tells the story of an Indian woman called Nandita. Nandita has been brought up by an English judge called Courtney Wickham. A the beginning of the play Wickham gives Nandita a Christmas present. It is a locket with a picture of them both inside and seems to symbolise how close they are to each other. She calls him 'Ma-bap' which, she explains, means mother and father.

In due course Nandita goes to work for a British Colonel as a nanny to his two young children – James and Elizabeth. Here she meets her cousin Tarun. He is the son of the Colonel's head servant, Ganesh, who is her uncle. Tarun has volunteered to join the British Army but in this scene his attitude towards his British masters becomes clear.

CHARACTERS

JAMES The young son of Colonel Gower.

TARUN An Indian servant who has just joined the British Army.

NANDITA An Indian servant. Tarun's cousin and James's nanny.

JAMES: I'm going to be a soldier when I grow up. I'm going to be a colonel. Do you think the War will last long, Tarun?

TARUN: I don't know.

JAMES: I hope it does. I don't want to miss it. I know, let's play wars.

TARUN: Why not? I need the practice.

JAMES: I'm my daddy. I'm the Colonel and you're the enemy. You're crawling round in the jungle.

TARUN groans as if in pain

Come on, Tarun, let's play. Tarun? Are you alright?

TARUN shoots at JAMES

TARUN: Got you!

JAMES: That's not fair.

TARUN: What's not fair?

JAMES: I wasn't ready.

TARUN: First lesson, Colonel Gower: the enemy strikes when you least expect him.

JAMES: You missed me.

TARUN: I didn't, James.

JAMES: Alright then, but I was only wounded.

TARUN: Alright.

They hide and start shooting at each other.

JAMES: Come out, you coward. Come out and fight like a man.

TARUN: Not on your life.

JAMES: Aw, Tarun, the enemy can't win. Look, you get scared and you make a run for it.

TARUN: Alright. Here I come.

TARUN runs out; JAMES shoots him; TARUN dies dramatically, ending up spread-eagled on the ground.

JAMES: That'll teach you. I know, I'll be my daddy and you be your daddy. I say, Ganesh, I couldn't half do with a gin and tonic. . . Hey, Vicky, has that fan broken down again? . . Ganesh? . . Where is that boy? . . I don't know, Vicky, these Indians, they're so slow, you need the patience of a saint. Ganesh! . . Well I'll just have to get shot of him . . . I mean, servants like him are ten a penny. . . Come on Tarun.

TARUN kneels up. JAMES presents his foot.

I say, Ganesh, my boots are filthy.

TARUN: Then clean them.

JAMES: That's not right. Ganesh wouldn't say that.

TARUN: What would he say?

JAMES: He'd say, yes sahib, and he'd do it.

TARUN: Show me.

JAMES: No.

TARUN: Why not?

JAMES: Because I'm not your daddy, I'm my daddy.

JAMES sits down; TARUN gets up and presents his foot. NANDITA enters unnoticed.

TARUN: I say, Ganesh, my boots are filthy.

JAMES: No!

TARUN: Give them a clean, there's a good chap.

JAMES: I don't want to be your daddy. *[He sees NANDITA.]* Nandita, where's Binkie?

NANDITA: In his kennel.

JAMES: *[to TARUN]* I'm going to play with my dog.

He exits.

NANDITA: You've upset him.

TARUN: He upset me.

NANDITA: He's only a child.

TARUN: So I should kneel at his feet and

clean his shoes?

NANDITA: It was a game.

TARUN: No, it is not a game. My father's on his knees, every day of his life, like his father before him. Well, it stops with me.

NANDITA: We all serve the British. I don't see what's wrong with it.

TARUN: It's our country. It should be in our hands.

NANDITA: Do you want the British to go?

TARUN: Look, my father says I should fight for the British because it's my duty to serve them. Well, I'll fight, but when it's over I shall say: I fought with you, side by side; now I have the right to stand beside you, a free man in my own country.

NANDITA: I don't see why you want to change things.

TARUN: Dita. Look on the ground, hold your tongue, know your place? That's got to change.

NANDITA: When do you have to go?

TARUN: Any day now.

NANDITA: You look very smart in that uniform. Are you scared?

TARUN: Yes.

He exits.

Understanding the text

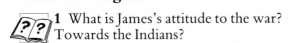

1 What is James's attitude to the war? Towards the Indians?

2 What do you learn about Colonel Gower's attitudes from this extract?

3 Why do you think James doesn't want to play at being Tarun's daddy?

4 What is Tarun's attitude towards James? Towards his own father?

5 In what way is Tarun's attitude towards the war different from James's?

Towards the end of the play Tarun deserts from the British Army, appalled by the way he has seen British soldiers treating other Indians. He hides in his father's house. As the war draws to a close many Indians start demanding independence from British rule.

As a result of the growing mistrust and nervousness amongst the British, Tarun is shot and his father, Ganesh, imprisoned for hiding him.

In this last scene, Nandita goes to ask Ma-bap, Courtney Wickham, to release her uncle Ganesh.

CHARACTERS

NANDITA An Indian woman who has left the service of the British.

WICKHAM An English judge. Foster father to Nandita.

SCENE TWENTY-ONE

NANDITA: I wasn't only going to Lahore to be near my uncle. I knew there was one person there who could still help us. I went to the courthouse to see Ma-bap.

Enter **WICKHAM**.

WICKHAM: Alright, alright, that's enough for today. Everybody go home. My office will be open again at 8 o'clock tomorrow morning.

He turns to go out, but is aware that someone is still there.

I said, everybody go home.

He turns back.

Well, well, well. Nan.

NANDITA: Ma-bap.

WICKHAM: You never wrote to me.

NANDITA: You didn't write to me either.

WICKHAM: True. But you know how busy I am. Anyway, how are you? How's your husband? You must have children by now.

NANDITA: I'm a widow.

WICKHAM: I'm sorry.

NANDITA: I've got a job here in Lahore, at an Indian laundry.

WICKHAM: Are you well, child? You're looking tired. Come on, let's have tiffin.

NANDITA: Ma-bap, I need your help.

WICKHAM: Of course. Anything, anything for you, Nan.

NANDITA: It's about my uncle, Ganesh

Dar. His son was a deserter. He was shot by the army. Then the police arrested my uncle for hiding him. He was tried in Amritsar and now he's in prison.

WICKHAM: What, here in Lahore?

NANDITA: Yes, ma-bap. He's always been a loyal servant to the British, but at his trial they called him a traitor.

WICKHAM: What does he say, this uncle of yours? Did he shelter the boy?

NANDITA: Yes, ma-bap.

WICKHAM: Did the boy force your uncle, against his will?

NANDITA: No, ma-bap.

WICKHAM: What does he say?

NANDITA: He says nothing.

WICKHAM: Now he must say something, if he's as loyal as you think he is.

NANDITA: He is.

WICKHAM: Well then, he must have had a very good reason for sheltering a deserter.

NANDITA: Yes, of course. He was the boy's father. He had to put his son first before everything. He had no choice. You must see that.

WICKHAM: No, Nan. He had a clear choice between a traitor and his king and country. And nothing and no one can come before them. If we let ourselves put personal loyalty first, then we'll have nothing. Law and order, the empire, our whole world will just crumble away in our hands.

NANDITA: You won't help him?

WICKHAM: If that's his only defence, there is nothing I can do.

NANDITA: He's not a traitor. He served the British faithfully all his life. He's an old man. Prison could kill him. I'm begging you . . . [kneeling] . . . on my knees to have mercy on him.

WICKHAM: I care for you, Nan. More than anything, except my king and my country. I'm sorry.

NANDITA *gets up and begins to leave.*

Come for tiffin.

NANDITA *removes the locket and gives it to* WICKHAM. NANDITA *exits.* WICKHAM *exits.*

Understanding the text

 6 What, according to Wickham, should Ganesh have done to avoid imprisonment?

7 How does Wickham show that he lives by the same rules he recommends for Ganesh?

8 What evidence is there to suggest that Nandita's and Whickham's relationship cannot survive this meeting?

9 What do you think the locket may be symbolic of?

10 From the two short extracts you have read, what would you say *Raj* is trying to make the audience think about?

Further development

 11 In pairs, improvise a scene in which Nandita goes to tell Ganesh what Wickham has said but add this extra piece of information.

If Ganesh is prepared to say that Tarun forced his way into the house and made his father hide him, there is a chance that he'll be released.

Will Ganesh be prepared to lie about his son?

12 In the play, Courtney Wickham is said to be well-respected by everyone for his fairness. Imagine a scene soon after India achieved its independence in 1947. All British nationals must apply for a visa in order to stay in India. In groups of four or five improvise the scene in which Wickham is being interviewed by Indian officials who will decide whether or not he can stay. What is their attitude towards him? What decision will they take?

13 In pairs, improvise a scene in which Wickham's son or daughter has tracked down Nandita years later. Wickham is dead but in his will he has asked that the locket be returned to Nandita. Will she accept it? What would the message of the play be

a if she did?
b if she didn't?

E Focusing on Issues

The tasks in this unit develop further the idea that dramas can make an audience think about something in a new way. Some plays go beyond making the audience generally aware of issues by asking the audience directly to consider what they might do in certain situations.

Dilemmas

You may have heard the term 'the horns of a dilemma'. Its origin provides quite a good explanation of what a dilemma is. Imagine someone being chased by an angry bull. Whichever way he turns at least one of the horns is sure to impale him!

Some sort of dilemma lies behind most dramas. Situations in which there are no easy answers are powerful because audiences sympathise with the feeling that there is 'no way out'.

Some dilemmas are on a vast scale.

● Should Britain scrap all its nuclear weapons in order to use the money elsewhere, and risk being invaded?
● Should the army be pulled out of Northern Ireland in the hope that this will reduce the violence there though there is a chance that this will lead to a complete breakdown of law and order?

A way of confronting audiences with such big dilemmas is to focus on what they might mean to individuals in particular situations. In *Raj* Ganesh, Nandita and Wickham are all faced with the same dilemma – what should come first? The people you love, or the country which apparently looks after them?

Young people frequently find themselves in a dilemma created by feeling torn between parents and friends. The diagram on the next page shows you how this central issue can be explored by devising a number of different scenes around it.

1 Suggest ideas of your own in order to complete the chart. Which particular scene do you think would present the most difficult situation? In appropriately sized groups, prepare the improvisation and share it with the rest of the class. Does everyone agree on what the most difficult situation is?

2 Look carefully at the idea for a scene in which the father discovers his daughter is taking drugs. Find ways of playing the scene so that
a the audience sympathises firstly with one character (eg the father is very gentle, the daughter selfish)
b the sympathies lies with the other character (the father always concentrates on work but spends no time with his daughter who is confused and gullible)
c it is apparent that other forces which neither character can control are really responsible for the situation (drug-taking is regarded as the 'in' thing to do, there are no facilities for young people in the town and the authorities are not strict enough on drug pushers etc).

3 All of the suggested scenes in the diagram tend to focus on the dilemma as experienced by the young person. Task 2 showed that the same scene can be 'turned around' in order to show the dilemma parents may experience when bringing up children. Try to tackle the scene you produced in Task 1 in this way, or if you don't feel that this is possible, choose another possibility as a starting point.

4 In threes – **A**, **B** and **C** – invent a situation which you think presents a dilemma. The dilemma must involve three people, each of whom sees the situation in a different way. For example:

A You have recently got on the wrong side of your mother/father. In order to pacify them, you decide to get them a birthday present. However, you have no money of your own, so you shoplift the present.

THE DILEMMA WHEEL

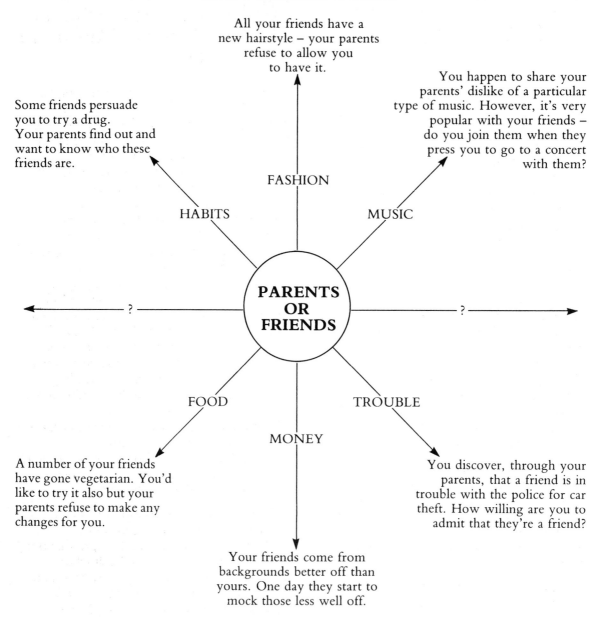

All your friends have a
new hairstyle – your parents
refuse to allow you
to have it.

You happen to share your
parents' dislike of a particular
type of music. However, it's very
popular with your friends –
do you join them when they
press you to go to a concert
with them?

Some friends persuade
you to try a drug.
Your parents find out and
want to know who these
friends are.

FASHION

HABITS

MUSIC

PARENTS
OR
FRIENDS

?

?

FOOD

TROUBLE

MONEY

A number of your friends
have gone vegetarian. You'd
like to try it also but your
parents refuse to make any
changes for you.

You discover, through your
parents, that a friend is in
trouble with the police for car
theft. How willing are you to
admit that they're a friend?

Your friends come from
backgrounds better off than
yours. One day they start to
mock those less well off.

B You witness your friend shoplifting. You know that **A** has been in trouble for this before and that **A**'s mother/father has a violent temper and will hurt your friend if it happens again. What do you do?

C You are a young shop assistant who knows both **A** and **B**. There has been a lot of shoplifting in your section lately and the manager has given you a severe warning about what might happen if it continues. You witness **A** stealing something and assume that **B** is an accomplice. What do you do?

Having devised a suitably tricky dilemma, write it down as clearly as possible or explain it to another group of three who must improvise the scene without preparation. The improvisation shouldn't last more than a few minutes. Try to avoid ending in a shouting match!

Reflection

5 When the improvisation has finished, the two groups – writers and improvisors – should discuss the scene together. Which character seemed most likely to gain the audience's sympathy? Was this because of the way the scene was acted or because of what you personally believe to be the 'right' thing to do in such a situation? Write up your conclusions in your working notebook.

Distancing

Raising and inspecting some issues can become a dilemma in itself. Because they are questions which haven't yet been answered, people tend to have different views on how they might be answered. Sometimes those views are so deeply held that the people who hold them are unwilling to consider any alternatives. Challenging such views head on often meets strong resistance and can create unhelpful conflict.

One way of tackling this problem is to 'distance' the issue by looking at it in a different **frame**. In practice this means finding some particular situation other than the one you really want to explore but which seems to contain the same sort of problem.

The extract in the next unit is an example of how an issue, which caused many people to stop listening to other opinions at the time, was opened up for further discussion.

STUDY EXTRACT TWO
Questions Arising in 1985 from a Mutiny in 1789

In 1985 there was a long and bitter miners' strike. The government planned to close several pits in order to make the mines more profitable. Unemployment was extremely high at that time and often already particularly bad in mining areas; to close the pits would mean throwing whole communities into poverty. The plan was bitterly opposed by the Miners' Union which was led by Arthur Scargill. The Union tried to win support for their case by picketing those coalmines still working. However, the government, led by Margaret Thatcher, had successfully introduced a law limiting such action. The miners considered they had no choice but to break the law if they were to save their jobs. As the union continued with their action, the government defended the working mines by sending large numbers of police to the 'trouble spots' and even setting up roadblocks to stop pickets getting too close. The strike became more violent and divided whole communities between those who supported the government's authority and those who thought it should be challenged.

A TIE company called Action Pie which was based in South Wales (one of the 'troublespots' in the strike) thought that the issues behind the strike needed further thought and discussion. To tackle it head on might have caused some members of the audiences to simply switch off. Others might have taken sides straight away without considering the points the company really wanted to make.

Action Pie's answer was to retell the famous story of the mutiny on the *Bounty* when the ship's Captain – Captain Bligh – was set adrift and another officer called Fletcher Christian took charge. By focusing on the issues which lay behind that incident, the audience would in fact be considering what might lie behind the miners' strike.

The play uses an unusual and interesting technique to help focus the audience's attention on certain things. In several places the story is stopped and the actors freeze in a tableau or 'depiction'. The effect of this is to give the audience a chance to study carefully what key moments might have meant to certain characters in the story.

This is the opening of the play. Read it through and then answer the questions on it.

NARRATION: This play was written in 1985 during the miners' strike. It is called Questions Arising in 1985 from a Mutiny in 1789.

The questions remain. *(Pause.)* Nearly two hundred years ago, a small sailing ship left Portsmouth for the Pacific. Its objective was to collect bread-fruit plants in Tahiti and transport them to the West Indies, where they were to be planted as a staple food crop for slaves. The ship never reached Jamaica; nor did it return to England. Although at this time the loss of a ship was not unusual, because of the circumstances of its loss, this ship became one of the most notorious in naval history. Its name was the *Bounty*. It was lost not because of storms, shipwreck or disease; but because its crew seized the *Bounty* from the captain by force.

Depiction of the Mutiny: **BLIGH** *stands in a launch, facing away from the ship.* **CHURCHILL**

is holding a musket, relaxed, and looks towards BLIGH. CHRISTIAN *stands by the mooring point, cutlass in hand. Disturbed.*

NARRATION: They put him in a launch with those who opposed the mutiny, and sailed the ship to an unknown island. And there the ship was destroyed. *(Hold.)*

CHRISTIAN *in mental pain cries 'Go-o-o' as he brings his cutlass down on the mooring line from the ship to* BLIGH'S *launch. The* NARRATOR, *as* BROWN, *holds an imaginary helm, and look straight ahead. Hold.*

We are not concerned with why the mutiny happened. That much is clear – conditions were intolerable. Fifty men cooped up for over two years with little space; food that a dog would refuse; working conditions more dangerous even than those of miners; a captain whose over-riding intention was to fulfil the aims of the voyage, no matter what it cost. But, really, there was nothing unusual in all this. No. It is more a matter of why there weren't mutinies on every ship! The questions we are asking are these: What did it feel like to be in a mutiny? How do people get to mutiny? What problems are people faced with on the way to doing it and when they've done it? These are the questions arising in 1985 from a mutiny in 1789 – the year of the French Revolution, that toppled a dictatorial government and began a new era in man's struggle for freedom, equality and brotherhood.

NARRATION: Break.

Depiction breaks. The actors prepare for the next scene.

We shall play many parts. All the people really existed but we have invented their characters. Each will wear a badge. Red for mutineer. Blue for non-mutineer. To show you at all times what he does not know himself until he does it. No one knows exactly how it was so we are not showing 'facts' in the narrow sense. In history, what is most interesting to future generations is rarely recorded!

But our job as actors is not the showing-of-facts, but imagining-the-real.

Depiction: CHURCHILL *is standing in the process of speaking, his finger pointing to the ground.* MUSPRATT *is kneeling looking to the space that* BURKITT *will occupy.* COLEMAN *is more inert but listening to the argument proceeding.* BURKITT *will join the depiction looking at* CHURCHILL *and about to speak.*

NARRATION: Question one. How did the crew see their situation before the *Bounty* left Portsmouth? Crew's quarters. Below decks. (BURKITT *joins the depiction.*)
BURKITT: That's what I'm saying! Everyone's been shifted to get them bloody plant racks in the Cabin area.
CHURCHILL: And who picks up the tab?!
BURKITT: We do.
CHURCHILL: What's going to happen if we get a dose of scurvy down here? This space we ain't got a chance. Go through like lightning. (MUSPRATT *is poking about to find some space.*) Get out of there Muspratt. That's mine. (MUSPRATT *retreats. Takes out his snake.*)
BURKITT: What do you think, Coleman?
COLEMAN (*to* MUSPRATT): *What the hell have you got there?*
MUSPRATT (*to all*): Snake.
BURKITT: Coleman.
COLEMAN: What?
BURKITT: I asked you a question.
COLEMAN (*still watching snake*): I think it's bad. What do you want us to say?
MUSPRATT: Burkitt, what am I going to do with Sloper? I ain't got. . .
COLEMAN: Eat it. Tastiest thing you'll get in two years.
CHURCHILL (*to* COLEMAN): What about the marines? Where are they supposed to go?
COLEMAN: Hanging over the side, what do you think! There ain't any.
CHURCHILL: What!
BURKITT: Right that's it. Hear that Churchill? No marines.
CHURCHILL: Yeah.
BURKITT: First they coop us up in less space than they'd give to the chickens. To offset

that they cut down on the crew – not on the officers mind –

CHURCHILL: Plenty of them!

BURKITT: – that means they're carrying less food. Now they expect us to do the fighting if we meet any savages.

MUSPRATT: We aren't gonna meet savages are we Burkitt?

BURKITT: Probably. *(No one says anything.)*

MUSPRATT: Sloper wouldn't like that.

CHURCHILL: No. Nor will you. *(Silence again.* CHURCHILL, BURKITT *and even* COLEMAN *brood on the situation.* MUSPRATT *handles the snake.)*

BURKITT: Alright lads, what we gonna do about it?! *(No response.)* Churchill?

CHURCHILL: What?

BURKITT: What do you mean 'what'? What are we going to do about it?

*(*MUSPRATT *listens again.)*

CHURCHILL: Nothing we can do, is there?

BURKITT: Course there is!

CHURCHILL: What?

BURKITT: Go up and tell 'em we're not having it?

CHURCHILL: You must be joking. They don't listen to us.

BURKITT: No? A mate of mine was on the *Venus.* Someone found out the boats were rotten. They all went up and told the Captain they weren't leaving Bristol till there were proper boats and they got 'em. Double quick.

CHURCHILL: Yeah that was boats though.

BURKITT: Same difference. We go up there and tell 'em.

CHURCHILL: They won't listen to us.

BURKITT: They'll have to.

CHURCHILL: Don't you believe it. *(He sits back.)*

BURKITT: Look at you. Plenty of that *(gesture of chatting)* but when it comes to doing something you just sit back and take it.

CHURCHILL: You do something if you feel so strongly about it.

BURKITT: Oh yeah!

CHURCHILL: Yeah!

BURKITT: Look we're all in this. What's the use in just me going up! Coleman, Muspratt. We've all got to do it. Go up on me own, I'll just get marked down as a trouble-maker. Let's do something. Before we leave.

MUSPRATT: Yeah. Come on then. *(He doesn't move.)*

BURKITT *(ignoring* MUSPRATT*)*: Coleman?

COLEMAN: No thanks.

BURKITT: Well that's just great, in it? Shout your mouths off, but no one wants to do anything.

COLEMAN: Why don't you get off your soap-box, Burkitt. You didn't have to come on this ship. It was your decision. No one press-ganged you. You don't like it, you go and tell him. Or just walk off again. We shan't miss you.

CHURCHILL: Oh shut up Coleman.

BURKITT: No. And no one's going to miss your trap if I put me boot in it.

COLEMAN *(shaping up)*: You wanna try it?

MUSPRATT *(to* CHURCHILL*)*: Is there going to be a fight?

BURKITT: Wouldn't waste my time. *(He looks to* CHURCHILL.*)*

CHURCHILL: They're too powerful, Burkitt. They've got all the aces. *(Pause.)*

MUSPRATT: Aren't we going to do anything?

BURKITT: No. It don't look like it. *(He stares at* CHURCHILL *and* COLEMAN.*)*
Depiction.

NARRATION: For a long time, people live under conditions they should not tolerate. It is not that they do accept them: but that they do not know they have the power to change them.
Break.

Depiction breaks. Change of stage properties.

Understanding the text

 1 Pick out any examples of lines which seem to tell the audience

    a what the story of the play is

b what the issues behind the story are.

2 Look carefully at the first two stage

directions which describe how the actors depict the moment when Captain Bligh is set adrift from his ship the *Bounty*. Which of the characters appears to be in the greatest dilemma? How is this shown and why might this be?

3 What reasons do various characters give for not complaining about the conditions on the ship?

4 What attitude do Churchill, Burkitt, Coleman and Muspratt seem to have towards

a each other?
b the organisers of the expedition?

Producing the scene

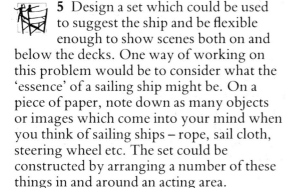 **5** Design a set which could be used to suggest the ship and be flexible enough to show scenes both on and below the decks. One way of working on this problem would be to consider what the 'essence' of a sailing ship might be. On a piece of paper, note down as many objects or images which come into your mind when you think of sailing ships – rope, sail cloth, steering wheel etc. The set could be constructed by arranging a number of these things in and around an acting area.

6 Working in small groups, develop a 'soundscape' in which you use your voices and bodies to create an image of the sea.

Arrange yourselves into the first two suggested depictions – firstly where Captain Bligh is set adrift and then where the able seamen meet below decks whilst the ship is still in port. How could you create sounds which suggest where each scene is taking place and what the atmosphere is like between the characters?

7 Working in groups of four, rehearse the last section of this extract from where Burkitt says
    'Look, we're all in this . . .'
to his last line
    'No. It don't look like it.'

How can you vary the pace, tone and volume of the voices to draw the audience's attention to the men's hopelessness and frustration?

8 Work through the same scene again. This time concentrate on the movement and positioning of the men. Try to suggest that they are in a cramped space and that they are uneasy with each other.

Reflection

 9 What do you think, just from this extract, the play is saying are the similarities between the situation of the men on the *Bounty* in 1789, and the miners in 1985?

As a whole class divide into three groups.

Group A You are the TIE company who have devised and presented this play.
Group B You are the audience of young people and teachers who have seen the play.
Group C You are a group of people who have heard about this play and object to what it appears to be saying.

Spend ten minutes in your separate groups discussing what your attitude is towards both the play and the other two groups. Try to develop particular characters within your role-play. You may or may not choose to know members of the other groups and you don't have to agree with the other members of your own group.

Set out some chairs to represent a suitable meeting place. Each group has been called to a meeting to discuss whether or not this show should continue to be allowed to tour local schools. Bring the three groups together in a meeting (Consider: How would they enter the space? Where would they choose to sit?) Elect a Chairperson and conduct the meeting in your chosen roles.

10 Are there any issues currently in the

news that you think need to be focused on but which seem to be causing heated disagreement? Discuss ways in which you could present the issues by telling a story which contains the same issues but is distanced from the current news item.

11 At the end of 1985 Action Pie had the grant that it existed on withdrawn by the local education authority and the Welsh Arts Council. The reason given was that the company's work was of a low standard. The company considered that this decision was more to do with the content of their work. In small groups, improvise a scene in which a theatre company who have devised what they think is an important and worthwhile show (it could be one that deals with the news item discussed in Task 10) have been told that unless they drop this particular show their grant will be cut. This will mean that the company will have to close down and its members be out of work. What do they decide to do?

12 What do you think about censorship? What sorts of thing do you think should be censored, and who should make the decisions? Imagine that you are writing a play about the issue of censorship. Write a speech for one of the characters. The speech may reflect your own ideas, or you may choose to write something that you feel would provoke a strong response from the audience. Try out your speech on the rest of the class, who should comment on both

a the ideas presented, and
b how dramatically effective the speech would be in the context of a play.

 Resolving Issues

To suggest that there is ever a simple solution to any issue could be a dangerous and foolish thing to do. Finding a resolution to a dilemma may depend on what particular perspective you have on it or the particular details of the situation.

'Never talk to strangers' is a common and sensible piece of advice to give to young children yet they are often also told to go and knock on the nearest door if anyone is chasing or threatening them! Which is right?

Perhaps the most useful thing to teach people is how to judge situations for themselves. Of course, some situations are easier to judge than others.

- Is it sensible to smoke even when you know that it damages your health?
- Is it right to bully children smaller than yourself knowing that you can cause them physical and emotional pain?
- Is it sensible to play chicken on railway lines knowing that express trains can seriously damage your health?

In these examples the 'correct' way of behaving becomes obvious because the result of not behaving 'correctly' is also obvious.

People often learn these things simply because they are told them. However, you may have noticed yourself that just because you're told something is no guarantee that you will take any notice of it! A lot of people believe that it is much more effective to learn through your own experience what is sensible and what is not.

What some TIE programmes attempt to do is show the groups they are working with a number of possible solutions, or help them find one they are happy to accept. What this generally means is that the audience must become active in some way and have their opinions and decisions taken into account –

they experience the problem and discover a suitable resolution.

Through the fiction of drama, children can, for example, learn what might happen if they play chicken on railway lines, without actually doing it.

The programme below is an example of how drama can be used to help children learn something the company thought was useful knowledge by actually involving them in the show.

Captain Nibbles where are you?

'Captain Nibbles' was the invention of a group of 5th year GCSE students.

The project started with a discussion on what sort of issues the group thought it would be useful to raise with children. A long list was drawn up. It included ideas such as:

The dangers of drugs	Eating sweets
	Never talk to strangers
Smoking	Looking after pets
Road safety	Litter

The group then decided that they particularly wanted to work with infant school children (aged 5–7). Returning to their list the group crossed out any ideas that they felt might be unsuitable or too difficult to handle with this age group – for example, they decided to cross out smoking and drugs because they thought the problem wasn't one that the children were likely to face for the time being. They also crossed out 'Never talk to strangers'. This was because they felt uncertain about their own ability to deal with the reasons why children shouldn't go with strangers, and also the possible exceptions there might be to this rule. After careful discussion of their own interests and what they thought they could handle safely, they decided that they would like to devise a play on the theme of pet care.

Their aim was simply to make the infants aware that cruelty to animals is as unforgivable as cruelty to other people.

Within this broad aim they hoped to teach the children about some of the specific needs various pets have.

The storyline for the play arose out of improvisations with a whole group of about 25 students. A **treatment** was written then each scene was constructed through further improvisation. A script was written later as a rehearsal guide rather than something that had to be stuck to rigidly.

A group of seven went on to actually perform the play in several infant schools.

Printed here is the treatment which was used as the foundation for the final play. Including the group discussion and interaction which was an essential part of the programme, the play lasted 40 minutes.

SCENE ONE

A few chairs placed to represent a classroom. Towards one side is a small table covered with a cloth. On the table is a hamster cage. Tommy is staring intently into the cage. His face shows, alternately, delight, wonder, fascination, curiosity. Grouped behind him are the other kids in the class. They sing, to the tune of 'Nick Nack Paddywack':

Tommy Dean, Tommy Dean
Always sits there in a dream
Stares at his hamster all day long
He gets every question wrong.

Tommy's trance is broken by the teacher asking him something to which, of course, he doesn't know the answer. A bell goes and the kids pile out leaving the teacher and Tommy. She tells him in a kindly but firm way that he must stop daydreaming. All his attention goes onto the hamster. It's as if, she says, he is actually talking to it! Tommy replies that that is exactly what he is doing. With a sigh the teacher tells him to go home and not to forget to collect some more hamster food from the pet shop.

Tommy addresses the hamster and complains how adults can't seem to see that animals are just like people and need attention. He gives, as an example, Mrs Floggem who runs the pet shop. She is a horrible, uncaring old woman who treats her animals terribly.

Tommy goes off. A strange sound (or lighting) effect changes the atmosphere. From behind the cage a hamster rises up. He talks to the audience and agrees with Tommy. He expresses horror at the conditions in Mrs Floggem's pet shop. He then explains that he always has his ear to the ground about such things so that he can help fellow animals in distress in the guise of . . . CAPTAIN NIBBLES!

SCENE TWO

The petshop. The animals, a rabbit, a kitten, a puppy and a tortoise, sit in cages made from upturned school tables. Tommy comes in and they greet him warmly. However, the entrance of Mrs Floggem changes the atmosphere. Tommy sheepishly buys the hamster food and nervously leaves. Mrs Floggem moans at the animals for not getting themselves sold. The trouble is, she says, they look too miserable. They had better perk up or she'll throw them out onto the street where the stray cats and dogs will soon finish them off.

She leaves and the same sound effect allows us into the world of the animals. We hear more about how they are treated and their fears of the wild outside. Pets aren't, after all, wild creatures but have been bred in such a way as to need attention from humans. The tortoise tells of a story he once heard about a superhero who, if called hard enough, rescues despairing pets like themselves. The others don't believe him and he enlists the support of the audience to convince them that CAPTAIN NIBBLES really does exist. They call together and sure enough he appears!

SCENE THREE

The petshop. CAPTAIN NIBBLES is listening to the pets' stories and checks out the truth of them with the audience. He decides they must be released at once but they explain that they can't survive on their own and have nowhere else to go. CAPTAIN NIBBLES tells them about his friend Tommy who might be able to help. They will need the help of Tommy's classmates. The animals cheer excitedly and Mrs Floggem, woken by the noise, enters in a terrible mood. They manage to escape in the nick of time but the poor old tortoise isn't quick enough. Mrs Floggem tries to find out where the animals have gone by threatening the tortoise. She says she will turn him on his back and leave him like it. As this is the worst thing you can do to a tortoise he gives in.

SCENE FOUR

The classroom. CAPTAIN NIBBLES leads the others in and tells them to wait quietly while he explains to Tommy. Tommy enters and hears the story. NIBBLES asks him if he thinks the other children in the class will help out. Tommy isn't sure so he asks them (ie the audience) if they will. The animals reveal themselves and are very nervous. NIBBLES and TOMMY ask the class to try to find ways of reassuring the animals.

The class is split into four groups, one for each animal (TOMMY and NIBBLES move around monitoring the next section). Each animal explains Five Golden Rules that people should know if they are to have a pet like this. Bit by bit the animals become more relaxed. This is a chance for the children to talk about their own pets and how they look after them whilst learning why such things are important.

After a suitable length of time on this activity, Mrs Floggem enters and tells them that she has turned the tortoise on his back and won't turn him over again until the rest of the animals give themselves up. The animals ask the children what they should do. Suggestions to encourage might include contacting the class teacher, police, RSPCA etc. Mrs Floggem is visibly frightened and they manage easily to chase her away.

The animals start to celebrate then notice that NIBBLES is missing. He returns with the tortoise whom he has just rescued. TOMMY announces that he has made up a song which might help everyone remember what they have learned. The cast teach the class the song, after which CAPTAIN NIBBLES announces that he hopes that the children in that school will treat pets well in future and tell their teacher or parents about anyone who doesn't. Unfortunately, there are still too many Mrs Floggems about who like to just make money out of animals or use them for their own purposes without really caring at all. For this reason he has decided to recruit four new helpers in his fight and introduces COURAGEOUS KITTY, DYNAMIC DOG etc.

As they whizz off into the uncaring world the actress playing the class teacher enters and notes that TOMMY looks a bit strange this morning. She asks what has been going on, and he replies that she should ask the class . . .

Practical problems

 1 What preparation would need to be done before the show actually took place in an infant school? Make a list of

a the resources you will need in order to perform
b ways the class's real teacher might help you
c ways in which you could make the songs and Golden Rules easier to follow and remember.

2 Design simple costumes or masks for the animals (the diagram below shows how to make a simple but effective animal mask out of card). The actors must be able to move and talk easily through them. An alternative to wearing naturalistic costumes would be to develop a way of talking and moving that reflected the animal. One advantage of this is that it clearly indicates to the children that these are not real animals at all but actors pretending for a purpose. Their task is not to appreciate how like animals the actors are but to concentrate on what the show is saying.

4 Features may be drawn, painted or glued onto the mask. Use round adhesive labels for eyes.

The actor looks under the mask, not through it. Bending the head forward exposes the animal features to the audience.

How to make an animal mask

12 cm

28 cm

1 Use a strong piece of paper, measurements approximately as shown here. If several masks are to be made, make a card template to draw around.

2 Cut the top part into eight equal-width strips.

3 Staple the strips together and secure the finished mask onto a paper headband to fit the head.

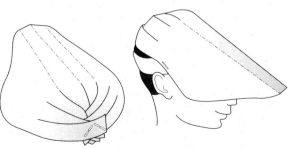

Some variations on the basic mask

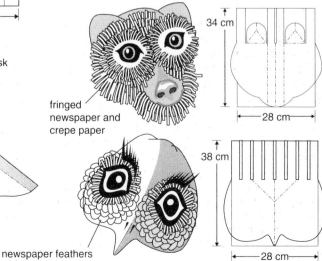

fringed newspaper and crepe paper

34 cm

28 cm

newspaper feathers

38 cm

28 cm

3 This programme requires involving the audience in a very direct way. Their ideas are important and shouldn't be dismissed just because they don't fit into the show. There is sometimes a tendency to fall into the 'He's behind you' syndrome in which an audience participates but can't really affect the outcome of the play. If you don't intend to use the audience's ideas it's fairer not to ask for them. If you are going to ask for them, you need to have a fair idea in advance of

a what they might be
b how you can usefully accommodate them in what you say and do next.

Look through the treatment again and select carefully those moments when the audience's ideas might be usefully asked for and used. Try to predict the sort of things they might say.

4 The advantage of using a treatment rather than a script for this type of work is that it can be more flexible. Note down four possible responses from an audience as to how they might deal with Mrs Floggem. Now improvise the last scene in four different ways, taking account each time of one of the suggestions.

5 The actors in a TIE programme are also in part teachers. If the class suggest, in the last scene, that the best way to deal with Mrs Floggem is to tie her up and burn her shop down with her in it, you will have to consider what to do. Is it a serious suggestion? To what extent are you prepared to let the audience have complete control over the events? Should you

a take the suggestion on board and do it?
b tell the child not to be so stupid?
c pretend you didn't hear?
d ask the rest of the group what they think?
e ask the child who made the suggestion why they made it and what they think the consequences might be?

Which of these do you think might be most effective? Have you any other suggestions?

A useful piece of research which can help with these situations is, of course, to ask the class teacher if there are any children in the class who might try to 'sabotage' the show and if so how they may best be handled. TIE companies need to work with the class teacher as much as possible in order to make their show as effective as possible.

Written tasks

6 Using a tune which you think everyone will know, write lyrics for the final song in which the children are reminded of what they have found out.

7 Devise a publicity sheet for CAPTAIN NIBBLES which explains to teachers what the purpose of the programme is and how it works.

8 Many TIE programmes are usefully accompanied by information or project packs relating to the show. Working in small groups or even as a whole class, assemble a project pack for CAPTAIN NIBBLES. It could include suggestions for

● work in Drama, Art, Creative Writing, Science and so on
● ideas for things to research into further
● poems, pictures, short stories relating to pets
● a questionnaire about the show.

9 It may be useful to script those parts of the programme where no audience interaction is required, in order to provide the actors with key reference points and serve as a limit on the running time of the piece. Find a scene which you feel would benefit from careful scripting and write the script.

SPECIAL ASSIGNMENT

To suggest that there is just one way of making a piece of TIE would be very shortsighted. However, you may wish to remind yourselves at this point what you have discovered in this chapter.

- The success of dramas tends to be measured by how much they entertain the audience.
- Some dramas seek to challenge the audience by raising or focusing their attention on particular issues. Some even offer possible solutions and invite the audience to choose what they think is the most appropriate one.
- A way of exploring an issue is to see it as a dilemma and to create a story around that.
- The audience need to be carefully targeted if they are to appreciate what the issue might mean to them.
- Research and discussion are vitally important both for finding a starting point, identifying your own values and perspectives and ensuring that you will effectively reach the audience you have targeted.

1 Select an issue which you feel needs to be raised and focused upon.

2 Agree on a suitable audience to target.

3 Devise a number of scenes which could reflect the issue you have chosen.

4 Discuss what perspective or perspectives could be most suitably used for an exploration of the issue.

5 Consider to what degree you want the audience to be involved in finding a possible solution to the issue.

6 Devise a treatment for the programme. Aim to keep the performance element of the programme *under 30 minutes*.

7 Prepare, if it would be appropriate, a 'project pack' which the targeted audience could use to explore the issue further after seeing the programme.

This Special Assignment could, of course, be realised in a programme which is actually used in your own school or taken out to a different venue, for example a primary school, old people's home, hospital and so on.

Before embarking on a visit to a venue outside your own school, it is helpful to draw up a checklist like the one below.

- Discuss the project with your own teacher.
- Contact the venue. Make sure that whoever is giving you permission to go has the authority to do so.
- Prepare details of the show to give to venues. The better presented and clearer they are the more confidence they will inspire – an important point if you want people to take your work seriously.
- Include in the details: brief description of the play, its aim, running time, setting-up time, ideal number of audience, any special requirements that the venue will need to help with.
- Make a preliminary visit to the venue to talk through the project with the appropriate person.
- Arrange transport. It's as well to keep set, lighting and effects etc to a minimum unless you have the facility to transport them easily.
- Allow time to set the show up carefully and get used to the new venue before the audience arrive.
- Allow time after the show for feedback either from the audience or the contact.
- Evaluate your work considering your organisation, ideas, presentation and to what extent you feel you tackled the issue you wanted to tackle.

Further Reading

Unfortunately, only a few TIE plays and programmes are actually published. However, you may have a TIE company operating in your area. You will usually find that they are very willing to help in any research you may wish to do into the construction, scripting or performance of TIE projects. The following books do contain excellent examples of some of the most successful pieces performed over the last 20 years.

Theatre in Education edited by Pam Schweitzer (Methuen).   There are three volumes of this:
>   *Five Infant Programmes*
>   *Four Junior Programmes*
>   *Four Secondary Programmes*

Each volume contains useful notes on the nature of TIE and how each play was devised and performed.

Sweetie Pie devised by Bolton Octagon TIE Co. (Methuen).   A play for teenagers about women in society.

Rare Earth devised by Belgrade TIE Co. (Methuen).   A play for juniors about pollution.

Six TIE programmes edited by Christine Redington (Methuen).   This is a collection of some of the best programmes developed recently, spreading across the school age range.

Killed devised by Belgrade TIE Co. (Amber Lane Press).   A play about the First World War (an extract is used in Chapter Two on 'Women in the War').

Raj devised by Leeds TIE Co. (Amber Lane Press).   A play for a mixed–race cast on the last days of the British occupation of India.

Learning Through Theatre by Tony Jackson (Manchester University Press).   This is a book aimed at teachers but it includes detailed descriptions of three interesting TIE projects.

In Search of Dragon's Mountain by Toeckey Jones (Nelson).   A play about a black girl and a white boy growing up together in South Africa under apartheid.

No Man's Land by Paul Swift (Nelson).   Set in the First World War, this play is about a young woman who has to fight for her rights while working in an armaments factory.

Anansi by Alistair Campbell (Nelson).   The story of how a young girl who has been taken by slavers learns, by listening to traditional stories, how to survive.

Forum theatre

Good drama provokes discussion. This project looks at how the technique called FORUM THEATRE can be used to discuss issues in an active dramatic way.

The work focuses on DISCOURSE in drama, that is, what is actually spoken. It shows how you can PRESENT ideas through speech and actively involve an audience in the discussion.

The stimulus for the activities is the true story of an unusual archaeological discovery.

The Lost Mosaic

The story which follows is true. It is about a Roman mosaic which was found in the grounds of a large house in Berkshire. Read it through then answer the questions that follow. They will help you start to develop a fictional drama from the factual evidence and uncover a range of issues which could then be explored through FORUM THEATRE.

Littlecote House in Berkshire owes part of its fame to a rabbit! In the grounds an almost perfect Roman mosaic is now open for inspection thanks to an extraordinary story of selfishness and good luck. In 1727 during some landscaping work within the grounds the mosaic was discovered by chance. The house and grounds were owned at that time by Edward Popham whose steward, William George, was a keen amateur archaeologist.

When the mosaic was uncovered, Mr George couldn't believe his luck but imagine how he felt when his master, Edward Popham, ordered it to be covered up again and its position on local maps to be altered in order to ensure that it would be lost forever. He ordered the planting of trees on the site in order to disguise it. However, Mr George took drawings of the mosaic and his wife embroidered a panel depicting it so that the beautiful design would survive even if the original mosaic was lost.

In 1976 a survey was taken of the grounds. Whilst looking for some remains of a medieval village known to have existed in the area, the archaeologists were inspecting the soil around rabbit holes (why dig a hole yourself to see what's under the surface when rabbits can do it for you?) What soon became apparent was that around some rabbit holes there were particles which were of Roman, not medieval origin. After careful excavation (no doubt to the chagrin of the bunnies) the lost mosaic was found once more. The mosaic has been reconstructed using William George's original drawings and various new elements of the piece have come to light.

One mystery remains though. A complete section noted in the 1730 drawings is missing. Not even the mortar bedding has survived. Has it been destroyed by natural means or was it removed before the site was hidden all those years ago? If so, where is it now?

Creating a fiction

1 Form into groups of four and take on the following roles:

A You are William George. You have been told by your master to cover up the mosaic but feel it would be a crime to do so. You will carry out your orders but cannot resist the temptation to remove part of the mosaic first to hide it away somewhere safe. However, you will need some help but you know you'll have to pay for it.

B You are a very poor workman working on the landscaping job. You need the money

offered by Mr George yet know that if you are caught the consequences will be dire.

C You are Mrs George. You know the mosaic is enormously important to your husband but also know that you have little money and if he is caught it will bring ruination to your family.

D You are Edward Popham. The finding of a mosaic on your land is a nuisance and you just want it rehidden as soon as possible. You demand absolute obedience from your servants and your patience is already being tried by your steward William George who keeps going on about this wretched mosaic.

Write down a few lines which you think will make it clear what your character's attitude is towards

a the mosaic
b the other characters.

Create a tableau in which all four characters appear. How could they be positioned to show who they are and what their relationship is to each other? When you have decided on the appropriate positioning, speak the prepared lines aloud as if they are what happens to be in each character's mind.

2 Note down as many combinations of these characters as you can, for example:

William + Wife   William + Workman
William + Wife + Workman   and so on.

3 Use these character combinations as the basis of a scene. Decide where the scene takes place and what reason the characters have for being there. Examples might be as follows.

● The mosaic site. It is the end of the day and all the workmen are going home. William finds some false reason for keeping one man behind and carefully suggests his plan.
● The Georges' house. Late night. The Workman has reluctantly come to hear more details of the plan. He and Mrs George are

The Roman mosaic at Littlecote House

sharing their worries when William arrives home.

4 By developing four or five of the character combinations you have noted into actual scenes, devise a short play which shows how William George manages to secretly remove and hide a part of the mosaic. The aim of the play is to reveal what the characters' attitudes are towards the mosaic and towards each other.

Reflection

5 What kind of man do you think Popham is? Is he right to order the mosaic to be rehidden? What arguments might he use to defend his decision?

6 Is William George justified in removing part of the mosaic? Is he justified in endangering his wife's and the workman's welfare in order to achieve his plan? What does his action suggest about him as a character?

7 How would modern-day archaeologists feel about

a Popham?
b William George?

8 Who, in your play, do you think came across as being 'in the right'? What was there about your play that made this so? Write a brief report in your working notebook.

B Forum Theatre

In Roman times the 'Forum' was a place where views could be exchanged and quarrels sorted out. 'Forum Theatre' is a technique which was developed in South America as a way of helping peasants who could not read or write to show what their lives were like and explore possible ways of improving things. The form is concerned with showing events in a way that can be stopped and commented upon. The drama itself is a discussion.

This unit illustrates one way in which Forum Theatre can be developed from a story to provoke a discussion about a number of issues underlying the story.

If the story about William George secretly removing part of the mosaic were true, imagine the following possibility.

> A researcher at the British Museum discovers some old papers left by William George which give a number of clues as to where the missing segment is. After extensive further investigation the researcher is convinced that the segment is under the floorboards of an old cottage near Littlecote. She visits the cottage which has recently been lavishly restored by a wealthy businessman. He allows her to take up a floorboard in the plush living room and there, sure enough, is the priceless segment beautifully set into the original flooring.
>
> The remarkable find is published. The British Museum, having invested in the research, suggest that the segment be taken to London for display.
>
> The owner of the house feels it should stay exactly where it is.
>
> The present owner of Littlecote House suggests it should stay in the area but be put back in its rightful place with the rest of the mosaic which is open to the public.

1 Form a circle. Moving around the circle, each member of the group states what they think should happen

to the treasure. Simply say, MUSEUM, LITTLECOTE, STAY.

2 TEAM TALK Divide the circle into three sections according to what you think should happen to the mosaic. Place three chairs in the centre of the drama room facing each other and elect a player from each 'team' to sit in a chair. One will play the Museum archaeologist, one the house owner and one the owner of Littlecote. The three characters are meeting for the first time. Their aim is to persuade the other two that they have the best claim on the mosaic.

3 TIME OUT If at any time the player of a particular viewpoint feels they are stuck for an argument, they simply say 'time out'. The improvisation is stopped and the 'players' may consult with the others in their 'team' for one minute as to what they should say or do next.

The 'time out' rule can also be used by any member of the team so that should they think of a good point to make during the scene, they can pass it on to their player.

4 SUBSTITUTION This is a variation on the 'time out' in which the player may be replaced by another member of the team who thinks they can see a better way of playing the situation. When the substitute takes the player's seat, they must adopt the same character. They may, of course, use any new arguments or information they wish but they must also accept what the previous player has said or done.

5 ASSESSMENT After keeping the improvisation going for ten minutes or so (judgement needs to be exercised depending on how well it seems to be going) re-form into a circle.

Everyone may then be given another chance to say what they think should happen to the mosaic as their opinion may well have been changed depending on the arguments they have heard.

6 FOCUSING ON ISSUES What issues appear to be coming out of the improvised

debate? Consider, for example, what the following possibilities might mean to you.

- All art/archaeological treasures are kept in private ownership.
- All treasures are centralised in London.
- Everyone has to pay in order to see such treasures.
- Owners have the right to hide or destroy treasures.
- Public money is spent on the discovery of treasures.

7 EXPLORING OUTCOMES As a whole class decide on who is most likely to win the argument over the ownership of the mosaic. What happens next?

Invent a scene which may follow this decision. For example:

- The British Museum pays the owner of the house £10 million for the mosaic. A number of organisations representing the poor and homeless protest and picket the museum on the morning of the mosaic's arrival.
- The mosaic is sent back to Littlecote House where it will be on view to the public but an entrance fee will be charged. The owner explains why this is necessary to an angry group at the gate.
- The businessman keeps it in his house. He arrives home one evening to find a gang of raiders in the process of removing it.

The improvisation should take place in the middle of a circle created by the rest of the group. Play the improvisation through until some kind of end is reached – this may simply be some sort of stalemate.

Discuss, as a whole class:

a What sort of issues were being raised in the scene that needed to be focused on more clearly? What was the content of the scene? **b** How well did the scene work as a piece of drama? How clearly were the characters coming across? What did the positioning of the actors suggest about their characters' attitudes? Was the form effective?

8 ACTION REPLAY The scene is replayed following, as closely as possible, the original pattern. This time any member of the audience may call 'substitution'. This could be because they feel the character has an opportunity of saying or doing something differently and so change the content of the improvisation. Alternatively, it could be because they feel the actor hasn't said or done something clearly enough – they haven't used the form well. When someone calls 'substitution' the improvisation is stopped and the caller explains helpfully and positively why they think the player could have done something better. They then enter the circle in that person's place and the improvisation restarts from a moment before the call was made.

Further Development

Although there are obviously issues to be explored in the story of 'The Lost Mosaic', you may feel that they are not the sort of issues that really concern you very directly. The South American theatre director Augusto Boal has used techniques of Forum Theatre in his work with people who, for whatever reason, have been oppressed by the laws under which they live, or by their personal or economic situation. The main purpose of Forum Theatre is to explore what the implications of a decision or event might be. In other words, 'If this happens, what will happen next?' Or perhaps, 'If this is the situation now, what can you do to change it?'

Look at the following scenes and think of each one as being the end-result of a sequence of events, then use the exercises below to explore how the situation might have been changed, or how the characters might deal with the situation once it has happened.

- A child lies unconscious and badly burned below an electricity pylon. A group of larger children are running away.
- It is 3.00am. A teenager creeps down the stairs of a house carrying a holdall. He quietly leaves by the front door. An adult has been watching him through the living room door. The adult has not been seen and does not say anything.

• Three youths in a room in a police station. Two of them are seated staring in anger at the third who is facing away from them.

• Two teenagers arguing. They are brothers/ sisters. One of them is holding a purse or wallet and angrily showing that it is empty.

SMALL GROUP FORUM

 1 In small groups, choose one of these scenes and position yourselves in the tableau. Hold your positions and carefully consider what your relationship with the other people in the picture might be. Keep in your positions but speak aloud what you think might be in your character's mind. (If there are more people in the group than in the picture, they could invent a new character who has something to do with the scene even though they are not present.)

2 Staying in the same groups, discuss what scenes went on earlier to bring about this final one.

3 Improvise one of these scenes with the appropriate characters. What could any of the characters involved in that scene do or say which might help avoid the final scene ever happening? Use the time out, substitution and action replay techniques to change the course of events.

LARGE GROUP FORUM

4 Forum theatre often works better with a large group where there are more people to suggest alternative ways of playing a scene and to offer different views about the **content**. Tasks 1–3 could be used by the whole class with an appropriate number of volunteers forming the tableau and everyone contributing suggestions as to what feelings and thoughts might be locked in it.

5 An alternative approach might be to devise, in small groups, a short and dramatic scene which is clearly the end result of a series of events. Each small group then takes

turns to present the piece to the rest of the class. The class may then hot-seat the characters and ask questions about who they are, what they are doing in the scene and why.

The class decide on which other scenes they would like to see to help them understand why this last one came about. The group try to improvise these. Time out, substitution and action replay can then be used to

a understand more completely the attitudes of the characters

b explore ways of changing the outcome.

Reflection

6 The whole purpose of Forum Theatre is to try to understand why situations develop and how their outcome can be altered. To what extent do you feel that working in this way

a helps you to explore a situation?
b helps you understand why people do the things they do?
c shows up possible solutions to problems?
d encourages you to take an active part in the discussion?
e helps you understand the way the others in your group think and feel?
f leads to arguments which go nowhere?
g gets bogged down and isn't active enough?

7 How much do you feel drama on the whole should

a provoke discussion about issues ie things that seem to matter to people?
b simply entertain people?
c try to explore issues in an entertaining way?

8 Has drama helped you personally to

a see issues more clearly?
b form an opinion and feelings about them?
c express your opinions and feelings to others?
Try to pick out those activities which you feel have particularly helped you in these ways.

Comedy for a change

 ## Stand and Deliver

1 *I say, I say, I say, what is the essence of good comedy?*

2 *I don't know. What is the essence of good com . . .?*

1 *. . . timing!*

It doesn't really work on paper, does it? The fact is, comedy is the most frustrating type of drama. It's very difficult to do well and very difficult to explain how it is done well. While most people would admit to enjoying a good laugh, there's no universal agreement on what is actually funny. What becomes obvious when you work with comedy is just how hard it is to identify what people do to make themselves funny. Two groups of actors can say the same lines and do pretty much the same actions, yet one will appear hysterically funny and the other just stupid and embarrassing. Perhaps more than any other type of drama, comedy shows up how, in the eyes of the audience, the way you perform is ultimately more important than what you perform; it's not just what you say and do, but the way you say it and do it.

This unit of work is not about learning how to become a stand-up comedian who can deliver jokes well, but it looks at how some of the techniques used by stand-up comedians can be used to make your own performances in drama sharper.

The King of Prussia

The extract below is from the opening of Nick Darke's play *The King of Prussia*. The play is based on the true story of a Cornish smuggler called John Carter whose successful career was destroyed when a rich but bored lady and a corrupt customs officer moved in on his operation. Carter comes across as a kind of eighteenth-century Del-boy, a 'loveable rogue' set against people richer and more influential than himself.

In pairs, read through this extract aloud. (Jack, Nantz and Geneva are types of brandy.)

JOHN CARTER *is received on deck by the* **CAPTAIN**.

CARTER Where y'from?
CAPTAIN China.
CARTER I don't want tea.

The hatchtop is replaced.

CARTER Did ye pick up any liquor on your voyage home?

CAPTAIN A few ton.

CARTER Let's feel the strength of it.

He watches the CAPTAIN *give orders to the* SUPERCARGO.

CARTER This is me brother's job but 'e's in gaol so I'm doin' 'is job on toppa my job which is two jobs too many don't ya think? What's your price?

CAPTAIN Five pounds?

CARTER Jack?

CAPTAIN Nantz.

CARTER Bugger five. Three.

CAPTAIN Three?

CARTER I wouldn't give ya five for Jack. I'd consider four for Geneva but Nantz? Three's generous. In fact you've talked me out of three. Two or nothing. Geneva three. Four for the Jack. What did we agree, one?

CAPTAIN Two.

CARTER That was Geneva. And three pound for Jack.

CAPTAIN Four pound the Jack.

CARTER So you have Jack!

CAPTAIN Yes!

A barrel is brought.

CARTER At two.

CAPTAIN Two?

CARTER Thass better. Two for the Jack.

CAPTAIN Three.

CARTER You offered me two! I heard you say it. Come along Cap'm I'm a busy man, willya shit or get off the pot?

CAPTAIN *hands a measure of brandy to* CARTER.

CARTER Whass this, Nantz?

CAPTAIN Jack.

CARTER (*studying the contents of the measure*) It ain't Geneva.

CAPTAIN No.

CARTER That we do know.

CARTER *drains the liquor and hands the measure back.*

CARTER Pound a tub.

CAPTAIN You said two!

CARTER Thass for Jack.

CAPTAIN This is Jack.

CARTER It ain't Geneva so we'm down to Jack and Nantz.

CAPTAIN Nantz?

CARTER I aren't so sure either Cap'm. Could be Nantz, could be Jack. Now I'm prepared to take the risk and pay y'a pound a tub for what might turn out on closer inspection not to be Geneva not to be Jack but Nantz.

CAPTAIN A pound!

CARTER Good! Thass more like it. (*He shakes the* CAPTAIN'S *hand*) Have y'never dealt with a free-trader before Cap'm?

CAPTAIN No sir.

CARTER First thing you gotta learn is a free-trader's an honest man cus 'e d'break the law. And if you break the law you gotta be honest. If I offer you a pound then a pound is a fair price.

Understanding the text

1 How experienced do you think the Captain is in dealing with smugglers like John Carter?

2 How would you describe the technique Carter uses to get a good deal from the Captain?

3 Carter suggests that 'free-traders' are honest men because they break the law. What does this tell you about his view of the law?

4 Nick Darke has tried to capture the Cornish dialect in the way that he has written Carter's lines. Carter was Cornish, but what effect do you think his use of language will have on an audience?

Producing the scene

5 Work through the scene in pairs. How quickly do you think the characters should talk? Should they both speak at about the same speed or is one faster than the other?

6 Carter seems to be able to twist what the Captain says. This could come across as comical or it could make Carter appear as hard and unsympathetic. Try playing the characters in a number of ways and decide which one works best. For example:

Carter as a villain Captain as a victim
Carter as a funny guy Captain as an idiot
Carter as a 'serious' businessman
Captain as an honest but rather innocent man

Talk about what different attitudes the audience will develop towards the characters depending on how they are played.

A Man in a Mess

A man walks into a pub with a newt on his shoulder, goes up to the bar and says 'I'll have a pint of beer and Tiny will have a whisky'.

So the barman says, 'That's an unusual pet. Why do you call him Tiny?'

'Well,' says the man, 'because he's my newt.'

1 Funny or not? Talk about just *how* this joke works. If you personally didn't find it funny, can you actually say why not?

It has been said that all drama is, in one way or another, about 'a man in a mess'. The 'mess' in comedy can come about through people in ordinary situations behaving in extra-ordinary ways, or ordinary people finding themselves in extra-ordinary situations. Either way, something is somehow out of place which makes it look 'funny'.

In the joke printed above the sound of the ordinary word 'minute' is used in a ridiculous way. A lot of comedy works by playing with words in this way (it's called a **pun**) but clearly the way the joke is told 'live' is a crucial factor.

The Last Laugh

Read this extract from Ben Payne's play *The Last Laugh*.

An empty horizon. A dotted line crosses the stage left to right.

SOLDIER 1 *and* **SOLDIER 2** *stand on guard. Beside them an old weatherworn sign which says* YOU ARE NOW ENTERING A FUN-FREE COUNTRY. NO LAUGHING FROM THIS POINT ON.

They march up and down the dotted line once, then stop, then face out.

Pause

SOLDIER 1 So Soldier Two – here we are. Here we are, week after week, day after day, hour after hour – guarding the border of our country . . .

SOLDIER 2 . . .border. . .

SOLDIER 1 And you know, Soldier Two, while we've been looking at this empty horizon I've been wondering. If there was a special award for doing the most boring job in the world would we get it? I mean, could we be any more bored than this?

SOLDIER 2 . . .border. . .

SOLDIER 1 Ah. So we're not of the same mind then, us two, Soldier Two. Because this is the most boring job I've ever done. And, let me tell you, I've done some incredibly boring jobs in my time. (*Pause*) Have I ever told you before about the incredibly boring jobs I've done in my time, Soldier Two?

SOLDIER 2 *nods twice, slowly, sadly.*

I once guarded the State Graveyard for Not Very Important Dead People. Tremendously boring that was. Didn't think there was a job that could get me . . .

SOLDIER 2 . . .border. . .

SOLDIER 1 . . .than that. Oh, but I was wrong. I was so good at guarding, our glorious leaders Gilbert and Gloria Grimm posted me here. And from then on I got . . .

SOLDIER 2 . . .border. . .

SOLDIER 1 . . .and. . .

SOLDIER 2 . . .border. . .

SOLDIER 1 until now all I can talk about is how much. . .

SOLDIER 2 . . .border. . .

SOLDIER 1 . . .I am than the last time I talked about it. So, of anyone, from one farthest-flung border to the other farthest-flung border of this glorious country which is so gloriously boring no one would ever think of coming here, I think we deserve that special award for doing the job that's the last word, the ultimate, the number one in all-time, big-time tedium: guarding the . . .

BOTH . . .border.

2 In pairs, try this scene out. You will need to play with the sounds of the words 'bored' and 'border' to make that particular joke work. Think also how you can get comedy out of:

> the way the soldiers walk up and down
>
> their facial expressions as they stare forward
>
> their tone of voice – should they both sound the same or can you make it funnier by having a contrast in the way they talk?

These apparently ordinary soldiers are in an extra-ordinary situation. Who ever heard of a 'fun-free country'? You have no doubt been in a situation when a teacher has said, 'No laughing from now on' – how easy was it to stop? Both soldiers seem unhappy with their job yet if it is performed well an audience will laugh. Perhaps not so much at them, but at the situation they are in.

Practical improvisation work

3 In pairs or threes, make a short improvisation based on one of the following ideas. All of these ideas form the basis of plays which are very funny if they are performed well.

● Two tramps are in a wasteland. There is just one small tree in sight and that appears to be dead. They have nothing to eat and nothing to do except wait in the hope that someone or something will come along and make their lives better. How do they pass the time?

Waiting for Godot by Samuel Beckett

● Two hit-men are in a dingy basement waiting for their victim to arrive. Neither of them knows who it will be but both have done this kind of work many times before. One of them is now beginning to feel a bit uncomfortable with his job.

The Dumb Waiter by Harold Pinter

● A woman decides to celebrate her success in business by inviting a number of other women to a dinner party. Her guests come from different periods of history and include a woman who successfully hid the fact she was a woman in order to become Pope, a knight's wife from an old English story, a Victorian woman explorer, and a hardy working woman from the Middle Ages who has survived everything from giving birth to several children, to the plague. What do they talk about?

Top Girls by Caryl Churchill

Reflection

In these plays the laughter comes out of seeing how the characters react to each other and the situation they are in (where nothing very much is actually going on). Some dramas, however, rely heavily on a complex situation being developed. You can see many examples of these situation comedies on television. For example:

> *Only Fools and Horses*
> *The Vicar of Dibley*
> *One Foot in the Grave.*

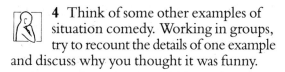 **4** Think of some other examples of situation comedy. Working in groups, try to recount the details of one example and discuss why you thought it was funny.

5 In what way do these comedies show a man (or a woman) 'in a mess'?

Situation comedies have a close relation in theatre, which is **farce**. The fun often comes from mistaken identities or other misunderstandings between characters. The hallmarks of English farce tend to involve young women losing their clothes through some ridiculous circumstances, vicars being caught with their trousers around their ankles, and generally a good deal of rushing about on the stage. Generally referred to as 'light entertainment', farces do not ask the audience to think about what is going on but to sit back and watch the antics. Some playwrights, though, have used the techniques of farce to make a serious point.

Practical improvisation work

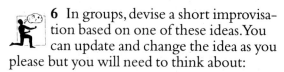 **6** In groups, devise a short improvisation based on one of these ideas. You can update and change the idea as you please but you will need to think about:

- how the situation is set up so the audience understand what is going on
- how to keep the tension going so that the situation isn't resolved straight away
- how comedy might develop from the way the characters behave in the situation.

Again, these ideas come from actual plays:

- Two young men have robbed a bank. The mother of one of them has recently died and her body is lying in a coffin in the front room awaiting burial. They decide to hide the money in the coffin, which means putting Mum in the cupboard. A police officer arrives who suspects the young men of the robbery.

Loot by Joe Orton

- A gang of confidence-tricksters have set up their operation and are promising to make people's dreams come true through magic. They have already told one person to wait in a cupboard for the Queen of the Fairies. Another man enters who appears to be Spanish so they feel free to say whatever they wish in English. Actually the man understands every word they say and has come to gather evidence that will expose them.

The Alchemist by Ben Jonson

- The people of a town hear that an Inspector is being sent from the government to look into the way they are running things. They are told that he will be travelling in disguise. When a stranger is seen in the local inn they all assume it is him and set about trying to impress him. Actually he's just a nobody but, realising that he's onto a good thing, he starts to take advantage of them.

The Government Inspector by Nicolai Gogol

Reflection

If this last idea looks familiar it may be because exactly the same storyline was used for an episode of *Fawlty Towers!*

Loot, The Alchemist and *The Government Inspector* all use elements of farce. They are also satirical. **Satire** is a type of comedy where the audience are invited to laugh at the weaknesses and vices of people.

 7 What sort of human weaknesses do you think are being put under the spotlight and commented on in the three examples above?

8 Can you think of any other television programmes, films or plays that are comical because of the way they focus on human weaknesses?

 Who Are You Laughing At?

Q: *How many actors does it take to change a light bulb?*

A: *100. One to go up the ladder and 99 to stand at the bottom and say 'It should have been me up there!'*

Trevor Griffiths' play *Comedians* is about a group of would-be comics. They have been taught by an old professional called Eddie Waters who has a very clear idea about the role of comedy. Unfortunately, the man sent to examine their acts (Burt Challenor) has a very different view.

Read these two extracts from the play. In the first, Eddie Waters is giving advice to his class of comedians before they perform for the first time in front of a live audience. In the second, Burt Challenor is commenting on their performances.

WATERS It's not the jokes. It's not the jokes. It's what lies behind 'em. It's the attitude. A real comedian – that's a daring man. He *dares* to see what his listeners shy away from, fear to express. And what he sees is a sort of truth, about people, about their situation, about what hurts or terrifies them, about what's hard, above all, about what they *want*. A joke releases the tension, says the unsayable, any joke pretty well. But a true joke, a comedian's joke, has to do more than release tension, it has to *liberate* the will and the desire, it has to *change the situation*. (*Pause*) There's very little won't take a joke. But when a joke bases itself upon a distortion – a 'stereotype' perhaps – and gives the lie to the truth so as to win a laugh and stay in favour, we've moved away from a comic art and into the world of 'entertainment' and slick success . . . A joke that feeds on ignorance starves its audience.

CHALLENOR (*to Connor*) You might find being an Irishman in England fascinating, there's no reason we should, is there? (*Pause*) Had a sort of . . . earnestness about it I didn't much take to. You know, as if you were giving a sermon. One thing you've gotta learn, people don't learn, they don't want to, and if they did, they won't look to the likes of us to teach 'em. (*Pause*) The sex was crude. I've nothing against it, but it requires taste, if you see what I mean . . . Still, you had your moments.

(*To Samuels*) First thing you want to do is ditch the first half of your act . . . S'too Jewish. What's a Jew nowadays eh? Who wants to know I mean . . . Fortunately, you pulled out of it and got very good. It was a different act, the wife, blacks, Irish, women, you spread it around, you can score, keep it tight they'll fall asleep on you. (*Pause*) Liked the Women's Lib bits.

1 Talk about the comedians you know. Which ones do you think make us see 'a sort of truth' and help change our attitudes? Which ones 'spread it around a bit' in order to win laughs by distorting the truth?

What do you think about comedians like:

Harry Enfield   Ben Elton
French and Saunders   The Two Ronnies
Chris Evans   Jeremy Beadle
Morecambe and Wise?

Dead Funny

Terry Johnson's play *Dead Funny* is about a group of friends who are fanatics about comedians – especially dead ones! In this scene they have come together to celebrate the life and work of Benny Hill who has just

died. Nick has come to the party dressed as one of Benny Hill's characters 'Mr Chow Mein'.

NICK You know a trubber with my wife?
BRIAN What's that then?
NICK Sometimes she strips and shows her bare behind up in the air.
BRIAN Oooh. Well.
LISA It's a joke, Brian. He's being funny.
BRIAN Mmm?
NICK She strips and shows her bare behind up in the air.
BRIAN Oh, I see.
LISA See?
BRIAN I beg your pardon, sir?
NICK She strips.
BRIAN She strips?
NICK And shows her bare behind . . .
BRIAN And shows her bare behind . . .
NICK Up in the air.
BRIAN Up in the air?
NICK At's right, at's what I said.
LISA That's enough, Nick.
NICK You deaf or sumfink?
LISA It's funny when Benny does it; when you do it it's just embarrassing.
BRIAN No, no no. She strips. . . ?
NICK She strips . . . strips . . . over the carpet!
BRIAN Trips over the carpet!
NICK And so her baby ends up in the air.

Enter **RICHARD** *with food.*

BRIAN She trips and her baby ends up in the air!
NICK That's right. That's what I said!! Strewf.
BRIAN Very good.
NICK Ahhhsoles.
BRIAN Must have taken you hours
LISA Well, little things please little minds.
NICK You have a good screw then?
RICHARD Sorry?
NICK You have a good screw, then? A good screw! For open a wine!
LISA Oh. Ha ha ha.
RICHARD Oh, a corkscrew! Here.
NICK Brimey o rirey!

2 In groups of three, try to act this scene out. What do you think is funnier:

- the joke Nick is trying to make?
- his impersonation of Benny Hill playing a Japanese man?
- Brian's inability to understand the joke?
- Nick's frustration at trying to make him understand?

Some people didn't find Benny Hill funny at all and would say that his humour was both racist and sexist. Nick tries to get a laugh from copying the way Benny Hill mocked the way Japanese people are 'stereotyped' by the way they are thought to speak. The lines are full of innuendo – that is, they make something that is quite innocent sound as if it has to do with sex.

Reflection

 3 What sort of jokes offend you? Is it the joke? The person telling it? The way it is told? The situation in which it is told?

Can you think of any comedians who tell jokes about things which you find offensive but still manage to make you laugh because of the way they tell them? How do they manage to do that?

4 Now read this information about the play *Dead Funny*.

Richard is married to Eleanor who hates his obsession with dead comedians. She desperately wants a baby but Richard seems entirely uninterested in sex. Lisa and Nick are married and have a small baby. Just before the scene above, Brian has come in and found Lisa and Richard having sex together! Richard knows that the baby actually belongs to him and not Nick.

How does this information affect the way the actors playing Brian, Lisa and Richard respond to Nick's jokes?

Does this information make the scene funnier for the audience or in some way tragic? Perhaps it does both. What do you think? Who, or what, are we actually laughing at in this scene?

The Sting in the Tail

The world is a comedy to those who think, a tragedy to those who feel.

The playwright Bertolt Brecht believed that plays could make people think about their own lives by making ordinary things look strange and strange things look ordinary. This is similar to what the English comic writer Joe Orton tried to do when he turned things that are normally treated as tragic into farces. (In *Loot*, for example, we are shocked to see the way Hal treats the body of his dead mother. Perhaps Orton is making us question the way we value money over life, or simply accept social rituals without question.)

In the extract from *Dead Funny* above, you can see that the comedy is working on different levels. All of the characters are in a situation that really isn't funny.

- Nick is a betrayed husband.
- Richard and Lisa are in fear of him finding out about them.
- Brian is in the difficult position of knowing about Richard and Lisa yet having to try to be 'normal' in front of Nick.

Layering the situation

The Italian playwright Dario Fo tries in his plays to make the audience think about serious situations by showing exactly how people can forget that they are in one. His characters tend to get so wrapped up in themselves and each other that even the most tragic circumstances lead to farce.

1 In groups, work through these improvisations in order and see if you can find a way of gradually adding new layers to the situation and turning a tragic situation into a comic one.

- A wealthy woman has shot her husband. He is dying. She is repenting what she has done. A male and female medic are desperately trying to save the man and comfort her.
- Try the same scene again but now add the fact that the medics are overworked, underpaid and very tired.
- Try it again, but now the medics are not only overworked but also not getting on with each other. They are lovers but one has recently discovered the other is having an affair.
- Try it again but in this scene it becomes obvious that the person whom one of the medics has been having an affair with is either the dying man or his wife.

2 Now use one of these starting points. Improvise the scene as it is described below first of all, then go through the same process of gradually building up tensions in the characters and the situation as you did in Task 1. Add new characters if you need to.

- A farmer and his wife have just been told by a vet that their herd is infected with BSE. Their son, who is present, realises that this means he won't be able to go to university. Their daughter tries to bribe the vet to keep quiet about the discovery.
- A couple of homeless people have been taken to police cells. One of them is very sick. A police doctor is called and discovers that the other has been beaten up by one of the policemen present.
- An old person has been involved in a road accident in which a teenager has been injured. The accident is clearly the teenager's fault. His friends are anxious to get away as they recognise the old man as someone they have recently mugged.

The DIY comedy kit

Look at the grid opposite.

 3 Work in small groups. From the grid, choose one setting, one situation, one central character and an opening line.

- Improvise the scene for a few minutes.
- Discuss where the best potential for comedy is. Is it in:

Setting	Situation	Character	Opening line
A mortuary	Someone is desperately in love	An important politician	'Excuse me, I wonder if you could help me'
Santa's grotto	Someone is feeling suicidal because of the way they have been treated	A boy scout or girl guide	'The time is now 10pm'
A nuclear bunker	Someone is feeling extremely guilty about something they have done	A complete maniac	'I know you from somewhere don't I?'
The gates of hell	Someone has just made a terrible mistake	A really bored teenager	'What an earth have you got in your hand?'
A school staffroom	Someone has lost something very important	A priest	'Here puss! Come on boy. Look what Daddy's got for you.'

– the situation in which the character finds him/herself?

– the way the characters are relating to each other?

– the way the characters are becoming so wrapped up with each other that they seem to be forgetting the situation they are in?

● Try the scene again, emphasising what you see as the main comic element.

● Show your scene to the rest of the group. Where do they think the comedy was coming from?

4 On your own, jot down a setting, situation, character and starting line on four separate pieces of paper. Place them in four boxes marked accordingly. Now, in groups, select four new ingredients and see if you can make a comedy out of them.

6 Is there anything that you think it would be impossible to make a comedy out of? Talk about the different ways in which using comedy could be dangerous.

7 Over the next week or so, think about the different types of comedy outlined in this Project and the different purposes comedy may have when you are watching television. Write a short review of two programmes which seem to you to use comedy in very different ways. Say which one you preferred and why.

Reflection

 5 In your working notebooks, write down

a what you have found most difficult about this work on comedy

b what you have learned about the reasons why people laugh at things

c how you think comedy can draw an audience's attention to serious issues.

Six

What's it all about?

Responding to plays

STUDY UNITS

This chapter looks at what is involved when talking about your own experience of plays.

It explores how PERSONAL RESPONSES are partly shaped by expectations and by the way an audience is actively POSITIONED.

The chapter offers guidance on how to write REVIEWS of plays seen and CRITICAL COMMENTARIES on students' own drama work.

Total Experience

What was the last play or film you went to see?

When did your experience of it start?

You might think the second question is a rather strange one. The answer seems obvious: 'It started when the lights went down in the auditorium and up on the stage' might be your answer. Working through the following tasks will give you some other answers which you should bear in mind when talking and writing about plays that you have seen, and when you are considering how other people have responded to your own work.

1 Work in small groups. One of you should start to tell the story of your last trip to the theatre or cinema. The job of the listeners is to ask questions that will seek out when the actual experience really started for you. So, for example, if you started by saying you have recently been to see a film called *Revenge of the Classroom Gerbils* you might be asked how you got to the cinema? Why did you decide to go to see it on that particular night? Why did you go to see it at all? What had you heard about the film? Where had you heard it?

The questioners should try to discover what the expectations and hopes of the person in the hot-seat were.

2 Look at the three posters opposite. If you could only go to see one of these plays, which one would you choose? What does your choice say about you as a person?

You might have many different reasons for going to the theatre or cinema – perhaps your teacher has made it clear that you ought to go to see a particular show! In this way your experience of the show will start long before the lights go down, and you will already have certain expectations of what you are about to see.

3 Talk about the things that might affect your enjoyment of the experience. For example:

> Who are you going with?
> Did you really feel like going?
> How did you feel about the cost?
> How much did you know about the play or film already?
> Where were you sitting? Did you have a good view of the stage?

If you don't end up enjoying the show it might be because of some of these things rather than the show itself.

Thinking about the 'total experience' of the theatre can help you prepare your own presentation work. In the first instance, you might usefully ask yourselves: 'What sort of audience do we want to see our work?'

4 Look again at the three posters. What sort of audiences do you think they are targeted at? How can you tell?

5 Think about a piece of practical work that you have recently been involved with. Sketch or jot down some ideas on the sort of poster that you would want to create if this work was to be developed into a public presentation. Write a note explaining how the images chosen for the poster would

a relate to the content of the drama
b appeal to a certain audience.

Taking care over how a play is advertised helps to position the audience so that they are more receptive to the style and content of the show than if they had just wandered in off the street. Positioning an audience carefully is very important: if their expectations of a show are not met the result is usually disappointment. Imagine, for example, going to see a show called *The Wizard of Oz* which is presented at your local theatre one Christmas, and discovering that it is actually about Satanic rituals in Australia!

Other paraphernalia such as tickets and programmes also help to position the audience. Theatre tickets are usually, let's face it, pretty dull things and at their simplest programmes simply tell you who is playing what part. Sometimes, though, tickets and programmes are used to add to the pleasure of the experience.

In the play about the Second World War called *When the Lights Go On Again* (an extract of which is printed in Chapter Two) the programmes were made to look like ration books. During the interval the audience had to present their ticket at a counter where they were told what they were allowed to eat and drink. They then had to queue at other counters where their ration books were ticked to make sure they didn't come back for any more!

A group of students presenting Stephen Lowe's play *The Sally Ann Hallelujah Show* (see Chapter Three) designed a programme that included instructions on how to fold it into a Robin Hood hatprint. Printed on suitable green paper, the show was stopped at one point so that all of the audience could become Merry Men!

---

6 As a class, gather together examples of theatre programmes. Discuss the different designs used and the sort of information they include. How useful and interesting is each one?

7 Look back at some of the other plays mentioned in this book and consider how tickets and programmes might have helped add to the whole theatrical experience.

8 Do you think that there are some plays where using the tickets and programmes in this way might be seen as no more than an unhelpful 'gimmick'? What types of play would you think this sort of thing would be inappropriate for?

9 When you next visit the theatre or cinema, keep a brief record of the total experience. Sort out what elements of the experience were beyond the control of those presenting the show, and how the presenters have actively tried to shape the experience for you.

Review Writing

No two people are likely to have exactly the same response to an experience for exactly the same reasons. The unit above will have helped you to see that your personal response to a play or film is shaped as much by very personal factors as by the show itself. What is certain is that you will have *some* sort of response to dramas that you see or are in yourself.

You might think that it is unfortunate that simply writing sentences such as 'I thought the play was really good because it made me laugh' is not likely to get you a very good mark in GCSE exams or coursework. On the other hand, you might see that analysing why you thought and felt what you did is genuinely useful because you can then use the experience as something against which you can check future work of your own. As pointed out above, you can never completely control what an audience is feeling when you start a presentation, but you can put into place those things that you think work dramatically: reviewing your own work and that of others will help you do this.

1 Reviews can be rather personal things and perhaps this is rightly so. Read the reviews that follow. Talk about which one you think

● gives you the most information about the play itself
● tells you most about the way the play is performed
● tells you most about the personal attitudes of the reviewer!

LYNNE KIRWIN ASSOCIATES ■ PRESS CUTTINGS
The Guardian, 6 March 1996

Michael Billington on Nick Darke's snappy *King of Prussia*, at the Donmar

Reality bites

NOT ALL THEATRE is instantly transportable. But Kneehigh Theatre's production of Nick Darke's *The King of Prussia*, which comes from Cornwall to the Donmar Warehouse, triumphantly survives the journey because of its expressive vigour and collaborative energy: it is bracing, and rare, to see a real company at work in London's West End.

Darke's play is short (90 minutes) but packed with incident. It is set in Cornwall and France, in the late 1780s. Smuggling, or free-trading as it's politely known, is a thriving local industry: one run by John Carter, the self-styled King of Prussia, but also one in which the wealthy wife of a marine biologist and even the Collector of Customs are implicated. Darke's point is that smuggling, for all its romantic trappings, is a dubious capitalist enterprise; and he reserves his admiration less for the buccaneering Carter than for Carter's brothers, one of whom becomes a Methodist preacher and the other a lobster fisherman.

The writing is brisk, snappy, volatile, and packed with Cornish references. But what really impresses is the unity of Mike Shepherd's production, recalling Peter Cheeseman's legendary 1960s musical documentaries based on Stoke-on-Trent's potteries. Actors switch roles in a second, play a variety of instruments – ranging from drum to Jew's harp – and manipulate a rotating central structure which becomes everything from ship's bowsprit to guillotine.

Tristan Sturrock, as the chief brandy-pusher, and Mary Woodvine, as a well-connected woman who stages a takeover bid, particularly shine. But it's a marvellous piece of group theatre that conveys the feel of 18th-century Cornwall – everything from the study of marine plants to visions of the apocalypse – while reminding us that smuggling was a form of profiteering hijacked by the gentry. Strongly recommended.

Western Morning News, 21 March 1996

Review: *The King of Prussia*

Right royal triumph

by SU CARROLL

KNEEHIGH Theatre has become an overnight success – and it only took them 15 years.

The West Cornwall-based company is much-loved in its native land where they fill venues from the Minack Theatre to the most modest village hall.

This month the company ventured up to the big city and took London by storm with its latest play, *The King of Prussia*, which formed the centre-piece of a Celtic Festival.

Plymouth audiences witnessed Kneehigh's triumphant return to the Westcountry, when Nick Darke's play opened in The Drum.

The story of free-traders in Cornwall may be set at the end of the 18th century but it is crammed with contemporary references. Jibes at the Royals, the odd dig at the Establishment, but at the heart the play is a celebration of Cornishness.

The men and women live by their wits and their inherent ability. Today, the free-traders would be multi-skilling and running a thriving black economy.

John Carter is the King of Prussia, a free-trader who takes a modest profit on his barrels of Jack brandy because it's all his customers can afford.

His brother Harry is trapped in a French jail, preparing to give up smuggling to follow a Wesleyan path as a preacher. Brother Edward also

wants to forsake the smugglers' life to fish for lobsters.

Suzanne Stackhouse is the wealthy but bored aristocrat who flirts with danger as she enters into a wager with The King about who will be first to corrupt upstanding revenue man John Knill.

Nick Darke's soulful script, Mike Shepherd's pacy direction, and the magnificent versatility and energy of the cast – Charlie Barnecut, Tristan Sturrock, Bec Applebee, Carl Grose, Mary Woodvine and Giles King – make this an absorbing and exciting piece of theatre.

Demand for tickets is great but there are plans for a revival next year.

The Times, 6 March 1996

This much fun must be illegal

The King of Prussia
Donmar Warehouse

OVER the next five weeks the Donmar is importing work from Ireland, Wales and Scotland; but it launches its 'four corners' season by introducing us to a company from a less obvious Celtic nook. Kneehigh Theatre has been touring Cornwall for the past 14 years without making any noise that has reached this particular pair of metropolitan ears. On the evidence of Mike Shepherd's production of Nick Darke's *King of Prussia*, that is my loss, and an indisputable gain for the land of caravans, lobster pots, defunct tin mines and retired pirates with parrots on their shoulders.

The title is the sobriquet of one John Carter, a late 18th-century smuggler and, in his way, as decent a man as ever left brandy in a helpful vicar's porch. He is more inclined to rescue a foe than kill him and takes his pole position in the local economy seriously. Village after village is dependent on his evading the punitive duties of the time, for person after person is involved in the booze chain; and he lets nobody down.

One of Kneehigh's qualities would seem to be a delight in story-telling. After a few moments in which I struggled to

get my bearings – brains are probably nimbler in the Cornish sea air than the Seven Dials fug – I found myself fully absorbed in Darke's tall tale of a King of Prussia who takes a bet with his rival in customs-busting, the less principled wife of the eccentric scientist and seaweed fancier who owns the local castle.

Whichever of them manages to bribe the apparently incorruptible revenue officer, John Knill ('the detestable practice of cheating King George is a crime, for the poor demented monarch needs all the money he can get') will receive £100 from the other. The money is duly exchanged, but only after betrayals, forays to revolutionary France, near-death experiences and, for Knill, a three-day period suspended in a length of canvas over a cliff. Thanks to an unexpected show of female flesh below, he manages to survive the experience without too much suffering.

In Cornwall, the piece may have resonances Londoners will miss. After

all, whole communities are dependent on a fishing industry they feel is imperilled by Brussels, and many people must wonder if Carter's attitude to the rules isn't the right one. But the point is put over with a sly wink, not a hammer. The mood is more merry than menacing – how could it be otherwise with a baker called Gilbert Giddy doing his bit for the smuggling syndicate? And yet things never get silly or facetious.

Clearly another of Kneehigh's qualities is agility of performance. Bill Mitchell's set consists of little more than an ad-hoc mast, a tarpaulin and the odd barrel, but that is enough. The six-person cast rattles purposefully along, turning on fresh characters as if with light switches, and picking up cues as if with electro-magnets. Let's name them all: Giles King, Bec Applebee, Mary Woodvine, Charlie Barnecut, Carl Grose and, as a bright, sharp, unpretentiously chivalric King of Prussia, Tristan Sturrock. And let's hope they make another visit to the smoke very soon.

BENEDICT NIGHTINGALE

2 Think about a drama that you have seen very recently. It could be a play or film but could just as well have been last night's episode of *Eastenders*.

a Retell the story in as few words as possible.
b Give a brief description of how well performed and presented the drama seemed to be.
c Write a few sentences about the circumstances under which you were watching the drama.

The ideal review to produce for GCSE should have all three of these elements.

Simply retelling the story of the play is a bit pointless as the person who will read your review probably knows it anyway. However, you will want to show that you were awake enough to know what the story was about, so should include a very brief synopsis of it. Similarly, simply talking about what a great evening you had, what mood you were in and who you were sitting next to will not prove much about your understanding of drama. Picking out other elements of your personal experience may be helpful, though. For example, you may justifiably feel that the ticket prices were far too high or that the advance publicity for the show was misleading; admitting that these things may have coloured your experience is no bad thing.

What is really needed in a piece of GCSE coursework or an examination answer is evidence that you can explain why you felt a piece of drama worked or not.

Useful Headings

There is a lot you can do to make sure that your own reviews tell the readers what they really want to know. Whether you are talking about plays you have seen at the theatre or your own presentation, making notes on very basic things will help you to see what sorts of thing will be more important to comment on than others.

1 Use this checklist to make some notes before even going to see your next play.

Title	What is the play called? What expectations does this set up for you?
Author	Who wrote it? Do you know anything about the writer? How does this knowledge affect your expectations?
Venue	Where is the play being performed? Does this suggest anything about how the play might be done and what sort of audience will be present?
Director/ company	Do you know anything about them?
Date	When is the performance? Is this in any way significant? For example, is it the sort of play that fits with the time of year, or a current news item?

2 As soon as possible after seeing the play, use the checklist on p 222 to jot down some details about what you actually saw. (You could try making notes during the performance but the trouble with this is that it will stop you getting deeply involved with what you are watching and you may miss bits.)

3 From these notes you should be able to write a full and interesting review, but they will need some re-ordering. Use the following as a guide to shaping your review.

Staging	What sort of stage was the play presented on? In the round? End on? In amongst the audience (promenade)?
Set	Briefly describe the design of the set. Was more than one set used? How well constructed was it? (Did the walls wobble when characters closed the doors?) Did it show a 'realistic' scene or was it an abstract design?
Plot	Say in as few words as possible what the actual storyline of the play was.
Themes	Were there any particular themes that were explored in the play? Was it about unemployment? Or the problems of a particular type of personal relationship?
Genre	Did the play remind you of anything else you have seen or read? Was it very obviously a comedy or tragedy or melodrama?
Costume/make-up	Did the costumes relate to a particular historical period? How good were they to look at? How did they fit in with the colours used in the set? Was the make-up used to add to the realism or was it in any way strange?
Lighting	Did the lights just illuminate the set and action or were there any special effects? Were certain characters picked out in spotlights? What effect did this have? Were any particular colours used to make some sort of dramatic point?
Sound	How was music used to help the atmosphere or make a particular dramatic point? Were the sound-effects simply functional (eg doorbells, telephone rings, etc) or were some of them strange in some way?
Acting	Were all of the actors believable or did this not matter in this particular play? Could you hear and see them clearly enough? Did any of them seem to stand out for you? Can you say why?

a Give your review a suitable **headline**. You might just choose to put the title of the play, where it was seen and when, or perhaps something snappier that captures the essence of your personal response, for example:

Something is definitely rotten in the State of Denmark!

Little Fumblings Amateur Dramatic Society present *Hamlet*

b Write a very brief outline of the **plot**.

c Next, focus on those **key aspects** of the production that stand out in your notes as being worthy of comment. Talk about what surprised you or what you found confusing

and what struck you as being well or badly done. Try to get a balance between what the play was about, how it was performed, and how the technical aspects of the production helped the experience.

d It might be worth mentioning any particular factors that affected your personal experience, such as the context in which you saw it. If you had already seen or read the play before, you could compare how this production matches up with your previous experience.

e Finally, write a brief **conclusion** to sum up your personal response to the production. The reader should be clear on whether or not you liked it, and why.

D Self-assessment

Devising a piece of your own drama or working towards the presentation of a piece of script can be rather like playing a game of snakes and ladders. For much of the time you will be moving steadily forward. Sometimes someone will have a great idea and you'll leap ahead, only to experience a major setback the following lesson. You will miss some good opportunities on the way – but then again, you'll spot some pitfalls in advance and be able to avoid them.

Look at the grid below which shows one group's experience of devising a play. Discuss where this group made mistakes and how they might have made their journey towards the final presentation a little easier.

FINISH				
Group makes a list of five key things to remember for next time.	Discuss with audience what they thought came out of the work.	Presentation runs smoothly but stumbled over some of the poem.	Final preparations go well. Ed has a good idea about lighting angles.	Keeping to strict timetable but decided to try out some scenes in different ways. Good ideas generated – hope it's not too late to make them work.
Discover lights chosen clash horribly with colour of costume and make masks look too sinister.	Dress rehearsal goes well. Rest of class make helpful suggestions about the masks which have been muffling our voices.	Group working well together. Ideas gelling. Rehearsals getting a bit boring now doing the same thing every time.	Decide to work with character voices. Successful session.	Studio in use by Sixth Form – can't do movement in classroom . . .
Agree on running order for scene created so far.	Discover a piece of music that suits the atmosphere. Good workshop using movement.	Try to make masks. Harder than we thought but still want to use them.	Come up with a storyline that ties the poem and the theme together.	Decide to keep notes on what we have done each lesson and set preparation tasks.
Group struck by 'flu. No one present has brought in the poem.	Go to see a theatre group which uses masks. Decide to use lots of masks ourselves.	Talk about costumes and make-up which show the characters.	Identify a major theme in the poem which excites us. Strange we missed it before!	Experimenting with the sounds of the words in the poem.
Improvising around the characters. Lots of laughs but we didn't write any ideas down.	Kirsty decides to change groups and takes the picture with her!	Invent some dialogue which suits the characters in the picture.	Manage to make a good still image to capture the essence of the poem.	Brainstorm ideas. Lots of time spent talking. All lesson in fact!
Task set: devise a 15-minute presentation based on a poem.	Recognise the poem as we've done it in English.	Gradually work out what the poem is all about.	Get into groups and discuss personal responses to the stimulus.	Persuade Kirsty to join group. She's brilliant at Drama and will be able to tell us what to do.
START				

Talking about your own work can be difficult. You may find that you are so wrapped up in it that it is hard to step back and comment on exactly what you have done and why. Starting from the basics will help. Whether you are keeping a regular 'log' book of your work or writing a final piece of coursework or examination answer, you will find that considering the following headings will make the process that you have been through clearer.

The task	What is the task you have been set? Does it relate to work you have been doing or is it entirely new? Does it involve a particular stimulus? What are the constraints?
Introduction	How was the task introduced? Through a workshop? Given out cold?
Initial response	What do you feel about the task? Do you like the material? Why? Where do you think the problems might be? What questions do you have about it?
Group response	How does the rest of the group feel? What ideas do they have about tackling the work?
Mediated response	Having heard the views of the group, do you feel differently? Have you any new ideas or questions about moving forward?
Group	Who are you working with? What particular strengths do they have?
Deadlines	Working backwards from the final deadline, what sort of timetable will you try to set yourselves for preparing the different elements of the presentation?
Snakes and ladders	This is likely to be the longest and most important section of your report. Pick out those moments when the group moved forward most quickly, and identify the specific problems you experienced. Try to focus more on the way the dramatic ideas came about rather than talking about how the group got on.
Final preparations	What are your aims for the final presentation? What effect do you want to achieve? How will your preparations help you to achieve them? What is left to be done?
Presentation	What worked (or not) in the final presentation? How did the presence of an audience affect it? What were the surprises and disappointments?
Audience response	Talk to members of the audience. To what extent did they pick out the messages you were trying to convey? Did they agree with you on where the strong/weak points were?
Conclusion	What have you learned from the experience? How has the process helped you identify things to build on or watch out for in the future?

Glossary

acting This involves not only adopting someone else's attitudes and beliefs as in **role-play**, but also developing a sense of their **character** by altering the way you speak and move.

audience Anyone watching the drama. This may be a group sitting in a theatre watching professional actors or the rest of the class watching a short piece of improvisation being presented. It may also include yourself while you are actually acting.

character A character in a play has a recognisable personality. Characters do things because of who and how they are as individuals rather than what they are. In this sense, *character* differs from *role*.

content What's in the drama. It may be mainly concerned with telling a story (see **plot**) or exploring a theme (see **focus**).

context The general situation within which something happens. Context does not just involve what is in the **frame** at the time, it also takes account of the things that have happened before.

conventions Suggest the 'usual' way of doing things. All types of language work through conventions in that we have to agree on the rules if we are to understand what is being said. Conventions don't stand still, though; they are constantly being developed and questioned.

depiction Literally, to show in words or pictures. This might involve making a **tableau** (freeze-frame, still image). Depiction involves inspecting one specific event by looking at it very carefully and considering how different **signs** have been used to convey a message.

design Anything needed to enhance the visual or audible quality of the drama must be designed in order to communicate the right **signs** and so help the **audience** understand. Lighting, costume, make-up, scenery, sound effects, posters and programmes must all be considered as adding to the total experience and message of a drama.

dialogue The words spoken between two or more people.

discourse All those aspects of the drama that seem to tell us something. This isn't just about spoken language, but also all those images that seem to make a point.

duologue This refers to a dramatic conversation between two people.

essence machine A particular exercise which explores and captures the key features of given situations.

focus The core subject that the drama is dealing with. The central issue, rather than the other elements that may be in the **frame**.

form The manner by which the **content** is expressed. The form might involve mime, dance, certain **styles** of acting etc.

frame The where and when of a drama. Think of a photograph which is taken at a certain time, in a certain place and only includes whatever information can be captured by the lens. Within this frame there will be something that the photograph is **focused** on.

gesture Those aspects of communication which rely on physical movement. This may mean a particular hand signal, facial expression or the shape and movement made by the whole body in order to communicate meaning.

hot-seating This is a technique in which a person in role is questioned in order to get a clearer idea of what they are thinking or to acquire more information about the story and themes the drama is exploring.

improvisation Making something up by using whatever is immediately to hand, ie your own ideas!

mapping A technique that can be used to give work a stronger structure. It involves laying out the different scenes and events, looking for links between them, and shuffling them around to find the most interesting order.

melodrama A **style** of drama in which the emotions are unrealistically heightened. Melodrama has a feeling of being 'over the top'.

monologue This means that just one person is speaking on the stage. He/she may be speaking their thoughts aloud (**soliloquy**), actually talking to the audience (**direct address**) or perhaps making some kind of speech to other characters.

narrative We usually think of narrative as simply meaning the story or **plot**. However, a still image has a narrative in that there is a **focus** and a **frame**: something is going on somewhere and our attention is being directed towards it.

naturalism A **style** of drama which attempts to accurately recreate the details of real life on stage.

plot The order in which a **narrative** is unravelled, the course the story takes. Plot is often used in such a way that it heightens the **tension** by deliberately keeping back bits of information.

positioning This can mean simply where people are standing on a stage but it can also refer to the way an audience's attitude is shaped. If you think of a drama happening in a frame then you might ask what angle you want the audience to see the play from – in other words, what view do you want them to have on the action?

realism A **style** of drama which attempts to make clear on stage the dynamics and meaning of real life rather than showing what it looks like on the surface.

rehearsal The repeated acting-out of a drama aimed always at improving the product by selecting and rejecting various ways of presenting it.

role-play Consciously adopting a role that isn't your own, pretending to be someone else in a fictitious situation. Playing a role doesn't necessarily involve changing the way you speak or move as in playing a character, but does involve adopting new attitudes and beliefs to fit the drama.

signs Signs in drama guide us towards a meaning in the same way that road signs guide us towards a destination. They must be clearly set out and easily read if the audience are going to follow the route we want them to. The way we look, talk and move and the setting in which we do that give strong signs to an audience about how to interpret the drama.

sound Music, sound-effects, chanting and even the way people breathe can carry special meanings in a drama. Included in sound must be silence, the very deliberate use of which can create considerable tension.

storyboard A device that involves sketching the different actions of a play in a sort of cartoon. Storyboarding will help you focus on what is really important in a scene or storyline.

style The special way in which a drama is written and performed. A drama can have the same **form** and **content** but still be presented in totally different **styles** – characters and incidents may be realistic, exaggerated, poetic, presented through music or movement etc. See **melodrama**, **naturalism**, **realism**.

tension Dramatic tension tends to depend on the consequences of actions. It's rather like gambling: the more money you put on the more you stand to win – or lose! Dramas that put characters in a situation which is potentially dangerous for them have more tension. This isn't to say that only dramas about murder or violence have tension. The tension may be because a relationship or belief is endangered.

text This may refer to the written script of a play. Increasingly though the word is used to refer to all of the **signs** in a drama; everything that is seen and heard which communicates meaning in the drama.

treatment The outline of a drama. The treatment may deal principally with either the **plot** or the **focus**. Treatment helps you see what the purpose of the drama is.

Activity charts

The charts that follow show the different skills that are dealt with in this book. The skills have been arranged under the headings of MAKING, PERFORMING and RESPONDING, though it is recognised that most of the tasks will, in practice, involve all three of these areas.

The letters along the top of the chart show you the Study Units within the chapter. The numbers in the table refer to the tasks in that Study Unit that focus on the particular skills (listed in the left-hand column). So, for example, you can see that Task 1 in Study Unit A of Chapter One principally involves Research.

The charts may be helpful if you want:

- **To find particular activities.** If you are having some difficulty understanding how a certain drama technique works you can look for similar activities elsewhere in the book.

- **To plan your own project around a particular skill.** As a piece of coursework you may wish, for example, to submit some design for the theatre. Use the chart to show you where in the book you will find different ideas and guidance for this.

- **To revise certain aspects of the course.** The chart will help remind you of the different work you have undertaken in the course. This is especially useful if you have to write about the processes you went through in acquiring your knowledge and skill in drama.

Where **SA** appears on the chart this shows you that there is a whole Special Assignment focused on that particular area of drama work.

The Project columns show the Unit and Task number together.

Chapter One Playmaking	A	B	C	D	E	F	G	H	Project 1	Project 2
MAKING										
Research	1/4	2/3/6	5						A1–3/5	C1
Discussion	3/5	1								
Devising	6		6	SA	1	1	1	10/12/13		C2–6
Improvisation and role-play	2	4		1–6	1	2	1/2	11/12/13	A6 B1–7 C 1–5	
Scriptwriting			1–4		7–9	3		14–16		B8 C2–6
PERFORMING										
Improvisation	7	5			2–6				A4 D1–4	
Presenting scripts	8					4				B5
Movement								10		
Design and technical										
RESPONDING										
Discussion	7/9/10	5/7			3	2/4		1–9 17–19	E1–2	B1–4/6
Written tasks				SA						B7 C 7–8

Chapter Two Characterisation	A	B	C	D	E	F	G	H	I	Project 3	Project 4
MAKING											
Research	1–6				SA	2					A1
Discussion		1–4	1-2/5	1–6	8						B1 C1
Devising			7	9–10	10	3/5				B11	A2/4 B2 C3
Improvisation and role-play		5–6	3–4		2 SA	1/4/5	1/3–7	7–11	7–9	A1/3–4 B10	C2/4–5
Scriptwriting						6			10–13	B12–13	A3 B3 D2
PERFORMING											
Improvisation			7	8–9						A1/3–4	C3 D1
Presenting scripts				7	1/9				4	B7–9	B4
Movement											
Design and technical			6						5–6/14		
RESPONDING											
Discussion		7	8–9	10	3–7/ 11–12		2/8	1–6	1–3	A2/5 B2–6	B4 C5 D3
Written tasks									15	B1/14–15	D1–2

Chapter Three Style	A	B	C	D	E	F	G	H	Project 5	Project 6
MAKING										
Research		1/6–7						SA6–8	A1–2 C4–6	A1–5 B1
Discussion		2–5/ 8–11/ 13/15–16							B1–21	A1–5
Devising			10	1–2		10	8		C4–6	C1–3
Improvisation and role-play			2/5–9	1			8		C1–3	B1 C1–3
Scriptwriting		12/14		3				10–11		
PERFORMING									C5	
Improvisation			3–4/ 10							
Presenting scripts	6				6–8	4/6–7		6 SA15–16		
Movement										
Design and technical					9–11	5		5/7–12 SA1–8/ 9–16	C9	
RESPONDING										
Discussion	1–6		10–11		2–4/ 12–14	1–3/ 8	1–7	1–4/ 8–9	C7–9	
Written tasks					1/5	9	9	SA17–18		C4–5

Chapter Four Movement & sound	A	B	C	D	E	F	G	Project 7	Project 8
MAKING									
Research	2	1–3/7		1/3	3–6		13	A1 B8 D1	D6
Discussion	1			1				A2–4	
Devising		4–6	9–11	2/5	SA1–2			E3–4	
Improvisation and role-play	1	8–9					12	D2–4	D1/4
Scriptwriting							12/17–20	E8	B4
PERFORMING									
Improvisation								E7–9	
Presenting scripts			7–8	9–10	10	10–11	7–11/13	B6 C4–6 E5–6	A1–4 B1–3/5–6 C1–3 D2–3
Movement	1/3–10	4–6/ 8–9	9–11	2/5	5–6/10 SA1–2		8–11/14	D2–4 E3–4	
Design and technical			5–6	7	3–9	7–9	6		A4
RESPONDING									
Discussion	11–12	10	1–4	4/8/11	1–2	1–6/ 12–13	1–5/ 21	B1–5/7 C1–3 E11	A2
Written tasks		11		6		2	3/15–16/ 20	E1–2	D5

Chapter Five Tackling issues	A	B	C	D	E	F	G	Project 9	Project 10
MAKING									
Research							1/5 SA1–2		
Discussion						10	SA4–5	A5–7 B1–8 C2	B1 C3
Devising							SA3/6–7	A4 C5	B6 D1–4
Improvisation and role-play	5–7		7–11	11–13		9/11		A1–3 B1–8 C1–4	B3
Scriptwriting			7			12	6/9		
PERFORMING									
Improvisation			12		1–5				D1–4
Presenting scripts						6–8/12	4		A5–6 B2 C2
Movement									
Design and technical						5	2		
RESPONDING									
Discussion	2–9	1–8	1–6/12	1–10	5	1–4	3	C5–7	A1–4 B4–5/7–8 C1–4 D6
Written tasks	1	7				12	7–8	A8	D5–7